Sects & Stats

To my beautiful wife and partner, Evelyn Dorothy Oliver, whose insightful conversations across the years have sparked many of the original ideas contained within these pages. Thank you for inspiring me to undertake this project.

Sects & Stats

Overturning the Conventional Wisdom about Cult Members

James R. Lewis

SHEFFIELD UK   BRISTOL CT

Published by Equinox Publishing Ltd.

UK: Office 415, The Workstation, 15 Paternoster Row, Sheffield S1 2BX
USA: ISD, 70 Enterprise Drive, Bristol, CT 06010

www.equinoxpub.com

First published 2014

© James R. Lewis 2014

All rights reserved. No part of this publication may be reproduced or transmitted in any form or by any means, electronic or mechanical, including photocopying, recording or any information storage or retrieval system, without prior permission in writing from the publishers.

ISBN-13 978 1 78179 107 3   (hardback)
         978 1 78179 108 0   (paperback)

British Library Cataloguing-in-Publication Data

A catalogue record for this book is available from the British Library.

Library of Congress Cataloging-in-Publication Data

Lewis, James R.
  Sects & stats : overturning the conventional wisdom about cult members / James R. Lewis.
      pages cm
  Includes bibliographical references and index.
  ISBN 978-1-78179-107-3 (hb) -- ISBN 978-1-78179-108-0 (pb)
  1. Cults--Research. 2. Cults--Statistics. I. Title. II. Title: Sects and stats.
  BP603.L53 2014
  209--dc23
                            2014010902

Typeset by ISB Typesetting, Sheffield, UK

Printed and bound by Lightning Source Inc. (La Vergne, TN), Lighting Source UK Ltd. (Milton Keynes), Lightning Source AU Pty. (Scoresby, Victoria)

Contents

	Preface	vii
	Introduction – Are Meaningful Generalizations about New Religious Movement Members Still Possible?	1

Part I
Quasi-longitudinal Approaches

1	Whatever Happened to Youthful Converts?	11
2	Social Networks and Conversion	31

Part II
Three Styles of Longitudinal Research

3	Increasing Complexity versus Prior Generalizations – Census Data and Longitudinal Approaches	49
4	Toward a Paradigm for Longitudinal Studies – The Order of Christ Sophia	69
5	The Movement of Spiritual Inner Awareness – Demographic Patterns, 1998–2011	83

Part III
Mixed Method Approaches

6	Demise of the Teen Witch Fad	99
7	Who Serves Satan?	111

| 8 | New Religious Movements and Gender – The Case of Scientology | 131 |

Part IV
Ex-Members

9	Post-Involvement Attitudes	143
10	Member versus Ex-member Profiles	159
	Afterword – Directions for Future Research	173
	Appendix – Anglophone Census and National Survey Data on New Religious Movements	177
	References	191
	Index	205

Preface

There are researchers who write books, and then there are researchers who write mostly journal articles (as well as book chapters for anthologies). I am decidedly a member of the latter tribe. Additionally, in my particular case, I often judge that topics suitable for monographs will work just as well or better as topics for anthologies – and as a consequence have been the organizer of numerous such collections.

I have also noticed that some academicians publish articles for several years, and then bring them together, along with a touch of new material into a semblance of a monograph. Thus, for example, the contents of Bruce Lincoln's recent (2012) book, *Gods and Demons, Priests and Scholars* (an evocative title!), includes, as he notes, roughly 50% recycled material including such pieces as his celebrated short essay, "Theses on Method." And while it is occasionally the case that articles become significant documents in themselves (e.g., Colin Campbell's "The Cultic Milieu," Anthony F. C. Wallace's "Revitalization Movements" and the aforementioned "Theses on Method"), it is more often the case – or at least in the areas of scholarship with which I am most familiar – that ideas typically do not become influential until after they have appeared in book form.

I mention this state of affairs as (probably unnecessary) justification for the present volume. A number of the following chapters have appeared before – though often in less developed forms, and sometimes containing significantly dated information that has been updated for this new incarnation. While some have been published in well-regarded academic periodicals, others have not. However, and unlike a few of the stitched-together monographs I have seen, this volume makes a coherent statement that is more than the sum of its parts. My overriding purpose in bringing these studies together under one cover is to address an issue that I view as a major stumbling block in the field of New Religious Movements (NRMs), namely the fact that many of our key generalizations about members of such groups are based on studies that were carried out more than a quarter of a century ago. Furthermore, as I will demonstrate, many of these generalizations no longer apply to current alternative religions.

In addition to deconstructing obsolete scholarship, I also want both to encourage researchers with mild cases of math phobia to undertake quantitative work, as well as to present some alternative models for undertaking such research. Over and above traditional longitudinal approaches, I will describe a post-facto approach (that is not really new) as well as a 'quasi-longitudinal' technique that some NRM specialists might find useful. I also call attention to census data that has been collected in four Anglophone countries which include useful demographic data on select alternative religions – data that can, in some cases, supplement conventional questionnaire data. In all of these approaches, including the utilization of census figures, my emphasis in a majority of chapters is on longitudinal methods – in other words, describing how the membership profiles of such groups change over time.

I should also say that this book arises out of many years of interacting with members of alternative religions and talking with other NRM specialists. Though it has often been said that scholarship is a cooperative endeavor, I become more acutely aware of this fact with every passing year. In addition to the thinkers and researchers to whom I refer in the body of this preface, I will begin my acknowledgements with a special word of thanks to my wife and partner, Evelyn Oliver, without whose support and input this book would not have been possible.

The research reported in Chapter Nine received support in the form of small grants from Syracuse University and from the Society for the Scientific Study of Religion. Additionally, the Australian census data referred to in many chapters was purchased by the acquisitions department of the University of Tromsø University Library. Finally, the core of my analysis in the Introduction and Chapter Three was formulated while working on a project funded, in part, by the Norwegian Research Council, the University of Tromsø and the Institute of History and Religious Studies at the University of Tromsø. Thanks, especially, to Fredrik Fagertun, Siv Ellen Kraft, Thorbjørg Hroarsdottir and Bjørg Hunstad who have helped me with funding and with funding applications since I arrived in Norway. Support from all of these sources and people is gratefully acknowledged.

At various stages in my ongoing research into the quantitative dimension of the New Religions phenomenon, I have received invaluable support and input from Helen Berger, David Bromley, Burke Rochford, Peter B. Andersen and my colleagues at the University of Tromsø. Thanks are also due to J. Gordon Melton, James Beckford, Olav Hammer, Asbjørn Dyrendal, Jesper Aagaard Petersen, Andreas Bauman, Liselotte Frisk, Carole Cusack, Diana Tumminia, Christine Johnson, Constance Jones, Michela M. Zonta, Dell DeChant, Sean Currie and innumerable other colleagues who have helped shape my scholarship, in ways large and small. I particularly want to thank my student, Inga B. Tøllefsen, for agreeing to contribute our jointly authored paper (Chapter Eight) and more generally for serving as a sounding board for some of my ideas.

I would especially like to thank the many people who responded to my questionnaires over the years, current members and former members alike.

A few of the research projects mentioned in these pages would not have happened at all without the cooperation of religious officials, leaders and certain key participants. At the risk of failing to mention important contacts, and in no particular order, thanks to Dani and Tami Lemberger, John-Roger Hinkins, Mark Lurie, Mother Clare Watts, Father Peter Bowes, Heber Jentzsch, Ben Shaw, Lynn Farny, Amina Olander Lap, Venus Satanas, Anton Long, 'Troll Towelhead,' Steven Gelberg and officials of the Unification Church and the Way International who a quarter of a century ago helped me with the research reported in Chapter Nine, but whose names have long since evaporated out of my brain. Finally, thanks to Chuck Beatty whose stubborn persistence prompted me to undertake more research on Scientology than I thought I should, and who contributed a key insight in Chapter Eight.

To acknowledge sources for many of the chapters in this book: Chapter Three is based on my and Andreas Bauman's "New Religions and the New Zealand Census: Are Meaningful Generalizations About NRM Members Still Possible?" that appeared in the *International Journal for the Study of New Religions* (2011) – though I should immediately note that my discussion has been considerably enlarged beyond New Zealand with the addition of data from the Australian, Canadian and British censuses. Chapter Two is based on my "Cracks in the Conversion Network Paradigm" that appeared in the *International Journal for the Study of New Religions* (2012), though I have dropped the original paper's penultimate section and added a completely new section earlier in the discussion. Chapter Six is an expansion of my article, "The Pagan Explosion Revisited: A Statistical Postmortem on the Teen Witch Fad," which originally appeared in *The Pomegranate: The International Journal of Pagan Studies* (2012). And Chapter Seven is a thorough rewrite of my "Fit for the Devil: Toward an Understanding of 'Conversion' to Satanism" that originally appeared in the *International Journal for the Study of New Religions* (2010).

The data and the methodology sections in Chapter Nine were drawn from a series of articles I authored and co-authored on former NRM members that were published in the mid to late 1980s in *Sociological Analysis* (subsequently renamed *Sociology of Religion*) and the *Journal for the Scientific Study of Religion* (refer to the Bibliography). The appendix is an updated rewrite of my now antiquated article, "New Religion Adherents: An Overview of Anglophone Census and Survey Data," which originally appeared a decade ago in the *Marburg Journal of Religious Studies* (2004).

Finally, one should note that all original human subject research reported in this book adheres to the guidelines drawn up by the Norwegian National Committee for Research Ethics in the Social Sciences and the Humanities (http://www.etikkom.no/).

Introduction –
Are Meaningful Generalizations about New Religious Movement Members Still Possible?

Back in the 1980s when I was a graduate student at Syracuse University, I had a conversation with a handful of other people at a regional American Academy of Religion (AAR) meeting that – like few other such conversations – managed to leave a residue in my memory. I have forgotten the precise context, but at some point I mentioned the need for quantitative, demographic research on members of alternative religions. The response to this remark from my conversation partners was mild incredulity. They smirked, as I recall, though quite subtly. I also felt they would have ridiculed the idea, had doing so not violated the canons of academic civility. Their consensus was that this was a task for Sociologists, not for scholars of Religious Studies (the latter, it seemed, should be above such mundane methods as collecting numerical data). I was much younger then, and did not feel up to challenging their attitudes. Their opinions also seemed set in stone, like an eleventh commandment that would fail to budge under the force of merely-human reasoning.

This is not, of course, to imply that all, or even the majority, of religious studies specialists adhere to this kind of disciplinary chauvinism. But there does appear to be an aversion to quantitative methods among many members of the religion academy. One consequence of this situation is that, as I shall argue throughout this book, our demographic profile of members of New Religious Movements (NRMs) is woefully out of date. Additionally, technological changes that influence the socio-cultural environment such as the advent of the Internet have impacted how people become involved in NRMs. And while these changes have not entirely been ignored, older generalizations about the people who join alternative religions persist into the present.

In part because I hope that many of the readers of this book will be people from Religious Studies backgrounds, I have intentionally kept the statistics I utilize here at a basic level. Among other things, I want to drive home the point that one does not need to have a sophisticated mathematical background in order to gather meaningful quantitative data, especially demographic data about NRM participants. Hopefully, the analyses in the following pages will encourage future researchers to collect the data necessary to bring New Religion studies back into attunement with the reality on the ground.

The Fundamental Problem

The solid data that NRM researchers have gathered in recent years on the size and composition of such groups is surprisingly meager, given that many hundreds of studies of new religions have been published every year for the past 20–25 years. NRM research is currently overwhelmingly based on analyses of texts (in the ordinary language sense of "text") and fieldwork, involving the gathering of comparatively little measurable data over the last several decades. Hence, as a field, the study of new religious movements now has a significantly inadequate quantitative empirical base.

Some of the problems with studies of NRM participants have been recognized within the field. For example, it has been generally acknowledged that the empirical research that has been conducted to date is clustered around a couple dozen of the most controversial groups. A more comprehensive approach that examined the many groups not locked in social conflict would likely provide a much different picture of the nature of these movements. Another problem is the lack of longitudinal studies. Yet another issue is the question of where to draw the line between religious groups that are NRMs and groups that are not. Though these problems are widely recognized, relatively few researchers have been prompted to address them in a systematic manner.

Another, less-frequently recognized issue with extant studies of NRMs is that our theoretical formulations and other generalizations are often based on unexamined assumptions, such as the assumption that, in terms of their demographic characteristics, the majority of alternative religious groups are more or less the same. Depending on which characteristic is being generalized, this assumption is often problematic – especially given the widely varying appeal and organizational structure of different NRMs.

Finally, the field has been criticized for its relative insularity. Thus, for example, several articles that have appeared in recent years have discussed the absence of dialogue between new religious movement researchers who study violent NRMs and terrorism researchers (e.g., Oleson and Richardson 2007). Additionally, in his book *Social Theory and Religion*, the prominent sociologist of religion James A. Beckford has called attention to the general problem of the NRM field's lack of integration into the larger discipline, pointing out that "students of religious movements have made highly selective use of social theories and have made relatively few attempts systematically to relate their empirical investigations to social theories" (Beckford 2003: 192).

However, there is a more fundamental problem with our generalizations about participants in new religions, namely that they are derived predominantly from research on NRM members that was conducted over a quarter of a century ago. These conclusions have in turn been projected onto later groups on the basis of the implicit assumption that members of most new religions are more or less the same, and the unconscious assumption that the social context of current NRMs is not substantially different from what it was three or four decades ago.

Current misperceptions about new religion participants derive from three processes:

1. New Religions specialists rarely voice concern over the lack of up-to-date quantitative data. This is in large part the result of changes within the NRM field itself. In the 1970s, alternative religions were studied primarily by sociologists who published in sociology of religion journals – journals that tended to feature papers with a quantitative emphasis. As the field developed, new researchers attracted to the study of NRMs were increasingly from religious studies rather than from social science backgrounds. Thus *Nova Religio*, a specialist journal in the field that began publication in 1997, was founded by researchers who were not predominantly social scientists. The consequences of this shift are evident in this journal's articles. Thus, for example, in 2010 and 2011, *Nova Religio* published only one article out of 39 with a quantitative dimension (Siegler 2010). And while fewer and fewer specialists have been engaged in this kind of empirical work, a new generation of NRM researchers has emerged that tends to rely upon quantitative generalizations established in the 1970s and 1980s.
2. As the field of NRM studies changed, so did conditions in the larger society. New religions initially attracted the attention of researchers when large numbers of former participants in the counter-culture of the 1960s began joining alternative religions in the 1970s. So at the time social scientists began studying them, the vast majority of NRM members fit the demographic profile of youthful counter-culturists. The characteristics of this generation then became the basis for generalizations about all members of alternative religions. However, over the years conditions changed so that the profile of

the typical participant has also diversified. Thus, for example, current members of – as well as recent converts to – new religions are, for the most part, no longer youthful (Barker 2010). Furthermore, the membership profiles of different new religions now tend to differ from each another, rather than being cut from the same cloth (as they were in the 1970s). For the most part, these changes have been missed because of the decline of quantitative studies in the field of new religious movements.

3. Finally, NRM researchers have noted that the Internet has changed the alternative religion environment (Cowan and Dawson 2004), particularly for decentralized movements like contemporary Paganism (Cowan 2004). Researchers have also called attention to more recent new religions that originated on the Internet and that continue to be Internet-based (e.g., Cusack 2010; Krogh and Pillifant 2004). However, they have generally failed to see how NRMs that are heavily Internet-oriented no long fit certain older, taken-for-granted generalizations, such as the conventional wisdom about conversion taking place primarily via social networks (Snow, Zurcher and Ekland-Olson 1980; Snow and Machalek 1984). The Internet has also fueled the growth of decentralized movements such as "religious" Satanism (Lewis 2011) and (neo)Paganism (Lewis 2007). In the case of Paganism, the dominant manner in which adherents interact with one another has changed from small face-to-face meetings to solitaries who interact with co-religionists primarily via the Internet (Lewis 2012a).

The first point of this three-pronged analysis has not (to the best of my knowledge) explicitly been recognized within NRM studies. With respect to the second point, a few recent papers have called attention to the aging of NRM members (e.g., Barker 2010; Bromley 2009), but the notion that new religions still *recruit* predominantly younger members continues to be presented as state of the art in major publications. Thus, for example, in the most recent edition of his textbook, *Comprehending Cults*, Lorne Dawson explains that, "[M]ost people convert to new religions when they are young, relatively free of other social obligations, and interested in experimenting with lifestyle options and alternative identities" (2006: 84). Another consideration is that almost everyone who has studied conversion to NRMs bases "their approaches, models, and conclusions on research among people under thirty" (Gooren 2010: 42). As a consequence, their studies explicitly or implicitly lend support to a model of conversion that highlights the youthfulness of recruits.

Survey of Contents

Chapters One and Two challenge two different generalizations about conversion to NRMs using a type of quasi-longitudinal method (projecting backward from current data) in both chapters. The youth-crisis model of conversion posited that new recruits were predominantly young people whose involvement could be explained as a function of their youth (e.g., as an adolescent developmental crisis). The first chapter presents statistics on recruits to seven different contemporary new religions that fundamentally challenge this item of conventional wisdom. Six out of seven data sets also embody a striking pattern of gradually increasing age across time for new converts.

One of the other standard generalizations about new religions is that people convert to NRMs primarily through preexisting social networks. In the second chapter, I examine data on a variety of new religions which demonstrate that social networks are not always the dominant point of first contact for new converts. Additionally, recruitment patterns change over time so that different factors become dominant at different points in a movement's development. Two reasons why this variability has escaped the attention of most researchers is an unconscious tendency to assume, as I have already noted, that the sociological profiles of members of different NRMs are essentially similar, plus the fact that such groups are typically studied synchronically rather than diachronically.

In the third chapter, I underline the point about the greater diversity of members of new religions by examining data from the New Zealand and Australian censuses – both of which, in contrast to Canada and the United Kingdom, hold censuses every five years instead of every ten years – though I will also periodically refer to census data from the latter two nations. Not only has the earlier profile of members of non-traditional religions reached in the 1970s and 1980s been superseded, but, further, it has become increasingly difficult to discuss NRM members "in general," as a class demographically distinct from members of other religious organizations.

In Chapters Four and Five, I examine data that I and others gathered on members of two NRMs, the Movement of Spiritual Inner Awareness (MSIA) and the Order of Christ Sophia (OCS). These two groups provide contrasting examples of longitudinal approaches, and in these two chapters findings from surveys are presented and discussed in terms of the parameters laid out by Lorne Dawson in his 1996 summary of NRM conversion research, "Who Joins New Religions and Why: Twenty Years of Research and What Have We Learned?" (later republished as a chapter in his 2003 reader, *Cults and New Religions*, and in his 2006 textbook, *Comprehending Cults*).

In 2005, 2008 and 2011, demographic questionnaires were administered to the membership of the Order of Christ Sophia, a "New Age" Christian group in the Holy Order of MANS tradition. In addition to analyzing the changes that have taken place in the Order between 2005 and 2011, the research project is presented as a paradigm for conducting longitudinal studies of other new religious movements in the future.

The Movement of Spiritual Inner Awareness is a medium-sized New Religion that can roughly be described as a blend of Sant Mat (Radhasoami) and "New Age" teachings. In 1998, a sample of 566 movement participants responded to a demographic survey administered by a colleague. Then again in late 2011, I administered a much longer, online questionnaire to MSIA's active North American membership, eventually gathering 531 respondents. Chapter Five compares the profiles derived from these two surveys. Though in many ways the average participant remained essentially the same between 1998 and 2011, in the intervening 13 years the membership excelled in terms of the classic indicators of achievement – education, income and professional achievement.

Two large, decentralized spiritual movements that show up in every census report are modern Paganism (in the sense of modern Neopaganism) and Satanism. Scientology also finds a place in all national census reports. I have made observations about all three of these movements that I subsequently modified as I was able to obtain a fuller statistical picture, especially via comparisons of census and survey data. The third section of the book examines each of these movements in turn.

Paganism's rapid growth was big news during the first decade of the new millennium. At the time, I wrote a piece on the "Pagan Explosion" that examined this growth through the lens of census data. By the end of the decade, however, it was clear that this rapid expansion had fallen off, and the movement appeared to have returned to something approaching a normal pattern of growth. What actually happened was that shortly after the turn of the millennium, the Teen Witch fad temporarily inflated total numbers of self-identified Pagans. After the fad ended, explosive growth also ended. In this chapter, I analyze what transpired via a juxtaposition of survey data and more recent census data.

With the exception of a certain subgenre of professional literature that focuses on the "problem" of adolescent Satanism, there have been no systematic analyses of how people become Satanists. Chapter Seven brings data from questionnaire research to bear on this issue, and draws on discussions of conversion to other alternative religions – particularly to contemporary Paganism – as lenses through which to interpret conversion to Satanism. The chapter's conclusion also raises the question of whether declaring oneself to be a member of an anarchistic Internet religion should properly be considered "conversion" or whether it would be more appropriate to regard the adoption of the label "Satanist" as being a form of identity construction.

As recently as the censuses that took place in 2006, Scientology seemed to be growing in all four of the Anglophone countries that record memberships in alternative religions. I initially analyzed this growth in a piece that appeared in 2009. However, more recent data from the Australian census and from the American Religious Identification Survey indicate a downturn in Scientology's growth while other, comparable movements continue to grow. Why? Additionally, why should more men than women join Scientology while almost every other religious group imaginable recruits more women than men?

One focus of this book is on overturning the conventional wisdom about the demographic profiles of current NRM members. In Chapters nine and ten, I turn my attention to the post-involvement attitudes and other characteristics of former NRM members which fly in the face of accepted stereotypes. My earliest quantitative work involved questionnaire research on former members of controversial New Religions. In a series of papers published in the 1980s, I contrasted the attitudes of ex-members and found a high correlation between negative, cult-stereotypical attitudes and exposure to anti-cult socialization. As part of later studies, I gathered more limited data from ex-members of MSIA and OCS, finding, in general, positive attitudes toward their former group. This later phenomenon is explainable, in part, by the ethic of seekership found in the West's alternative spiritual subculture. In the Afterword, I summarize and discuss the larger implications of this research. What should be done in the future, and to what extent do the studies in this book provide paradigms for future research?

Part I

Quasi-longitudinal Approaches

1 Whatever Happened to Youthful Converts?

Sometimes it makes the most sense to present an analysis in terms of a narrative about how one's own understanding has evolved and changed. With respect to the conventional wisdom about the youthfulness of religious converts, I have been both observer and subject. For these and other reasons, it seemed natural to work my way into this topic via an account of my ongoing experiences, research and reflections. I began questioning this item of conventional wisdom seven or eight years ago, and developed components of the critique presented here in the context of several other discussions. Thus, at certain junctures in the following discussion, I will be repeating points made in earlier publications.

The analysis undertaken in this chapter is, in a certain sense, a discovery narrative. It is also a story about how quickly our generalizations become coagulated and outdated. Some might even say that it is a narrative about the pitfalls of armchair research, about speculative generalizations made in a field of study that lacks a broad foundation of quantitative empirical studies. Additionally, it is a tale with a moral, namely that we are living in a world that is changing so quickly that what might have been true in one decade can be overturned in the next – and that if we blink, we can miss the fact that the situation on the ground has changed in fundamental ways.

To avoid possible misunderstandings, let me preface my analysis by emphasizing that in the following discussion I will *not* primarily be arguing *for* any particular interpretation of the data. Rather, the focus is on arguing *against* one of the more commonly accepted items of conventional wisdom in the field of new religious movements (NRMs).[1] Though a correlation between converts' ages and the time periods during which they joined will be described and discussed, no attempt will be made to systematically explain this correlation.

---

1. Like the parent term "religion," "new religions" or "new religious movements" are difficult if not impossible to define. For an analysis of this expression, refer to my discussion in "New Religious Movements" (Lewis, forthcoming).

The Youth-Crisis Model of Conversion

Raised on the central west coast of Florida, I was the oldest child in a reasonably typical middle-class family. After finishing community college and switching majors several times, I went on to pursue a Philosophy degree at the University of South Florida (USF). Through a complicated process I shall not recount here, I dropped out of USF and moved from Tampa to Orlando to live in a semi-communal residential and yoga teaching center as part of Yogi Bhajan's Healthy, Happy, Holy Organization (3HO). This group has received a moderate amount of attention from scholars, some of it quite recent (e.g., Tobey 1976; Khalsa 1986; Dusenbery 1988; Elsberg 2003; Laue 2007; Jakobsh 2008; Lewis 2010b). After a year in Orlando, I was sent to Tallahassee to start an ashram there. In my capacity as a local 3HO leader, I organized a small community that, at its height, included 18 people living together in a single large house, plus a larger number of informally affiliated participants in the Tallahassee, Florida, area. Through a gradual process (that I recount in Lewis 2010b), I became disaffected from 3HO after a three-year membership period. I was in my early 20s at the time.

I went back to school several years after leaving 3HO, eventually specializing in the study of new religious movements. I was attracted to this specialty in large part because of my personal background as a former member of a new religion. Some of the key generalizations about conversion I learned were formulated in the context of that particular time period. Specifically, there had been an explosion of alternative spirituality in and around the early 1970s that drew its membership out of the declining counter-culture of the late 1960s. As a consequence, this cohort of new spiritual seekers was constituted by people who were predominantly adolescents and young adults, and a number of the characteristics that came to be generally attributed to NRM recruits reflected traits of youthful converts during this era. Thus, to take two prominent examples, people who join new religions are said to have (1) fewer social ties and (2) fewer ideological alignments than non-joiners. (Dawson 2006: 78–80) These traits are far more characteristic of adolescents and young adults than of the population in general.

A standard approach to NRM conversion that built upon the youthfulness of recruits during that period was the so-called youth-crisis model (YCM). The youth-crisis model of conversion to NRMs was explicitly articulated as a developmental issue in J. Gordon Melton and Roger L. Moore's *The Cult Experience: Responding to the New Religious Pluralism* (1982) and in Saul V. Levine's *Radical Departures: Desperate Detours to Growing Up* (1983). The simple hypothesis of this model was that most recruits to non-traditional religions were young because conversion to such religions represented a way of dealing with the crisis of maturation: one had left home, but was not yet completely ready to be on one's own. As a consequence, one became attracted to an intensive religious group that provided the recruit with, in effect, a new family. Levine's research found that the average convert was between 16 and 26 years of age, that s/he stayed in a NRM for two years, and then left voluntarily.

Levine, a psychiatrist, asserted that such conversions "are desperate attempts to grow up in a society that places obstacles in the way of the normal yearnings of youth" (1983: 11). Further, "Virtually all joiners eventually leave their groups" and "they are able to use their radical departure in the service of growing up" (1983: 13). In contrast to Levine's approach, most researchers who study new religions are sociologists who proffer sociological rather than psychological explanations. Thus, for example, in the first edition of his popular textbook, *Comprehending Cults*, Lorne Dawson observes that, "Part of the reason for the disproportionate representation of adolescents and young adults in NRMs is simply that this segment of the population is relatively free of other social and economic commitments. They have the time and the opportunity to indulge their spiritual appetites and to experiment with alternative ways of living"[2] (1998: 81).

This is not to assert that all or even the majority of contemporary theorists posit youthfulness as the key factor in understanding conversion. Clearly this is not the case (refer, e.g., to surveys of conversion theories in Gooren 2010; Bromley 2006; and Lamb & Bryant 1999). However, whether psychologically or sociologically oriented, almost everyone who has studied conversion to NRMs bases "their approaches, models, and conclusions on research among people under thirty" (Gooren 2010: 42). As a consequence, their studies explicitly or implicitly lend support to the notion that such recruits are generally youthful.[3] In part for the sake of convenience, throughout the balance of this chapter I will utilize the designation 'youth-crisis model' as a general label for all approaches to conversion that highlight the youthfulness of recruits, whether or not a given approach posits a developmental crisis as providing the interpretive key for understanding conversion.

---

2. Though it should be obvious, let me be clear that in this and other chapters I am utilizing Lorne Dawson's summary of NRM conversion studies merely as a point of reference for my analysis. I am not criticizing Dawson's work *per se*.

3. Thus, for instance, I have seen Eileen Barker's influential study of youthful converts to the Unification Church (Barker 1984) cited in support of the youth-crisis model – despite the fact that Barker herself does not put forward an explanation in terms of stages of psychological development.

At the time it appeared, *Radical Departures* was a controversial book because it undermined the stereotype of "brainwashing cults." And, though there were things I disagreed with in Levine's analysis, I had to admit that I fell into the same general age range as Levine's subjects and that I was a member of 3HO for approximately the right period of time to fit the pattern. I was also a critic of the notion of "cult mind control," so I welcomed Levine's scholarship for the support it provided (i.e., if joining a new religion is the result of a developmental crisis, it leaves little room for "brainwashing" modes of explanation – as Levine himself makes clear).

Though few other researchers were willing to reduce conversion to a developmental crisis, Levine's more general observation that "radical departures" (his expression for sudden conversions to NRMs and related movements) were, "with few exceptions, a phenomenon of late adolescence and early adulthood" (1983: 28) expressed a consensus view, both inside and outside of NRM studies. Moreover, the notion that converts tend to be predominately youthful continues to be generally accepted. To cite just a few recent examples: in the latest edition of his new religions textbook, *Comprehending Cults,* Dawson observes that converts to new religions are "disproportionately young" (Dawson 2006: 83). Similarly, in *Religious Conversion and Disaffiliation*, a volume that addresses both NRM and non-NRM conversion, Gooren concludes that, "Contemporary conversion in the United States, Western Europe, and Latin America still happens mostly during adolescence and young adulthood" (2010: 135). And finally, in a study of the religious lives of adolescents, Smith, Denton, Faris and Regnerus note that "Adolescence and young adulthood is…the life stage when religious conversion is most likely to take place" (Smith et al. 2002: 597).

Because of the paucity of quantitative data collected in more recent decades, researchers have been compelled to speculate about the demographic profiles of contemporary NRMs. These projections sometimes note that although the ages of participants have risen, the average age of NRM members remains low because of high turnover – meaning that (1) older members tend to drop out, and implying that (2) new recruits continue to be young. Thus, for example, in her classic study of the Unification Church, Eileen Barker observed that, though the average age of the membership has risen, "it does not rise by nearly as much as a year each twelve-month [period], since there is a high turn-over rate and the new recruits continue to be mainly in their early twenties" (1984: 206). More recently, Lorne Dawson has similarly noted that, with respect to the ongoing youthfulness of converts to New Religions:

> As some of the NRMs of the 1960s have aged, these figures have shifted. But many people drop out of these organizations by the

time they are middle aged. This is especially true of NRMs that are more communal in structure and more exclusive in their commitments. The demands they make on members often conflict with the demands of family life and raising children (Dawson 2003).[4]

For the greater part of my academic career, I had no particular reason to doubt the continuing relevance of the youth-crisis approach. In the early 1990s, I collected basic demographic data on members of the Movement of Spiritual Inner Awareness (MSIA), but did not seek to determine at what ages they had joined (Lewis 1997). Most of the participants with whom I interacted over the course of that study were older, but they had been involved for decades – and had presumably joined in their youth – so I saw no reason to raise questions about the YCM. Also, in 2000 and 2001, I collected demographic data on Satanists (Lewis 2001a). Because so many of the people who self-identify as Satanists are adolescents and young adults, this seemed to confirm rather than to challenge the ongoing validity of the youth-crisis model. It was not until 2005, when I began to study the Order of Christ Sophia that I first questioned the general applicability of this model.

The Order of Christ Sophia[5]

As I discuss in more detail in Chapter Four, I collected data on the membership of the Order of Christ Sophia (OCS) in 2005, 2008 and 2011. Though some of the Order data supported generally-accepted conclusions that researchers had drawn from earlier studies of new religious movements, on certain points the data called into question prior generalizations, including the youth-crisis model. The average age of the 2005 sample was 40, while the 2008 average was 42 years. In 2005, the average length of membership was two-and-a-half years; by 2008, this had increased to four years. In both cases, this meant the average age at recruitment was approximately 37 years old. This finding sharply contrasted with the conventional wisdom

---

4. In more recent papers, Barker has called attention to the ageing of NRMs (e.g., Barker 2010). I should also note that, in this same passage, Dawson goes on to speculate that, "There is some reason to believe that the new religions that are more segmented and plural in their commitment expectations (like Scientology, Eckankar, Nichiren Shoshu, etc.,) will maintain a better spread in the age distribution of their members as the groups grow older" (Dawson 2003).
5. The information in this section essentially repeats the initial discussion found in Chapter Three of my and Nicholas Levine's *Children of Jesus and Mary* (2010), to which readers are referred for more information.

about youthful converts to NRMs. For example, in her study of the Unification Church, Barker found the average age at which people joined was 23 years old (1984: 206). Similarly, Burke Rochford found that more than 50% of the members of the Hare Krishna Movement had joined before their 21st birthdays (1985: 47).

I suspected that the 40/42-years-old figure might be somewhat deceptive. My impression had been that the Order of Christ Sophia was a blend of baby boomers and a younger (relatively speaking) set of seekers. If this informal observation was accurate, I reasoned that 40/42 represented a median figure between two different age groupings. When the age data was broken down into five-year intervals, the findings from both the 2005 and the 2008 questionnaires did, in fact, reveal two groups instead of a single bell curve – though the contrast between the two groups was statistically much less dramatic than anticipated.

The slight statistical spike I found in the early 1950s/late 1940s can, in fact, be explained as a function of a handful of members who were baby boomers. In contrast, the data for members born in the 1960s, 1970s and early 1980s could not really be called a "spike." Instead, what was striking about this group of members was the relatively even distribution of birth years across two-and-a-half decades (refer to Tables 4.1a–c in Chapter Four). Also, this younger group was not really "young" compared with the youthfulness of recruits reported in earlier studies of the Unification Church and the Hare Krishna Movement. Their average age worked out to be the mid-30s, meaning the mean age at which they affiliated was in their early 30s. These figures stand in sharp contrast to the age profile of the original Holy Order of MANS (the predecessor group to the Order of Christ Sophia), which drew its recruits almost exclusively from counter-cultural youth (Lucas 1995).

Retrospectively, I now realize that one of the factors that made the older ages of recruits stand out to me was the youthfulness of the organization. The Order had been founded in 1999, meaning I had started to study the group only six years after it began. Perhaps had the Order of Christ Sophia been around since the 1970s like the Movement of Spiritual Inner Awareness, I would not have noticed the age issue.

Paganism

In 2009, I teamed up with Helen Berger to undertake a follow-up to her first survey of contemporary (neo) Pagans that was conducted in 1993–95, and later published as *Voices from the Pagan Census* (2003). She had named the first survey as the Pagan Census, so the second was designated as the Pagan Census Revisited (PCR). Berger took the lead, both in designing and distributing the PCR. The questionnaire was quite lengthy, containing a total of 82 items that collected a wide variety of demographic and attitudinal data. It was posted online via Survey Monkey, an online questionnaire hosting service. We had a large sample, so I decided to determine the ages at which respondents began self-identifying as Pagans. (The relevant question was, "How long have you been a practicing Pagan?")

The PCR was open from 5 September 2009 to 15 October 2010, and received more than 8000 responses. By midnight 31 December 2009, there had been 6000+ responses. Because of the different ways in which we had worded the age and affiliation questions, restricting the sample to respondents from one year or the other made calculations significantly easier. The figures in Table 1.1 are for 2009.

Table 1.1 Ages at Which People Become "Practicing Pagans"[6]
[From the 2009 Pagan Census Revisited]

5-yr periods	Mean Age	No.*
2005–2009	30.51	1049
2000–2004	27.35	1235
1995–99	24.32	1339
1990–94	23.06	917
1985–89	21.97	773
1980–84	19.85	484
1975–79	18.27	301

[*No. = Number of Respondents per Five-year Period.]

Though I had expected something like this pattern, I was surprised to find a near perfect correlation between time period and age. Observers other than myself have noted that the characterization of NRM *members* as youthful is no longer applicable (e.g., Bromley 2009; Barker 2010), but no one thus far seems to have straightforwardly rejected the generalization that alternative religions continue to recruit youthful *converts*. Furthermore, to the best

---

6. In all of the tables in this chapter, I have not included supplementary figures for median age, standard deviation and the like – which I find sometimes clutter rather than clarify. The correlations between age and time period in Tables 1.1, 1.2, 1.3, 1.4, and 1.5 were all statistically significant ($p < 0.05$). For more details on the PCR, refer to Helen Berger's recent conference papers (2010a, 2010b, 2011).

of my knowledge, no one has called attention to the incremental increase in mean age of converts across time. I will refer to this steady increase in age across time as the *Eve correlation*, or, more simply, as the E-correlation. A relationship like this one between age and time period is obviously self-limiting, but I have yet to see a set of data indicating a fading of this correlation in recent years.

In addition to the E-correlation, the data also described a bell curve in terms of rate of growth. Numbers of new Pagans grew during each five-year period, and then began falling off by 2000–2004.[7] Whatever the causal factors might have been, the growth of Paganism had slowed early in the new millennium. This decline is confirmed by data from the 2006 Australian Census, the 2006 New Zealand Census, and the 2008 American Religious Identification Survey (ARIS). This decreasing rate of growth is perhaps best captured by Australian and New Zealand Census figures, which reflect the slowing rate of expansion between 2001 and 2006, in contrast to the markedly higher rate of growth between 1996 and 2001 (in this regard, refer to Tables 6.3 and 6.5 in Chapter Six).

I also wondered if recent Pagans were, like Order of Christ Sophia recruits, composed of two cohorts, namely a set of baby boomers plus a younger group. However, examining the birth years for people who most recently became practicing Pagans, I found a remarkably even age spread from younger to older (refer to Table 6.7 in Chapter Six).

Adidam

Thus far, I have focused on elaborating the E-correlation among people who become self-identified Pagans. In order to make a statement about NRMs

---

7. In my "Pagan Explosion" chapter in Hannah Johnston's and Peg Aloi's *The New Generation Witches: Teenage Witchcraft in Contemporary Culture* (2007), I presented survey data from the United States and census data from four other Anglophone countries which indicated that Paganism experienced explosive growth around the turn of the millennium. I attributed this rapid expansion to two factors: the advent of the Internet and the "Teen Witch" fad. I more recently concluded that I was mistaken about the latter because, as indicated by the PCR data, the mean age of new Pagans did not drop during the last decade. However, based on an examination of relevant statistics from the New Zealand census (Lewis and Bauman 2011: 191–93), it appears instead that my mistake was in assuming that the majority of these youthful converts would stick with Paganism after they matured. I discuss this at length in Chapter Six.

more generally, it is obviously necessary to demonstrate that this pattern can be extended to other new religions.

In connection with a larger research project on Adidam – a spiritual group devoted to the teachings of American-born adept and founder, Adi Da Samraj – I have been collecting demographic and attitudinal data on Adidam members. I adapted some of the items from the PCR questionnaire, dropped others, and added a selection of new items specific to this group. The resulting questionnaire ended up containing 69 items. It was posted on Survey Monkey in mid-Spring of 2011 and garnered responses until the end of the year. The pattern of the data on Adidam recruits reflects the E-correlation quite clearly (refer to Table 1.2).

Table 1.2 Ages of Adidam Recruits

5-yr period	Mean Age	No.
2005–Present	49.27	15
2000–2004	**37.35**	**20**
1995–1999	39.27	22
1990–1994	35.69	26
1985–1989	35.13	32
1980–1984	32.81	33
1975–1979	28.11	27
1970–1974	26.90	10

The one outlier is the average age for 2000–2004, which I have marked in bold. It is possible that this break in pattern would disappear with a larger sample. In contrast with the Pagan data, Adidam's mean recruitment age per five-year period is substantially higher, but not high enough to be in the baby-boomer range. Despite this difference, the same overall pattern of increasing age across time holds.[8]

---

8. As I have already indicated, one of the generally-recognized problems among NRM researchers is the lack of longitudinal studies. The backwards projection of the ages of current members is, at best, a quasi-longitudinal approach that I am utilizing in the absence of data from earlier periods. (For further discussion of this approach, refer to footnote 10). If, several decades ago, someone had collected data from a sample of Adidam adherents and then calculated the average age at which they joined/started self-identifying as participants, then we would have a much more adequate basis from which to draw conclusions about changes in recruitment age. Specifically, having stats from an earlier period would have addressed the problem of the ages of participants who died or disaffiliated over the course of those decades.

One characteristic of Adidam that sets it apart from a group like the Order of Christ Sophia is that Adidam has been around (under a succession of different names) since the early 1970s. This allows one to examine the group's recruitment history across four decades. A far smaller group than contemporary Paganism, at present the sample size is modest – about 185 respondents – though this is a reasonably good sample, given that it represents 20%–25% of the total core membership of Adidam.

Hare Krishna Movement

After finding comparable patterns in these two quite different groups – a decentralized, anarchistic movement and a structured, guru-centered organization – I hypothesized that it should be possible to find the same or similar patterns in yet other new religions. I subsequently contacted certain NRM scholars I knew who had carried out demographic research on specific alternative religions.

Burke Rochford at Middlebury College was one of the first people to respond. He noted that in his 1995–96 Prabhupada Centennial Survey he had asked two questions that would allow one to calculate the age at which they joined. (For details on the Prabhupada Centennial Survey, refer to Rochford 2007). Rochford then very generously calculated the ages-at-recruitment of Western devotees (Tables 1.3a and 1.3b).

The period from 1984 to 1989, which I have indicated in bold typeface, constitutes an outlier in both the international and the American table. Nevertheless, the E-correlation is still evident in both sets of figures. When

---

Along these lines, in a Question & Answer session following a public presentation of an earlier version of this chapter, Mark Chaves raised the issue of a hypothetical 70 year-old who joined the Pagan movement decades ago. This hypothetical Pagan would likely have made his transition to the Summerland long before the time of the PCR. And, if a significant percentage of early converts to Paganism had been crones and aged wizards who had already passed on, this could indicate that the E-correlation was little more than a mathematical artifact arising from my quasi-longitudinal approach. Though I agree that this is a serious consideration, I also think that it is significantly less problematic for the NRMs that originated in and around the heyday of the counterculture. These groups generally *did* recruit youthful members in the 1960s and 1970s, likely making the impact of older deceased NRM converts statistically insignificant. Additionally, this consideration has no bearing whatsoever on my findings about the higher average ages of recent recruits, which is the core consideration in my critique of the youth-crisis model of conversion.

Table 1.3a Ages of Recruits to ISKCON International*

5-yr period	Mean	No.
1990–1995	24.22	539
1984–1989	**24.74**	**312**
1978–1983	23.54	225
1972–1977	21.89	229
1966–1971	20.09	109

Table 1.3b Ages of Recruits to ISKCON North America*

5-yr period	Mean	No.
1990–1995	25.96	57
1984–1989	**26.22**	**46**
1978–1983	23.69	75
1972–1977	21.87	133
1966–1971	20.00	73

[*ISKCON is an acronym for the International Society for Krishna Consciousness. Tables exclude Indian members, those born within ISKCON, and children under 13 years at the time of ISKCON membership (the latter were children who joined ISKCON with their parents)]

Rochford sent me his calculations, he offered the following explanatory information:

1. The International Society for Krishna Consciousness (ISKCON) during its early days may differ from some of the other groups you are looking at. It was communal and involved a transformation in lifestyle for those joining ISKCON. Not surprisingly this appealed to young unattached people without family obligations, etc.
2. As ISKCON changed, structurally becoming less communal and more open to the outside (early 1980s), it also became more appealing to somewhat older people who didn't have to forsake jobs etc., to become ISKCON members. In time these less committed people also came to be accepted as "legitimate" members.
3. In the early days, as I have written in various places, family was denigrated by the renunciate leaders and hence those with families who tended to be a bit older found it difficult to seriously consider ISKCON membership. This too changed beginning in the mid-1980s. Today the nuclear family is the foundation of ISKCON's social organization. The temple and ISKCON community are less

important to Western ISKCON members (and more important to Indian congregational members). Many of the latter worship at home or with other devotee families who live nearby.

4   Age may also be related to how people were recruited into ISKCON and the other NRMs you are considering. For example we know that social networks became more important to recruitment as ISKCON began opening up to the outside society (see *Hare Krishna in America*, [Rochford 1985]). While more data analysis is required, it is also the case, as these tables indicate, the age of new members in North America was increasing during the 1980s as the Hare Krishna Movement (HKM) was becoming more inclusive and "accepting" of the larger society.

5   ISKCON continues to recruit among the young (at Rainbow festivals, college campuses) though not all that successfully. I suspect many more people are taking up Krishna Consciousness because of devotees they meet at work or in other non-ISKCON related settings. (But of course it is the Indians where all the action is and they are considerably older and more established; refer to Rochford 2011).

As I was careful to note in the introduction to this chapter, my purpose here is not to offer a general explanation for what I am calling the E-correlation. While it is safe to say that the increasing age of converts is, in part, a function of the decline of the youth culture of the 1960s, this observation does not explain why – to take but a single contrast found in the data collected thus far – the average new Pagan is currently in her or his early 30s whereas the average new convert to Adidam is almost 50.

As I indicated earlier, one of the problems with the field of new religions is that we have too readily extrapolated findings from one or from a few NRMs to all NRMs. This tendency is based on an unconscious assumption that new religious movements – particularly converts to such groups – constitute a monolithic phenomenon. There are, of course, parallels and shared characteristics among different new religions and particularly among the memberships of such groups. But these generalizations need to be balanced with the kinds of specifics that Rochford provides for interpreting the ageing of converts to the Hare Krishna Movement.

Scientology

Peter B. Andersen at the University of Copenhagen was similarly generous with data that had been collected on members of the Church of Scientology

Table 1.4 Ages of Scientology Recruits

5-y period	Mean Age	No.
1996–1998	30.68	22
1991–1995	**25.70**	**63**
1986–1990	29.58	183
1981–1985	26.02	273
1976–1980	23.48	232
1971–1975	23.25	177
1966–1970	24.13	90
1961–1965	25.00	22

in Denmark.[9] Andreas Baumann, a graduate student in the Department for Cross-Cultural and Regional Studies at the University of Copenhagen, calculated the relevant figures (Table 1.4).

If we temporarily set aside the first two five-year periods, we once again get the E-correlation – though with yet another outlier, in this case during the 1991–1995 period.

The pattern of age decline in the first three periods of Table 1.4 – from 1961 to 1975 – is, I believe, a reflection of the impact of the 1960s youth culture on the ages of people interested in Scientology. If this hypothesis is correct, then the early 1970s represent a nadir point, when the average age of recruits stopped declining and began rising.

---

9. Calculated on the basis of data materials filed at the Dansk Data Arkiv: http://www.sa.dk/dda/
   DDA 01494: Scientology som identitet og institution: kernemedlemmer, 1986–1987, primary investigator Merethe Sundby-Sørensen.
   DDA 01605: Scientology som identitet og institution II: Opfølgning, 1991–1992, primary investigators Merethe Sundby-Sørensen and Jesper Demian Korsgaard.
   DDA 05680: Scientology som identitet III, 1999, primary investigator Peter B. Andersen.
   DDA 13095: Scientology som identitet I, II og III, 1986–1999.
   Andersen had earlier used this same data base for a piece he contributed to my edited volume on the Church of Scientology (Andersen and Wellendorf 2009). For a summary description of the series of surveys that were administered to members of the Church of Scientology in Denmark on file at the Dansk Data Arkiv, refer to Andersen and Wellendorf 2002; Andersen and Wellendorf 2009.

Movement of Spiritual Inner Awareness

In November and December of 2011, I administered an online questionnaire to members of the Movement of Spiritual Inner Awareness (MSIA). As mentioned earlier, I had researched this group in the mid-1990s (Lewis 1997). MSIA is a contemporary spiritual group founded by John-Roger Hinkins in 1971. Though MSIA is sometimes classified as "New Age," its sound current practices are closely related to practices found in the Indian Sant Mat tradition. (I discuss MSIA at greater length in Chapter Five).

In cooperation with the MSIA organization, I adapted some of the items from the Adidam questionnaire, dropped others, and added a selection of new items. The resulting instrument contained 76 items. By the 31st of December, 531 respondents had taken the online survey, with 519 answering the item about age at recruitment. Once again, the resulting pattern reflects the E-correlation quite strongly (Table 1.5).

Out of 2662 potential respondents who were contacted via MSIA, 531 respondents represent a response rate of 20%, which was quite good considering the intimidating lengthiness of the questionnaire.[10]

---

10. Because I administered a basic demographic survey to MSIA participants in 1995, I was able to make a simple test of the accuracy of my "quasi-longitudinal" (by which I mean projecting backwards in time from current data) approach that I use to represent the age-at-recruitment data for Paganism, Adidam, and MSIA. Examining the figures from the first MSIA questionnaire (deriving an approximation from the figures in Table 7.1 in Lewis 1997: 165), the average age of respondents to the original questionnaire was somewhat less than 48 in 1995 (estimated mean birth year: 1947.71). By comparison, the average age of the 346 respondents to the 2011 questionnaire who had *joined MSIA prior to 1996* was marginally less than 48 in 1995 (mean birth year: 1947.98) – quite close to the figure from the original sample. Similarly, the gender proportions in the data from the 1995 survey were 65% female to 35% male – quite close to the proportion among the 346 respondents from the 2011 survey who joined prior to 1996, which was 63% female to 37% male.

These few findings do not, of course, demonstrate that this approach to MSIA will be as accurate for other parameters beyond age and gender, nor do they decisively demonstrate that this level of accuracy can necessarily be extrapolated to similar approaches to Paganism or Adidam. The findings are, however, suggestive, and indicate that the methodology I am here terming *quasi-longitudinal* could be accurate enough to utilize in certain situations where longitudinal data in the proper sense is lacking. I apply the same approach to a different issue in the next chapter.

Finally, to avoid possible confusion, it should be noted that the designation "quasi-longitudinal" is generally applied to retrospective studies in which

1 *Whatever Happened to Youthful Converts?* 25

Table 1.5 Ages of MSIA Recruits

5-yr period	Mean Age	No.
2010–Present	45.48	23
2005–2009	41.21	56
2000–2004	40.93	55
1995–1999	35.72	46
1990–1994	35.45	49
1985–1989	34.35	79
1980–1984	30.79	80
1975–1979	26.80	59
1970–1975	23.55	55
Before 1970	25.07	15

Though the MSIA organization was not formally established until 1971, Hinkins began attracting people to his teachings as early as 1968 (Lewis 1997: 22), which is why 15 respondents were able to say that they had joined MSIA prior to 1970. In Table 1.6, this handful of respondents has been separated from the others because they represent a break in the E-correlation. I have intentionally situated this discussion of findings from the MSIA survey immediately following the Scientology section because this exception to the overall pattern of increasing age of recruits can be explained in the same way I interpreted the falling ages of Scientology converts between 1961 and 1975, namely the increasing impact of the 1960s youth culture on participants recruited between the 1960s and early 1970s.

It should finally be noted that the 2010–Present interval in Table 1.5 represents respondents who became involved only in the past two years. When this exception to the size of the Table's other intervals (which are 5-year periods) is taken into account, there appears to be a pattern of increasing numbers of participants beginning in 1995–1999. This growth cycle follows a period of declining numbers of new members that began in the early 1990s in the wake of negative media coverage of MSIA (Lewis 1997: 187–89).[11]

---

respondents are asked to supply information from memory (Hakim 2000: 120–23).

11. The data on the Hare Krishna Movement, which indicates even younger converts in the late 1960s, is an obvious exception to the pattern found in the Scientology data and the MSIA data. I had also anticipated finding older people converting to Paganism in the 1960s in the Pagan data. However, so many older respondents indicated that they became Pagans when they were born – a reflection of the popular notion that true Pagans are "born Pagans" rather than converts (especially as this notion was articulated in Adler 1979)

EnlightenNext

How much further beyond these five groups can the E-correlation be generalized? I hypothesize that this pattern holds in a majority of Western new religions that have their roots in and around the "NRM period" of the early 1970s and which drew their initial memberships from former counter-culturists. At this juncture, we are in a position to ask the further question of whether the E-correlation can be found in more recently-formed spiritual groups.

In his chapter on affiliation/disaffiliation in the first volume of Gallagher and Ashcraft's *Introduction to New and Alternative Religions in America*, David Bromley (2006), repeats the standard generalization about the youthfulness of NRM converts, though he relegates this characterization to the earliest stages of a new religion's development:

> Particularly given the high membership turnover rates that characterize most NRMs, successful recruitment means that the movements are populated by eager young recruits for much of their early history (2006: 44).

He then goes on to discuss the problems new religions encounter retaining their second generations. The issue of the age of newer (post-early history) *recruits* to established NRMs is never addressed, as if to imply that such movements no longer attract converts after the passing of their energetic initial phase. This is not, of course, Bromley's intention. But this way of dealing with the age of more recent NRM recruits by not mentioning them at all is not uncommon, given the lack of up-to-date data that would allow an observer to make informed comments on the current situation. The above statement also appears to imply that more recently-formed NRMs would – similar to their predecessors – attract "eager young recruits" in the initial stages of their development. However, as reflected in the higher mean ages of converts to spiritual groups that emerged subsequent to the 1970s, this is not the case.

EnlightenNext (EN) – formerly the Impersonal Enlightenment Fellowship; formerly the Moksha Foundation – is an alternative spiritual group founded by Andrew Cohen in the second half of the 1980s. In cooperation with this organization, participants responded to an online questionnaire similar to my earlier questionnaires during the spring and summer of 2012. The survey eventually received 130 responses. This constitutes a

---

– that my various attempts to measure the ages of pre-1970s recruits were frustrated. I should note that the portrayal of Paganism as being "a religion without converts" has been criticized by a number of scholars (e.g., Gallagher 1994; Berger and Ezzy 2007; Reid 2009).

1 *Whatever Happened to Youthful Converts?* 27

Table 1.6 Ages of EnlightenNext Recruits

5-yr period	Mean Age	No.
2008–2012	43.00	46
2003–2007	42.39	33
1998–2002	35.58	19
1993–1997	35.27	15
1992 & before	31.47	17

reasonably good sample, given that the active body of current EN students is in the 400–500 range. Breaking the age-at-affiliation data down into five 5-year periods gives us Table 1.6.

In this case, the sample is too small and the overall time period too short for the data to be statistically significant. However, placed alongside the earlier tables in this chapter, we can legitimately hypothesize that a parallel process is at work in the age-at-affiliation pattern of EnlightenNext participants.

I should finally mention that I tried to find the E-correlation in the data from the Order of Christ Sophia. The Order, which has been around for a bare dozen years, tends, as mentioned earlier, to attract older seekers. In addition to the two OCS surveys described above, I also once again administered an online questionnaire to the full membership in 2011 and received 154 responses. Though I was unable to find a significant E-correlation in the data, the average age at recruitment for the 37 respondents who had been involved for more than six years was 33 and-a-half, while the average at recruitment for the 111 respondents who had been involved for six or fewer years was slightly more than 39 years of age. So while the data is far from being statistically significant, it again seems to point in the same direction as the E-correlation.

To tentatively extrapolate from the OCS data and the EN data, it appears that alternative spiritual groups founded in the 1980s and 1990s did *not* begin by attracting primarily younger members. Rather, both of these movements – and, by implication, other groups founded in the decades following the 1970s – began by attracting mature participants in their 30s. Thus, with the exception of certain true youth religions such as Internet Satanism, conversion to the more recently formed "new new religions"[12] cannot be explained as a function of the youthfulness of recruits.

---

12. I am here adapting an expression coined by the Japanese sociologist of religion Nishiyama Shigeru (Hardacre 1999: 273, note 14). Japanese researchers originally referred to the new religions that arose in the wake of the Second World War as *shin shukyo* (literally, "new religions"). When a newer crop of such movements emerged in the 1970s, they came to be referred to as *shin shin shukyo* ("new new religions").

Discussion

The E-correlation is an observed relationship between the mean age of new converts to NRMs and the period of time subsequent to the beginning of what some have referred to as the *NRM period* (the 1970s). Specifically, the further one moves forward in time, then the older, on average, converts become. Though self-limiting, the E-correlation had not yet exhausted itself by the end of the first decade of the twenty-first century.

In the current study, this pattern was uncovered in membership data from five different new religions – six if one counts EnlightenNext. Data from a seventh group, the Order of Christ Sophia, also contributed to the analysis. I participated in designing the Pagan questionnaire, the MSIA questionnaire, the Adidam questionnaire and the EnlightenNext questionnaire, which were all administered online. Though one might raise issues with my approach or with the online method of delivery for these surveys, the other two data sets were collected by different researchers at different time periods via traditional pencil-and-paper questionnaires – with the same result. Though it would be possible to question a generalization based on only one or two of these data sets, taken together they add up to a compelling case for the robustness of the E-correlation.

How much further beyond these groups can we generalize this pattern? The single exception I have found thus far is the Art of Living Foundation. The initial data Inga Tøllefsen recently collected on the Art of Living Foundation (Tøllefsen 2012) indicates that over the past two decades the average age at which Norwegian participants began practicing AoLF's core technique has fairly consistently been around 36, whether they first became involved in the early 1990s or in 2011. With the possible exception of groups like Calvary Chapel which grew out of the Jesus Movement, I am also reasonably certain the E-correlation is not a factor in conversions to traditional Christian denominations. Finally, I doubt this pattern manifests in religious communities outside the Western world that did not experience the religious ferment of the late 1960s and 1970s.[13]

One of the intriguing aspects of the E-correlation is that, despite the commonality of this pattern, mean ages vary considerably from group to group. Thus, for example, the average age of new Pagans rose from 18 and-a-half

---

13. In the course of researching this chapter, I came across one study which found that native British converts to Islam became Muslims at an average age of 30 (29.7). The author did not say anything about changing conversion ages across time, but he did emphasize that such conversions were more likely to occur post-adolescence (Köse 1996).

in the period 1975–79 to 31 in recent years, whereas the age of new Adidam devotees rose from almost 26 in 1970–1974 to a current average of 49. The data also reflects a disparity between time periods during which recruitment peaked. For instance, the increasing rate of conversions to Paganism peaked during the period 1995–1999, whereas conversions to the Church of Scientology in Denmark peaked in 1981–1985. In contrast, after a period of decline, MSIA currently appears to be growing, as does EnlightenNext.

These variations make it difficult to put forward a single compelling explanation for the E-correlation that adequately covers all NRMs. One could develop different specific explanations for the rising ages of recruits to each group as Rochford did for ISKCON, but there is clearly also a more general socio-cultural process at work. The Scientology data and MSIA data were also useful for providing a nadir point which, if my hypothesis is correct, reflects the increasing impact of the counter-culture on the declining ages of converts during the 1960s. Ages of new recruits to Scientology and MSIA then rose in the later 1970s, presumably as a consequence of greater distance in time from the 1960s counter-culture. Though this correlation is clearly relevant, it fails to explain the widely varying age ranges among the different groups. So to fall back on the oft-repeated caveat of empirical researchers, "more research is needed."

While I am unable to offer a general explanation for the E-correlation beyond pointing out that it is clearly linked to the decline of the 1960s counter-culture, it is possible to derive certain corollaries from this pattern that profoundly undermine a number of established explanations of conversion to alternative religions. Specifically, we can reject the psychological notion that joining a contemporary new religion is primarily a response to an adolescent development crisis. Similarly, we can dismiss sociological efforts to explain NRM involvement in terms of young people's greater availability to experiment with alternative lifestyles because of their relative freedom from social and economic restraints. Indeed, with the exception of true youth religions such as Internet Satanism, any attempt to interpret conversions to contemporary new religions as being a function of the imputed youthfulness of recruits must be consigned to the ash heap of social-scientific history. These approaches may have been relevant 30 or 40 years ago, but clearly they can no longer function as comprehensive explanations for conversions to current alternative religions.

Conclusion

Though interesting, the E-correlation in itself is a transitory, self-limiting pattern. For the field of NRM studies more generally, the more significant finding of the present study is that the primary audience for most alternative religions has changed: not only is it no longer youthful, but it appears to be growing older with each passing decade. However, a more fundamental question is how the characterization of NRM recruits as adolescents and young adults was allowed to persist for decades in the face of the changing situation on the ground?[14] This brings us back around to the issue that was discussed in the Introduction and that will be discussed further in Chapter Three, namely that the empirical research conducted by the great majority of new religions specialists over the last few decades simply lacked substantive quantitative dimensions.[15] As has already been pointed out, if one peruses the pages of contemporary academic NRM journals, one rarely finds quantitative studies – a symptom of the general absence of quantitatively-oriented researchers in our field of study. Given this situation, it is thus actually not surprising that we missed an important development that could have been detected with a little basic survey research.

---

14. Following a public presentation of an earlier version of the data in this chapter, Jim Beckford commented that the literature on social movements had already addressed the ageing of participants in non-NRM social movements – hence what I had discovered in NRMs was neither new nor original. However, when I examined sample references he later sent (Jennings 1987; Byrne 1988; Mattausch 1989), I found that these authors discussed the *ageing of a particular cohort* of participants *already involved* in the Campaign for Nuclear Disarmament. In contrast, the present analysis focuses on the ages of *new converts* rather than on ageing NRM members who joined their respective groups back in the 1960s and 1970s.

    I have found Beckford's specific misinterpretation to be not uncommon. I had a similar misunderstanding with another colleague. After contacting a variety of different new religions researchers to see if anyone else was working on the same or on a similar project, the colleague in question emailed me back and assured me that, yes, a number of people had already written about the ageing of NRM members. He thoughtfully attached a manuscript copy of one of his publications to his emailed response, noting that he had dealt with this very issue in that particular piece. However, upon reading his file, I found nothing about the ageing of recent converts to new religions. Instead, I found a discussion of the ageing of NRM members who had joined their respective groups in their youth. Like the playing card experiment in which subjects perceive red spades as hearts and black hearts as spades, this line of enquiry is apparently so unanticipated that it gets mistakenly re-perceived in more familiar terms.

15. Part of the problem is that, currently, the majority of NRM researchers come from religious studies rather than from social science backgrounds, meaning that such researchers often lack training in quantitative approaches. For further discussion of this issue, refer to my discussion in the Introduction.

2   Social Networks and Conversion

In addition to youthfulness, another item of the conventional wisdom about converts is that individuals are recruited primarily (though not exclusively) through people they already know (e.g., Bibby and Brinkerhoff 1974; Dawson 2003; Snow and Machalek 1984; Snow, Zurcher and Ekland-Olson 1980). This is stated clearly in *Comprehending Cults*, where Lorne Dawson notes that "studies of conversion and case studies of specific groups have found that recruitment to NRMs happens primarily through preexisting social networks and interpersonal bonds. Friends recruit friends, family members each other and neighbours recruit neighbours"[1] (2006: 77). This widely-accepted tenet of new religion studies was originally established on basis of studies that were conducted over a quarter of a century ago. (See especially Snow, Zurcher and Ekland-Olson 1980 in this regard).

The present chapter presents statistics on the memberships of four different new religions that fundamentally challenge this generalization. Not only do some religious movements not recruit primarily through social networks, but also conversion patterns can change, so that social networks can be the primary initial contact point for recruits at one point in an organization's life, but later drop in importance to become a secondary factor.

Different Meanings of Social Networks in the Study of Conversion

Before examining the data, it is first necessary to clarify a certain ambiguity in the notion of social networks. Dawson's statement of the issue quoted in the opening paragraph of this chapter makes clear that the issue is about recruitment via *preexisting* social networks. However, in some of the literature on conversion networks, social networks that antedate conversion are collapsed into the social networks that developed only after recruits began to participate in the community life of the relevant new religion.

---

1. As I have already noted, I am utilizing Lorne Dawson's summary of NRM conversion studies merely as a point of reference for my analysis, and that I am not criticizing Dawson's work per se.

For example, in Rodney Stark and William Sims Bainbridge's "Networks of Faith" (1980), the first two case studies given to illustrate the role social networks play in recruitment to alternative religions are contrasting rather than convergent cases with respect to this specific point. The initial example they provided was a "Doomsday Group" that in the early 1960s took refuge in underground shelters in response to a prophesied nuclear holocaust. Three-quarters of the group constituted a kind of extended family clustered around the leadership (Hardyck and Braden 1962). Gradually, defectors began leaving, until the leader received a new revelation that God was merely testing the faithful. What the data showed was that followers with family ties to the leadership had the lowest rate of defection (only 14% left the shelters). Members who had family ties with the group's extended family but not directly with the leadership had a higher rate of defection (25%). And members with no family ties to the core kinship group had the highest rate of defection (67%). Stark and Bainbridge remark that, "Clearly, this group formed by spreading along well-established interpersonal bonds" (1980: 1383). Furthermore, it was the bonds within the preexisting kinship network that seemed to prevent a greater number of members from defecting.

The article's next example, however, inadvertently makes a related but different point. Stark and Bainbridge examine findings from the small sample (28 members) gathered by Nordquist in his study of Swami Kriyananda's Ananda Cooperative Village. The great majority of these members were social isolates before joining. For instance, prior to their involvement with the community, 82% said they never or hardly ever went to parties or other kinds of social gatherings. In response to Nordquist's queries about why they stayed in the community, 61% responded that "fellowship with other devotees" was primary, while another 25% responded that their relationship with Kriyananda was primary. These responses were chosen over the ideals, lifestyle and religious practices of the group. Stark and Bainbridge conclude this section of their paper by observing that, "Over time many persons who were prepared to accept mysticism drifted through the Ananda village. Those who remained were those who formed interpersonal ties" (Stark and Bainbridge 1980: 1384–85).

This is a very different example from the Doomsday Group. In their first example, the social network that was the focus of their analysis was a *pre-existing* kinship network. In the second example, the focus was on the social bonds formed *after* recruits came into contact with the Ananda community. In both cases, interpersonal bonds were important for understanding conversion – or, at least, for understanding commitment. But in the second example, the social network explanation fails to address the issue of how recruits *initially* became interested in Ananda. My focus in this chapter is on understanding how people first come into contact with a religious group rather than on the processes that take place after first contact has been made (a distinction discussed in Snow and Machalek 1984: 182–84). With respect to social networks, I am thus interested only in *preexisting* social networks in the following analysis.[2]

Social Networks and Conversion

The discussion of how people become involved in alternative religions was stimulated by the Lofland-Stark model of conversion, which was developed in the context of a study of the early Unification Church in the United States in the 1960s (1965). This model has been heavily criticized, but it has been quite useful because it put forward a set of variables involved in affiliation that were subsequently scrutinized by later researchers. The variable with the most empirical support is that new members most often become involved through family and friends. Based on evidence from a variety of studies, Dawson notes that "the majority of recruits to the majority of NRMs come into contact with the groups they join because they personally know one or more members of the movement" (2003: 119). This generalization applies to the Movement of Spiritual Inner Awareness (MSIA), a group I studied in the 1990s (refer to Table 2.1, taken from Lewis 1997: 183).

Only 3.6% of the people who became involved in the Movement of Spiritual Inner Awareness did so via impersonal media such as posters, flyers or news media treatments of the group. It might also be noted that only two respondents (0.4%) mentioned the movement's books (some of which had been on *The New York Times* bestseller list) as being primary factors attracting them to MSIA (Lewis 1997: 105).

To bring this pattern up to date with some recent figures on a different movement, the data collected by Inga Tøllefsen on the Art of Living

---

2. It could, of course, be argued that interactions with members are always involved in the conversion process – even in the context of conversions to Internet religions – and thus social networks *in the broadest sense* are always keys to conversions. But this kind of argument would miss an important aspect of my analysis. In his *Religious Conversion and Disaffiliation*, Henri Gooren discusses the various factors involved in conversion in terms of *points of initial contact:* "The converting subject has many ways to make first contact with the religious groups, but the main avenues are those based on one's social networks, on contacts with the mass media, or on chance encounters with missionary agents from religious groups" (2010: 135). My focus in the present chapter is on these first contact points rather than on the entire conversion process.

Table 2.1 Introduction to MSIA

Initial Contact	%	No.	Initial Contact	%	No.
Impersonal/Media	3.6	18	MSIA Book(s)	0.4	2
Friends/Relatives	55.4	227	Other	5.8	47
Insight Seminar*	28.4	142	No Response	2.8	14

[*An MSIA-inspired weekend seminar similar to est and Lifespring].

Table 2.2 Introduction to Art of Living Foundation

Initial Contact	%	N	Initial Contact	%	N
Friend	45.0	76	Magazine	4.7	8
Co-Worker	8.3	14	TV or Movie	2.4	4
Partner/Spouse	6.5	11	Flyer; Poster	10.1	17
Relative	18.9	32	Student group	1.2	2
Website	4.7	8	Other	11.2	19
Book	1.8	3	Non-Response	4.0	7

[Data provided courtesy Inga Tøllefsen].

Foundation (AoLF is a South Asian NRM similar to Transcendental Meditation) indicates that involvement is most often via family and friendship networks (refer to Table 2.2):

The AoLF data clearly supports the generalization that people become involved primarily through family and friendship networks. Even a half-dozen of the respondents who answered the open-ended option "Other" were recruited via family or friends, as indicated by their written responses: "A few of my friends took this program and recommended it to me," "Parents," "Cousin," "Parents introduced me into Art of Living," "My brothers," and "My father's friend's wife" (Tøllefsen 2012).

Researchers are sometimes tempted to make sweeping generalizations on the basis of limited data. In the case at hand, data from two different new religions gathered at different points in time seem to provide strong support for the generalization that converts are recruited primarily via family and friends. However, this generalization falls apart when other new religions are examined, particularly when certain NRMs are examined at different points in their development.

Satanism

In Henri Gooren's recent study of conversion, he concludes that, "First contact with new religious groups is nowadays more often established through the modern mass media than through personal agents" (2010: 141; also refer to Einstein 2008). The primary new medium through which potential participants are recruited is the Internet. The twenty-first century has also witnessed the emergence of Internet-based religions. Two new religions which antedated the Internet but that have become predominantly online religions are "religious" Satanism (Petersen 2009b), particularly in the form initiated by Anton LaVey, and contemporary (neo) Paganism, which in recent years has been dominated by solitaries who interact with co-religionists primarily via the Internet (see the discussion in Lewis 2012b).

When I first began researching religious Satanists, no serious academic books had been written on this form of Satanism (at least not in English; refer to Schmidt 1992). What existed were a few articles and book chapters (e.g., Moody 1974), plus a number of volumes on the ritual abuse scare. With the exception of some minimal data on Temple of Set members that had been collected by Graham Harvey (1995), there were no available demographic data on self-identified Satanists.

To address this lack, I conducted a survey in 2000–2001 which I retrospectively referred to as "Satan Survey One" (SS-1). Eight years later, in June 2009, I initiated a more ambitious survey of contemporary Satanists which I referred to as "Satan Survey Two" (SS-2). (These are discussed in more detail in Chapter Seven).[3] The pattern of responses to a similar questionnaire item in SS-1 and SS-2 was significantly different. If we combine book and website readings, more than half of the respondents to SS-1 (57%) indicated that they were introduced to Satanism by something they read. This figure jumped to 79% for respondents to SS-2 (refer to Table 2.3).

The percentage of respondents introduced to religious Satanism via books remained at 45% for both SS-1 and SS-2 (adding together the percentages from *The Satanic Bible* and Other Reading categories in SS-1). Thus the growth in overall percentage of respondents who initially encountered Satanism via something they read came from website readings, which expanded from 12% to 34% as a conversion factor. Paganism experienced a similar expansion in the percentage of new recruits whose initial point of contact has been the Internet.

---

3. Because of the nature of the 'Satanic milieu' – to use Jesper Petersen's suggestive designation (2009a) – it is simply impossible to gather a statistically random sample of Satanists.

Table 2.3 Introduction to Satanism*

SS-1			SS-2		
Initial Contact	%	No.	*Initial Contact*	%	No.
Friend	17	24	Friend	18	45
Satanic Bible	21	30	Co-Worker	2	4
Other Reading	24	34	Relative	2	5
Website	12	17	Website	34	86
Music	1	2	Book	45	113
Other	20	28	Music	12	31
NR	4	5	Other	22	56
			NR	4	9

[*In SS-1 the categories were constructed retrospectively from responses to open-ended questions. In SS-2, respondents could check more than one answer to this particular item, which is why the total percentage adds up to more than 100%].

Paganism

In the previous chapter, I mentioned Helen Berger's and my research project, the Pagan Census Revisited (PCR), conducted in 2009–2010. The questionnaire was lengthy, containing 82 items that collected a wide variety of demographic and attitude data. Like the Satanism questionnaire, it was also posted online via Survey Monkey. It contained a similar grid asking respondents how they first came into contact with Paganism (refer to Table 2.4).

Friends and relatives totaled 38%. The percentage of responses that could legitimately be reclassified as family or friends from the "Other" responses was 2.5 -3.0% of the total. If one adds together friends, relatives, co-workers and partners/spouses plus an additional 3% from Other,

Table 2.4 Introduction to Paganism (Synchronic)*

Initial Contact	%	No.	*Initial Contact*	%	No.
Friend	30.0	2352	TV or Movie	2.7	215
Co-Worker	2.1	166	Flyer; Poster	1.7	135
Partner/Spouse	4.7	370	Student group	2.4	191
Relative	8.0	623	In Prison	0.3	22
Website	17.3	1352	Other	21.6	1694
Book	36.8	2880	Non-Response	3.1	248

[*This questionnaire item permitted respondents to check more than one answer, which is why the total percentage adds up to more than 100%].

we come up with almost half of all respondents (47.8%) being recruited via social networks.

Unfortunately, there was no similar questionnaire item in the original Pagan Census with which to make comparisons. We can, however, utilize the PCR data to make comparisons between different time periods using the same quasi-longitudinal approach I took in Chapter One. An item in the PCR questionnaire asked respondents when they started self-identifying as Pagan. The sample can then be divided into subsamples according to when they "converted" (a problematic term in the Pagan subculture) to Paganism. Using only the first seven items in the "first contact" grid and arranging the data into five-year periods produces Table 2.5.[4]

Table 2.5's backwards projection from a sample of current members is, at best, a quasi-longitudinal approach that is only being utilized here in the absence of adequate data from earlier time periods. If someone had systematically collected relevant data from large samples of Pagans at different points in the past (not just data collected at a few Pagan festivals), then we would have a much more adequate basis from which to draw conclusions about changes in recruitment across time. Specifically, having stats from earlier periods would address the problem of missing data on participants who died or disaffiliated over the course of those decades. However, the situation is that we simply do not have that information. While recognizing its limitations, the above data nevertheless paints a very interesting picture of changing conversion "gateways" to a dynamic movement across the course of 45–plus years.

For respondents who had been self-identified Pagans for 45 or more years, 43.9% indicated relatives and friends had originally introduced them to Paganism. Adding co-worker and partner/spouse categories brings the social networks total up to 47.7%. For more recent converts, relatives and friends declined to 33.0%, though an interesting development within the social network category was how relatives became progressively less important and friends became more important across time. Adding co-worker and partner/spouse categories brings the social networks total up to 41.5% for the most recent recruits. The primary non-personal introduction to Paganism has been books, a factor that is more significant than friends in all periods. And though the influence of partners/spouses and the entertainment

---

4. Though not exactly the same, a similar idea informs Table One in Rochford's article. (1982: 401). The Pagan Table in the current chapter documents a gradual demotion of the importance of social networks for recruits until they become a secondary factor. The Rochford Table presents data that reflects a fluctuating pattern between the dominance of social networks and the dominance of non-network recruiting.

38 Sects & Stats

Table 2.5 Introduction to Paganism in Different Five-Year Periods (Diachronic)*

No. of Yrs. Involved	45+		40–44		35–39		30–34		25–29	
	%	No.	%	No.	%	No.	%	No.	%	No.
Friend	12.1	16	18.4	27	23.9	49	23.9	70	28.6	137
Relative	31.8	42	19.0	28	13.7	28	11.3	33	9.4	45
Co-Worker	0.8	1	0.7	1	2.0	4	1.7	5	2.9	14
Partner/Spouse	3.0	4	1.4	2	0.5	1	2.0	6	4.8	23
TV or Movie	0.8	1	0.0	0	1.0	2	1.4	4	1.3	6
Book	21.2	28	34.0	50	40.0	82	32.1	94	38.2	183

No. of Yrs. Involved	20–24		15–19		10–14		5–9		4–0	
	%	No.	%	No.	%	No.	%	No.	%	No.
Friend	31.3	238	31.8	286	33.3	437	33.9	409	28.2	289
Relative	7.6	58	6.5	58	6.9	91	5.2	63	4.8	49
Co-Worker	1.7	13	2.0	18	2.3	30	2.6	31	2.0	20
Partner/Spouse	3.7	28	4.8	43	4.6	61	5.5	66	6.5	67
TV or Movie	2.0	15	1.7	15	3.6	47	3.0	36	4.8	49
Book	39.9	304	41.5	373	36.5	479	35.5	429	33.2	340
Website			8.2	74	19.5	256	26.1	315	31.5	323

$G = 321.48$, d.f. = 45, $p < 0.001$
Cramér's $V = 0.12$, $p < 0.01$

[*Note:* As I did with the Satanist statistics, "Book" and "Website" were collapsed into a single "Reading" category for the purpose of making these calculations. For further discussion of the quasi-longitudinal approach, refer to footnote 8 in Lewis 2014.]

* Andreas Baumann, a graduate student in the Department for Cross-Cultural and Regional Studies at the University of Copenhagen, calculated levels of significance for this and subsequent tables.

media show steady growth, the real rising star is the Internet, which appears to be on the edge of out-influencing every other factor.

As I will discuss in Chapter Seven, a large segment of contemporary Paganism has gradually been evolving into an Internet religion, though to a lesser extent than contemporary Satanism. One could thus respond to the decreasing importance of social networks for understanding these two movements by categorizing them as being somewhat different phenomena from religions based primarily on face-to-face interactions. In other words, the generalization that the majority of converts to most NRMs (i.e., the non-Internet-based varieties) are recruited via preexisting family and friendship networks is not undermined by the examples of contemporary Satanism and Paganism. It is thus necessary to examine data from other kinds of NRMs in order to fundamentally challenge this generalization.

The Hare Krishna Movement

In the Snow, Zurcher and Ekland-Olson article which helped establish the generalization that most NRM converts were recruited through social networks, the Hare Krishna Movement was mentioned as an exception (1980: 791). Two years after this piece appeared, Burke Rochford published a paper in which he discussed the specific social context of the late 1960s (particularly in San Francisco) which made the Hare Krishna Movement the exception to the rule (1982). Toward the end of his article, he also noted that "we expect that recruitment will increasingly occur through pre-established social ties" (1982: 408). This observation has the effect of bringing the Hare Krishnas back into the conversion-via-social-networks fold, and tends to obscure one of the more general points of Rochford's argument, namely that "as external social forces change, a movement's recruitment strategies, ideology and organization also change" (1980: 400). This observation is one of the lessons of the present chapter as well.

Rochford's first table (reproduced here as Table 2.6) presents a diachronic picture of different sources of new converts from the late 1960s to 1980. Though the categories are different – and though he utilizes longitudinal data (longitudinal in the proper sense, rather than quasi-longitudinal) – his table embodies the same sort of approach that was taken in Table 2.5.

The "Public Places" category refers to converts whose original contact with ISKCON was an encounter with Hare Krishna devotees. Despite the centrality of the social interactions that facilitated conversion in such instances, one *cannot* properly classify such conversions as being the consequence of pre-existing social networks any more than one can classify the Ananda Cooperative Community members interviewed by Nordquist as having been recruited via a pre-existing social network. Henri Gooren makes this point clear in his recently published study of conversion and disaffiliation where he analyzes the various factors involved in conversion. In his discussion of how the "converting subject [makes] first contact" with a religious group, Gooren is careful to distinguish between "those based on one's social networks" and those based "on chance encounters with

Table 2.6 Mode of Recruitment by Year of Entry*

Year Entered ISKCON	Devotee Networks[a]	Non-Member Networks[b]	Public Places	Other[c]	Total	
1967–1971	29%	7%	54%	10%	100%	(40)
1972–1974	16%	33%	38%	13%	100%	(44)
1975–1976	18%	26%	46%	10%	100%	(50)
1977–1978	23%	40%	31%	6%	100%	(35)
1979–1980	30%	12%	40%	19%	101%	(43)
Mean Percent	(23%)	(23%)	(42%)	(12%)	(100%)	(212)

Notes:
a. Devotee networks are contacts leading to membership initiated through social ties with persons who are already ISKCON members.
b. Non-member networks are contacts initiated with movement sympathizers which lead to persons taking up membership with ISKCON.
c. Contacts coded as "other" include being picked up hitchhiking by ISKCON members, visiting a Krishna community for a school project, and meeting the devotees at an anti-nuclear rally. Since only 6% of the devotee respondents indicated that they initiated contact with the movement on their own (i.e., attended a Sunday feast at a local temple or read ISKCON's literature) we have grouped them in the "other" category.

$G = 22.62$, d.f. $= 12$, $p < 0.05$
Cramér's $V = 0.12$, $p < 0.05$
Kruskal-Goodman λ (PRE) $= 0.54$

[*Reproduced from Rochford (1982: 401) with permission of author. ISKCON stands for the International Society for Krishna Consciousness].

missionary agents from religious groups" (2010: 135). An encounter with devotees clearly falls into the latter rather than into the former category.

With respect to my present argument, the most significant part of Rochford's table is how it captures the fluctuating importance of social network conversions, ranging from a total of 36% in 1967–1971 to a total of 63% in 1977–1978 (total network percentages were derived from adding figures for devotee networks to figures for non-member networks). However, the implications of this aspect of Rochford's analysis seem to have been largely missed at the time due to the fact that 30 years ago the collective attention of NRM and social movement researchers was focused on the conversion-via-social-networks approach as an alternative to earlier psychological models of conversion.

In any event, the Hare Krishna data indicates that a movement does not need to be a decentralized Internet religion in order to explain why social networks are not always the primary source of recruits. Rochford's findings from the early 1980s are further reinforced by Eileen Barker's findings on converts to the Unification Church (1984) during approximately the same period of time. Barker found that personal networks were not a factor in the conversion of most recruits. In his discussion of the role of personal networks in NRM recruitment, Dawson characterizes Barker's research as being an apparent exception to the rule:

> Eileen Barker denies that existing personal networks account for the majority of converts to the Moonies in Britain. But her claim is somewhat ambiguous since she notes that networks do account for over a quarter of the British membership and in a footnote she provides evidence that they also account for a third of the membership in the rest of Europe. Moreover, she does not clearly identify an alternative way in which the largest number of recruits are derived. By implication it would appear that she has in mind 'by-chance' encounters between recruiters and individuals in the streets (Dawson 2003).

It is precisely this kind of "chance" encounter that Gooren discusses in his analysis of conversion.

A different kind of pattern is provided by the example of Scientology. In large part because of the organization's general resistance to being studied in etic terms (Cowan 2009), no one outside of the Church of Scientology has thus far collected quantitative data on how members first become involved. However, we have enough information about how the Church works to know that recruiters – termed "body routers" within Scientology (Reitman 2011) – regularly approach strangers with offers of books, courses, and Scientology's famous personality test (Rigal-Cellard 2009: 330). The Church also regularly advertises in the mainstream media, and donates its books to libraries of every sort. Preliminary data from an ongoing research project on which I have been working indicates that approximately half of all Scientology converts' initial point of contact is one of these various avenues rather than through a social network. This means that at least three of the "classic cults" of the 1970s and 1980s – ISKCON, the Unification Church, and Scientology – have, during certain junctures in their organization's existence, recruited significantly from non-network sources. The conclusion that the Internet need not be invoked to explain non-network conversion is also reinforced by recent data from two other non-Internet-focused NRMs, Adidam and the Order of Christ Sophia.

Adidam

The Adidam questionnaire mentioned in the previous chapter also collected "first contact" data. The pattern of the conversion data on Adidam recruits can be seen in Table 2.7.

Additionally, nine respondents (or about 5% of the total) in the Other category were recruited via social networks. The friend and relative categories add up to 36.2%. With the additional 5% from Other, we get 41.5%. Finally, adding the partner/spouse category brings the total up to 48.8% recruited via personal networks.

Adidam has been around (though under a succession of different names) since the early 1970s. This allows one to examine the group's recruitment history across four decades. A far smaller group than either contemporary Paganism or the Hare Krishna Movement, the sample size was still modest at the time I made "first contact" calculations – about 192 respondents – though this is a fairly good sample, given that it represents approximately 25%-30% of the total core membership. Because Adidam has been a viable organization for decades, we can subdivide the sample according to length of membership as we did with Paganism and as Rochford did with ISKCON. However, rather than using five-year periods, ten-year periods are better suited for Adidam because of the relatively small sample size.

Interestingly, in an inversion of the pattern found among Pagans, 28.9% of respondents who joined Adidam more than 30 years ago reported that their initial point of contact was a friend (no relatives). Adding co-worker and partner/spouse categories brings the social network total up to 39.5%.

Table 2.7 Introduction to Adidam (Synchronic)*

Initial Contact	%	No.	Initial Contact	%	No.
Friend	32.5	62	Magazine	5.2	10
Relative	3.7	7	TV or Movie	1.0	2
Co-Worker	4.2	8	Flyer; Poster	9.4	18
Partner/Spouse	7.3	14	Student group	1.0	2
Website	1.0	2	Other	18.8	36
Book	36.6	70	Non-Response	1.0	2

$G = 35.8$, d.f.$=21$, $p < 0.05$
Cramer's $V = 0.24$
Kruskal-Goodman λ (PRE) $= 0.17$

[*This questionnaire item permitted respondents to check more than one answer, which is why the total percentage adds up to more than 100%].

Table 2.8 First Point of Contact with Adidam per 10-year Period (Diachronic)

	31–40		21–30		11–20		1–10	
	%	No.	%	No.	%	No.	%	No.
Friend	28.9	11	21.2	14	42.9	21	43.2	16
Relative	0.0	0	1.5	1	4.1	2	8.1	3
Co-Worker	5.3	2	7.6	5	0.0	0	2.7	1
Partner/Spouse	5.3	2	6.1	4	8.2	4	10.8	4
Book	52.6	20	43.9	29	24.5	12	24.3	9
Magazine	7.9	3	7.6	5	4.1	2	0.0	0
TV or Movie	2.6	1	0.0	0	2.0	1	0.0	0
Website	0.0	0	0.0	0	2.0	1	2.7	1

Instead of a personal contact, the majority were initially recruited via an impersonal medium, with half (52.6%) saying they first came into contact with Adidam through a book they had read (presumably a book written by Adi Da Samraj, Adidam's founder).

In contrast, the initial point of contact for more than half of respondents (51.3%) who joined Adidam more recently was a friend or relative. Adding co-worker and partner/spouse categories brings the social network total up to 64.8%. Only one-fourth (24.3%) of the sample checked "book," meaning that friends/relatives and books basically switched places percentage-wise. Hence, the notion that conversion comes about primarily via interpersonal networks applies to recent Adidam converts but not to earlier converts.

An examination of the data from contemporary Paganism, from Adidam and from Rochford's study demonstrates not only that patterns of initial contact for conversion can change over time, but also that these patterns can change in significantly different ways, depending on the specific movement. Additionally, the data shows that new factors such as the Internet can emerge and have different impacts on different groups. Thus a complex picture emerges from juxtaposing but a single characteristic – conversion "gateway" (i.e., first point of contact) – of only three NRMs, plotted as a variable across time.

In Chapter Four, I will be examining longitudinal data on the Order of Christ Sophia (OCS). One of the findings from that study was that – once again, plotted as a variable over time – the OCS gradually moves from an organization dependent primarily on social networks to recruit participants to an organization recruiting new members via other means. Additionally, in Chapter Seven, I will further be discussing Internet Satanism, as well as the gradual shift from social network conversion to Internet conversion in Paganism.

44   *Sects & Stats*

Concluding Remarks

A generation of new religions researchers have repeated the notion that NRMs recruit primarily via social networks as if it was a sacred mantra we received when we were initiated into the guild of new religion researchers. This may explain why no one has called this generalization into question, despite the changes that have taken place "on the ground" since it initially came into currency decades ago. We have also unconsciously assumed, as I have already noted in the Introduction and in the previous chapter, that NRM members were sociologically all more or less the same, and that more or less the same processes were involved in conversion – despite the many differences that exist between different new religions. It is this monolithic assumption that allows us to make broad generalizations on the basis of a relatively limited set of case studies.

Also, though new religions researchers are aware that NRMs are always changing, many of us have tended to study them as if they were static entities.[5] A common pattern within the field that reinforces this problem is that researchers will study one particular new religion, write a monograph on that specific group, and then begin the cycle all over again with another NRM. In contrast, for understanding how such groups develop across time, some of the best work has been done by scholars who study one movement for many years, such as Burke Rochford's work on the Hare Krishna Movement (Rochford 1985; Rochford 2007) and Gordon and Gary Shepherd's research on The Family International (Shepherd and Shepherd 2010). So in addition to undermining the generalization that NRMs recruit primarily through social networks, it is hoped that this chapter will drive home something we already know, namely that new religions are dynamic organizations that change over time and that different new religions change in different ways.

To conclude with this theme, I was struck by the tables that were produced by subdividing various conversion factors according to the time period in which respondents were recruited. For both Paganism and Adidam, I labeled Table 2.4 and Table 2.7 "synchronic" in contrast to Table 2.5 and Table 2.8 – the "diachronic" tables – that were produced by separating the data into subsamples according to different time periods. I was similarly

---

5.   I have elsewhere analyzed another aspect of this problem, namely the gradual decline of quantitative studies within the field of new religious movements and our subsequent reliance on research conducted over a quarter of a century ago (Lewis and Bauman 2011: 181–83). I have repeated this analysis in the Introduction.

struck by Rochford's Table 2.6, which combines synchronic and diachronic data.[6] For researchers with an interest in conversion, this approach could be a suggestive model for future studies that examine the variation in the gender, education, and the like of recruits across time.[7]

---

6. There is a lucid discussion of "longitudinal," "diachronic" and related terms in Barley 1990.
7. In Chapter Four, I examine the Order of Christ Sophia in terms of a properly longitudinal approach. The latter part of that analysis will also address the issue of recruitment through social networks.

Part II

Three Styles of Longitudinal Research

3 Increasing Complexity versus Prior Generalizations – Census Data and Longitudinal Approaches

I realize that the analysis of the recent history of NRM studies outlined in the Introduction – an analysis which fundamentally challenges some of the conventional wisdom about new religions – is radical. So as a preface to future empirical work on members of alternative religions, it will be helpful to examine data from a relatively neutral source that strongly confirms this seemingly radical analysis, namely census figures.

National census data is an important though neglected source of information bearing on adherents to alternative religions. The censuses of four English-speaking countries – New Zealand, Australia, Canada and the United Kingdom – collect information on religious membership. The kinds of data collected are relatively limited, from age and gender to income and education, but these categories are nevertheless sufficient to undermine certain important generalizations about current members of non-traditional religions.

As anyone who has worked with this kind of information knows, census data is sold rather than provided to researchers free of charge. If one wants to purchase data on multiple religions across a series of different census years, this quickly becomes quite expensive. I initially found the New Zealand (NZ) census to be the most reasonable, and purchased a broad variety of data for four censuses, 1991, 1996, 2001, and 2006. I was also going to obtain 2011 figures, but the most recent census was pushed back to 2013 because of the Christchurch earthquake (the New Zealand Census Bureau is located in Christchurch) that took place in early 2011. The number of NRMs measured by the New Zealand census across all four of these periods is actually quite limited. Up until 1991, the only alternative religions to appear in the census were "older" new religions, such as the Church of Jesus Christ of Latter-day Saints (LDS, popularly called Mormons). In 1991, New Zealand added Satanism, Spiritualism, Scientology, a vague New Age Religions category, and a similarly vague "Nature and Earth Based Religion" category. By 1996, recognizably Pagan traditions such as Druidism and Wicca had been added, as well as a number of other new religions such as the Hare Krishna Movement and a number of newer Christian movements such as the Vineyard Christian Fellowship.

Like New Zealand, Australia holds censuses every five years. Australia (began collecting data on minority religions in 1996. Thanks to the library acquisitions department at my university, the University of Tromsø, I was able to obtain basic Religion X Sex X Age data. In some ways, the data sets from New Zealand and Australia are complementary in the sense that New Zealand tracks data on Moonies, Hare Krishnas and the Vineyard Christian Fellowship (which the Australians do not) while Australia tracks data on groups like Eckankar, Religious Science and Theosophy (which the New Zealanders do not). Another difference, which will be evident in the below frequency tables, is that the New Zealand age categories only go up to 65, while the age categories used in Australia go up to 95 or 100, depending on the specific census year. Based on prior work with this kind of census data – studies that discovered similar patterns in different Anglophone countries (Lewis 2004; Lewis 2007) – I believe it is possible to cautiously project findings from the New Zealand and Australian censuses to other Anglophone countries, and perhaps selectively to certain other Western industrialized nations.[1]

The five-year pattern of New Zealand and Australia contrasts with Canada and the United Kingdom, which hold censuses every ten years. The United States, which one might normally want to prioritize because of its size, does not, unfortunately, include a religion self-identification item in its national census. I have to say that Canada's approach to collecting religion data is rather odd. In the 1991 and the 2001 censuses, the Canadian census bureau asked only one out of five people about their religious identity. They then multiplied these responses by five to obtain a national estimate. Canada also uses a rather limited set of religion categories that excludes certain major religions such as, for example, Christian Science and includes only the most controversial NRMs, such as Scientology and Satanism. The Canadian census then sells this truncated data for several times the asking price of the other Anglophone countries. Because of this high charge, any reference I make to data on Canada is from free information that at one time or another has been available on the Statistics Canada website. Also note that the way in which Statistics Canada gathered religion (and certain other) data in 2011 was different than in prior years, meaning – as it has been explained to me – there is a potential for significant differences between data from 2001 and from 2011.

---

1. The New Zealand census automatically rounds all cells to base 3, which is why all numbers in the census can be divided by 3. This is explained in Rule 4, Random rounding, at: http://www.stats.govt.nz/Census/about-2006–census/methodology-papers/2006–census-confidentiality-rules.aspx
The purpose is to protect respondents so that no one can be identified from census data.

3 *Increasing Complexity versus Prior Generalizations* 51

The UK did not start collecting religion data until 2001, meaning there have been only two usable census years. Additionally, the UK census only allowed one to "tick" one of the major religions; for any of the non-Christian NRMs, one had to tick "other" and write in one's religious identity. The UK census also does not provide data beyond age and sex on specific NRMs – which means that it is still okay for certain comparative purposes, but not for any sort of comprehensive analysis. I will occasionally be referring to census data from the England and Wales component of the British census. I will preface my discussion of census data on NRMs in New Zealand and Australia with an examination of New Zealand census data on the Anglican Church and the LDS Church.

Christians in Australia and New Zealand

The Anglican denomination, with its roots in the Church of England, is the closest religious body New Zealand has to a state church. New Zealand census data clearly reflects an aging, declining religious body that dropped a fourth of its total membership between 1991 and 2006. Table 3.1 is a little cramped and thus potentially confusing, so I have placed a few key items in boldface type. Total figures, which decline from 732,045 members in 1991 to 554,925 in 2006, can be seen along the very bottom of the table. And though the numbers of parishioners in the 65+ age bracket stay rather steady across all four years (which indicates that 30,000–40,000 Anglicans pass away every five years), the percentage of the total membership these elders represent gradually increases from 17.8% in 1991 to 25.1% in 2006. The numbers of new Anglicans being born into the faith, as represented by the 0–4 years of age category, indicates a precipitous decline.

The Anglican Church in Australia exhibits a similar pattern, though the decline there is far less pronounced: from 3,903,324 Anglicans in 1996, to 3,881,162 in 2001, to 3,716,377 in 2006, and 3,678,004 in 2011. In other words, whereas New Zealand Anglicans declined by almost a full 25% between 1991 and 2006 (a period of 16 years), Australian Anglicans declined by less than 6% between 1996 and 2011 (another period of 16 years).

I have chosen to include the table for New Zealand Anglicans rather than the table for Australians here because the various components of the overall pattern of a mainstream church's decline are easier to see in the New Zealand data. When one combines these figures with the fact that many of these respondents are likely non-practicing Anglicans, it is clear that this denomination's long range prospects are not bright.

The Anglican Church is not the only mainline Protestant denomination on the decline. Presbyterianism, for example, exhibits the same pattern, though

Table 3.1 Census Data for New Zealand Anglicanism, 1991–2006

NZ Anglicanism	1991		1996		2001		2006	
	No.	%	No.	%	No.	%	No.	%
0–4 Years	40,692	5.6	30,498	4.8	23,349	4.0	19,311	3.5
5–9 Years	42,561	5.8	37,608	5.9	32,271	5.5	26,091	4.7
10–14 Years	47,220	6.4	37,542	5.9	36,303	6.2	31,317	5.6
15–19 Years	49,071	6.7	31,341	5.0	26,688	4.6	25,128	4.5
20–24 Years	44,127	6.0	29,250	4.6	19,758	3.4	16,770	3.0
25–29 Years	46,197	6.3	34,338	5.4	23,112	3.9	16,452	3.0
30–34 Years	50,541	6.9	41,331	6.5	32,892	5.6	24,354	4.4
35–39 Years	51,141	7.0	45,702	7.2	40,209	6.9	33,405	6.0
40–44 Years	57,183	7.8	46,374	7.3	45,069	7.7	41,109	7.4
45–49 Years	48,630	6.6	51,963	8.2	45,150	7.7	44,907	8.1
50–54 Years	43,392	5.9	44,172	7.0	50,094	8.6	44,631	8.0
55–59 Years	39,111	5.3	39,591	6.3	42,291	7.2	49,671	8.9
60–64 Years	42,090	5.7	35,142	5.6	37,896	6.5	42,444	7.6
65 Years+	130,095	**17.8**	126,912	**20.1**	129,708	**22.2**	139,335	**25.1**
Male	335,406	45.8	347,571	55.0	258,918	44.3	244,638	44.1
Female	396,645	54.2	284,193	45.0	325,875	55.7	310,287	55.9
Total	**732,045**	100.0	**631,761**	100.0	**584,793**	100.0	**554,925**	100.0
Average Age*	38.63		40.99		42.84		45.46	

[Courtesy of New Zealand Statistics.]

* In this and all subsequent tables, I have averaged the 65 Years+ category to 70 years- old. Because the average member of the Anglican Church is significantly older than the other religious groups examined here, this way of proceeding likely misrepresents the membership profile of this particular denomination.

this group's decline is somewhat less precipitous than the Anglicans in New Zealand. Thus the 1991 New Zealand census reported 553,386 Presbyterians, 470,412 in the 1996 census, 431,139 in 2001, and 400,839 in 2006. There appears to be a similar decline in Australian Presbyterians between 1996 and 2006 when overall numbers sank from 662,685 in 1996 to 583,394 in 2006. However, total numbers actually started rising again – though only slightly – by 2011, to 584.818 Presbyterians. In Canada, the number of Presbyterians dropped off sharply from 636,295 members in 1991 to 409,830 in 2001, but then rose again to 472,385 members in 2011 – so recent numbers are positive, but not significant enough to make up for the post-1991 drop. However, the Presbyterians are surviving better than the Anglicans.

The Church of Jesus Christ of Latter-day Saints (LDS), on the other hand, appears to be holding steady in New Zealand. After a gradual decline from 1991 to 2001, the 2006 census reflected a certain measure of growth. As indicated by the double-digit percentages (which I have placed in bold) of Mormons who are children or teenagers, the denomination appears to be maintaining itself by replenishing its membership from within (refer to Table 3.2). The emphasis on growing the membership by having children is clearly a successful strategy as long as the group can retain its children – which seems to be the case here. I would nevertheless refer to the Mormon situation in New Zealand as one of "treading water," by which I mean that the LDS is not sinking, but it has not – or, at least, has not yet – shifted into a true expansion mode.

In terms of growth, future prospects are much brighter in Australia where the LDS has enjoyed steady growth across all four of the Australian censuses we have been considering: Starting with 42,158 self-identified Mormons in 1996, membership rose to 48,775 in 2001, 52,145 in 2006 and 58,838 in 2011. Growth is also evident in Canada, where Mormon totals went from 93,890 in 1991 to 104,745 in 2001 and to 105,365 in 2011. However, the rate of growth in the most recent decade was less than 1%, indicating that Canadian Mormons have switched to treading-water mode as well.

Not all Christian religious bodies are static or declining. In common with most other areas of the world, Pentecostalism is growing in New Zealand. Thus in the last four censuses, the number of census respondents in the generic "Pentecostalism" category has expanded from 49,596 in 1991, to 51,150 in 1996, to 67,182 in 2001 and to 79,155 in 2006. The Vineyard Christian Fellowship is a young American Pentecostal denomination with its roots in the Jesus movement of the 1960s and 1970s that is sometimes classified as a new religion. This group has expanded explosively in New Zealand where it doubled between 1996 and 2001, and then doubled again between 2001 and 2006.

Table 3.2 Census Data for New Zealand LDS, 1991–2006

NZ LDS	1991		1996		2001		2006	
	No.	%	No.	%	No.	%	No.	%
0–4 Years	5,526	11.5	4,794	11.6	4,227	10.6	4,206	9.7
5–9 Years	4,779	9.9	4,848	11.8	4,500	11.3	4,437	10.2
10–14 Years	5,409	11.3	4,356	10.6	4,668	11.7	4,827	11.1
15–19 Years	5,058	10.5	4,152	10.1	3,642	9.1	4,353	10.0
20–24 Years	4,749	9.9	3,402	8.3	3,120	7.8	3,018	6.9
25–29 Years	4,515	9.4	3,402	8.3	2,952	7.4	3,039	7.0
30–34 Years	4,077	8.5	3,285	8.0	3,054	7.6	2,994	6.9
35–39 Years	3,381	7.0	3,024	7.4	2,841	7.1	3,144	7.2
40–44 Years	2,718	5.7	2,481	6.0	2,583	6.5	2,898	6.7
45–49 Years	2,070	4.3	1,995	4.8	2,196	5.5	2,607	6.0
50–54 Years	1,647	3.4	1,518	3.7	1,761	4.4	2,259	5.2
55–59 Years	1,308	2.7	1,206	2.9	1,314	3.3	1,761	4.0
60–64 Years	1,065	2.2	951	2.3	1,074	2.7	1,320	3.0
65 Years +	1,716	3.6	1,758	4.3	1,980	5.0	2,676	6.2
Male	22,383	46.6	18,936	46.0	18,186	45.6	20,052	46.1
Female	25,629	53.4	22,233	54.0	21,729	54.4	23,487	53.9
Total	48,009		41,169		39,912		43,536	
Average Age	25.72		26.18		27.37		29.01	

[Courtesy of New Zealand Statistics.]

3 Increasing Complexity versus Prior Generalizations 55

Table 3.3 Census Data for New Zealand Vineyard Christian Fellowship, 1996–2006

NZ Vineyard	1996		2001		2006	
	N	%	N	%	N	%
0–4 Years	39	**11.5**	87	**11.2**	156	<u>9.7</u>
5–9 Years	51	**15.0**	105	**13.6**	177	**11.0**
10–14 Years	45	**13.3**	87	**11.2**	180	**11.2**
15–19 Years	9	2.7	33	4.3	126	7.9
20–24 Years	24	7.1	36	4.7	114	7.1
25–29 Years	36	**10.6**	69	8.9	108	6.7
30–34 Years	39	**11.5**	81	**10.5**	162	**10.1**
35–39 Years	39	**11.5**	90	**11.6**	156	<u>9.7</u>
40–44 Years	27	8.0	81	**10.5**	147	<u>9.2</u>
45–49 Years	15	4.4	48	6.2	117	7.3
50–54 Years	9	2.7	21	2.7	60	3.7
55–59 Years	3	0.9	15	1.9	45	2.8
60–64 Years	6	1.8	15	1.9	18	1.1
65 Years +	3	0.9	6	0.8	21	1.3
Male	162	47.8	384	49.6	762	47.5
Female	177	52.2	390	50.4	846	52.7
Total	**339**		**774**		**1,605**	
Average Age	24.29		25.90		26.58	

[Courtesy of New Zealand Statistics.]

What I find interesting about the Vineyard pattern is that the age range remains relatively constant across all three censuses. Unlike the LDS, where it was clear that the predominance of children indicated the Mormons were replenishing their membership from below, the concentration of children here might also mean that whole families have been joining the Fellowship. The second concentration of members in the young middle-age range would support this hypothesis. I have once again placed the double-digit percentages in bold and I have underlined the "almost" double-digit percentages to make the age pattern more visually striking (refer to Table 3.3).

The Australian census does not include a separate item for the Vineyard Christian Fellowship (VCF), but the Canadian census does. In the Canadian case, the number of self-identified members of the VCF doubled between 1991 and 2001, from 1200 to 2595, but then fell off substantially to 1585 by the time of the 2011 census. I do not have any hypothesis to explain this pattern, except that it might be part of the long-term fallout from the schism of the Toronto Airport Vineyard Church which left the Vineyard movement in 1995 (Skjoldli 2014). However, it might be interesting to note that the Canadian Vineyard pattern was the inverse of the generic Pentecostalism pattern in Canada, which fell from 436,435 in 1991 to 369,475 in 2001, but then rose again to 478,705 by the 2011 census.

Spiritualism exhibits a different pattern. Unlike the Anglicans, who are declining, and New Zealand Mormons, who are treading water, Spiritualism, like Vineyard, is growing – quite remarkably. A religion with significantly more female than male adherents, the dominant proportion of women to men actually grows larger (though only slightly) across time. And unlike what one might expect from studies of new religions, converts to Spiritualism are mostly not youthful. In fact, if one focuses on the column of double-digit percentages in the 1991 census (between 30 and 49 years of age) and then traces it across to 2006 (where it ends up between 35 and 59 years of age), one gets a visual sense of a gradually aging religion attracting older converts, at least between the 1996 Census and the 2001 Census (refer to Table 3.4). If, in contrast, a significant number of younger people were becoming Spiritualists, then the average age would be declining rather than rising (a phenomenon we will observe in Census data on Wicca).

Spiritualism exhibits a similar pattern in Australia, where Spiritualist membership rose from 8143 to 9279 to 9844 to 11,554 members in the 1996, 2001, 2005 and 2011 censuses, respectively. In Canada, however, membership dropped between 1991 and 2001 from 3735 to 3295 self-identified Spiritualists, but then rose to 4315 by the 2011 census. Because Spiritualism is a non-Christian religion, at this point it is possible to refer to data from the British census. (As mentioned earlier, members of the major "world religions" clicked "Buddhist" or "Christian" or whatever in the UK census, meaning no data was collected on Christian denominations). According to the census data from England and Wales (Scotland and Northern Ireland collected census data separately), the number of self-identified Spiritualists rose from 32,404 in 2001 to 39,061 in the 2011 census.

Compared with the other religions we have been examining, the Church of Scientology (CoS) is quite small. It has been growing in New Zealand, though not at a spectacular rate. CoS was also growing in Australia until the 2011 census indicated that membership had declined by about 14% from a high in 2006. Also, in sharp distinction from Spiritualism, there are far more males than females in CoS, by a ratio of two-to-one in New Zealand and a ratio of three-to-two in Australia. The consistent predominance of males undercuts the generalization that more women than men join new religions (Machalek and Snow 1993), though back in the 1970s Roy Wallis was already reporting that more men than women joined Scientology (Wallis 1977). CoS also appears to attract a fairly wide range of new recruits, from youthful to middle-aged. In terms of age, both Australian and New Zealand Scientology appear to have frozen around 35 years of age, in part because

Table 3.4 Census Data for New Zealand Spiritualism, 1991–2006

NZ Spiritualism	1991		1996		2001		2006	
	No.	%	No.	%	No.	%	No.	%
0–4 Years	96	3.1	132	2.6	114	1.9	129	1.7
5–9 Years	96	3.1	183	3.6	201	3.4	180	2.3
10–14 Years	72	2.3	132	2.6	153	2.6	204	2.6
15–19 Years	138	4.5	153	3.0	201	3.4	213	2.7
20–24 Years	192	6.2	327	6.4	279	4.8	339	4.4
25–29 Years	258	8.4	462	9.1	432	7.4	429	5.5
30–34 Years	318	10.3	570	11.2	573	9.8	618	8.0
35–39 Years	354	11.5	573	11.2	684	11.7	846	10.9
40–44 Years	357	11.6	588	11.5	669	11.4	909	11.7
45–49 Years	309	10.0	570	11.2	654	11.2	930	12.0
50–54 Years	240	7.8	414	8.1	627	10.7	876	11.3
55–59 Years	192	6.2	318	6.2	480	8.2	780	10.1
60–64 Years	162	5.2	240	4.7	294	5.0	510	6.6
65 Years +	303	9.8	444	8.7	489	8.3	777	10.0
Male	894	29.0	1,410	27.7	1,563	26.7	2,064	26.7
Female	2,190	71.0	3,687	72.3	4,293	73.3	5,676	73.3
Total	3,084	100.0	5,097	100.0	5,856	100.0	7,740	100.0
Average Age	39.76		39.55		40.96		43.36	

[Courtesy of New Zealand Statistics.]

Table 3.5 Census Data for Australian Scientologists, 1996–2011

AU Scientologists	1996		2001		2006		2011	
	No.	%	No.	%	No.	%	No.	%
0–4 Years	92	6.2	81	4.0	56	2.2	78	3.6
5–9 Years	78	5.2	114	5.6	80	3.2	53	2.5
10–14 Years	89	6.0	121	5.9	130	5.2	78	3.6
15–19 Years	59	4.0	161	7.9	229	9.1	169	7.8
20–24 Years	131	8.8	151	7.4	345	**13.8**	247	**11.4**
25–29 Years	160	**10.7**	174	8.6	289	**14.0**	217	**10.0**
30–34 Years	224	**15.0**	227	**11.2**	206	8.2	187	8.6
35–39 Years	191	**12.8**	252	**12.4**	231	9.2	163	7.5
40–44 Years	158	**10.6**	212	**10.4**	237	9.5	191	8.8
45–49 Years	97	6.5	204	**10.0**	219	8.7	190	8.8
50–54 Years	55	3.7	105	5.2	195	7.8	180	8.3
55–59 Years	35	2.3	62	3.0	106	4.2	91	4.2
60–64 Years	33	2.2	44	2.2	63	2.5	65	3.0
65–69 Years	37	2.5	36	1.8	37	1.5	27	1.2
70–74 Years	21	1.4	34	1.7	34	1.4	31	1.4
75–79 Years	13	0.9	26	1.3	23	0.9	19	0.9
80–84 Years	10	0.7	18	0.9	15	0.6	11	0.5
85–89 Years	7	0.5	6	0.3	9	0.4	3	0.1
90–94 Years	0	0.0	6	0.3	3	0.1	0	0.0
95+ Years	0	0.0	0	0.0	0	0.0	0	0.0
Male	843	57.7	1166	57.3	1522	60.7	1273	58.9
Female	647	43.3	868	43.7	985	39.3	889	41.1
Total	**1490**		**2034**		**2507**		**2162**	
Average Age	32.72		34.11		34.30		34.62	

[Based on Australian Bureau of Statistics data.]

CoS is losing some of its older members and in part because it attracts, on average, somewhat younger recruits. Both because the numbers of Scientologists in New Zealand are so small (357 in the 2006 census) and because of the interesting dip in membership in Australia, Table 3.5 is taken from the Australian Census.

Examining Table 3.5, it appears that an influx of new members in their twenties and early teens fueled the expansion of CoS in Australia between the 2001 census and the 2006 census, but then people of all ages defected from the Church of Scientology between the 2006 census and the 2011 census.

I was actually anticipating a membership dip similar to Australia's in the 2011 censuses in both Canada and the United Kingdom. However, in Canada,

3 *Increasing Complexity versus Prior Generalizations* 59

CoS has grown from 1215 to 1525 to 1745 self-identified Scientologists in the 1991, 2001 and 2011 censuses. Similarly, in the United Kingdom in the 2001 census, 1781 people self-identified as Scientologists in England and Wales, whereas in the 2011 census, 2418 respondents reported being Scientologists. Critics, however, note that whereas the Australian census specifies *Church of* Scientology, figures for the British census resulted from respondents writing "Scientology" into an "Other" box provided on the UK census form. So at least some of the growth might be accounted for by an increase in numbers of independent Scientologists (a rapidly expanding subgroup, given the large number of defections in the past dozen or so years).

It has also been pointed out to this writer that, if one had only the ten-year figures from the Australian census from 2001 to 2011, the data would appear to indicate growth (from 2032 members to 2162 members) rather than a decline. The implication of this observation is that had the UK and Canada held censuses in 2006, perhaps one would find a comparable decrease in numbers of Scientologists in Canada and in England and Wales between 2006 and 2011. I have to confess, however, that I do not find this argument compelling.

Table 3.6 Census Data for the New Zealand Hare Krishna Movement, 1996–2006

NZ Hare Krishnas	1996		2001		2006	
	No.	%	No.	%	No.	%
0–4 Years	18	7.0	30	8.3	30	8.1
5–9 Years	30	**11.6**	36	9.9	30	8.1
10–14 Years	12	4.6	33	9.1	30	8.1
15–19 Years	30	**11.6**	33	9.1	24	6.5
20–24 Years	24	9.3	36	9.9	42	**11.3**
25–29 Years	36	**14.0**	30	8.3	33	8.9
30–34 Years	33	**12.8**	45	**12.3**	36	9.7
35–39 Years	27	**10.5**	42	**11.6**	33	8.9
40–44 Years	24	9.3	36	9.9	33	8.9
45–49 Years	12	4.6	24	6.6	33	8.9
50–54 Years	6	2.3	21	5.8	24	6.5
55–59 Years	3	1.2	6	1.6	12	3.2
60–64 Years	0	0.0	6	1.6	6	1.6
65 Years +	9	3.5	3	0.8	15	4.0
Male	135	52.3	198	54.5	192	51.6
Female	123	47.7	162	44.6	180	48.4
Total	258		363		372	
Average Age	27.05		27.61		30.23	

[Courtesy of New Zealand Statistics.]

Though quite different from Scientology, the Hare Krishna Movement is another "classic" new religion. Unlike Scientology, gender is balanced in the movement, though there is still a predominance of males. However, like the LDS in New Zealand, the New Zealand Hare Krishnas appear be "standing still" age-wise, losing older members and attracting a few younger members, plus, as indicated by the 0–4 category, replenishing its membership from within (refer to Table 3.6). In contrast, the Hare Krishna Movement in the United Kingdom grew from 637 in 2001 to 834 in 2011. The Australian census does not, as mentioned earlier, collect separate data on Hare Krishnas who thus appear to have been subsumed within Hinduism. Ditto with respect to the Canadian census.

Whereas the Hare Krishna Movement shows up in the New Zealand census but not in the Australian census, Eckankar – a kind of New Age group (not unlike the MSIA group we will encounter at different stages throughout

Table 3.7 Census Data for Australian Eckists, 1996–2011

AU Eckankar	1996	%	2001	%	2006	%	2011	%
0–4 Years	27	3.3	9	1.2	8	1.2	12	1.8
5–9 Years	47	5.7	24	3.2	14	2.1	16	2.4
10–14 Years	52	6.3	30	4.0	27	4.0	14	2.1
15–19 Years	38	4.6	31	4.1	33	4.9	21	3.1
20–24 Years	36	4.4	25	3.3	16	2.4	17	2.5
25–29 Years	40	4.9	33	4.4	31	4.6	19	2.8
30–34 Years	72	8.7	37	4.9	33	4.9	28	4.2
35–39 Years	101	**12.3**	60	7.9	32	4.7	24	3.6
40–44 Years	107	**13.0**	92	**12.2**	64	9.4	34	5.0
45–49 Years	76	9.2	104	**13.8**	79	**11.6**	62	9.2
50–54 Years	71	8.6	83	**11.0**	91	**13.4**	75	**11.1**
55–59 Years	54	6.6	76	**10.1**	66	9.7	99	**14.7**
60–64 Years	43	5.2	51	6.8	73	**10.7**	74	**11.0**
65–69 Years	27	3.3	43	5.7	58	8.5	71	**10.5**
70–74 Years	24	2.9	26	3.4	26	3.8	54	8.0
75–79 Years	8	1.0	18	2.4	19	2.8	28	4.2
80–84 Years	0	0.0	6	0.8	10	1.5	19	2.8
85–89 Years	0	0.0	6	0.8	0	0.0	7	1.0
90–94 Years	0	0.0	0	0.0	0	0.0	0	0.0
95+ Years	0	0.0	0	0.0	0	0.0	0	0.0
Male	351	**42.6**	343	**45.5**	286	**42.1**	294	**43.6**
Female	472	57.4	411	54.5	394	57.9	380	56.4
Total	823		754		680		674	
Average Age		37.9		42.2		45.9		51.6

[Based on Australian Bureau of Statistics data.]

this book) – is recorded in Australia but not New Zealand. And while the Hare Krishna Movement is gradually growing, Eckankar appears to be slowly declining. This decline is easy to follow in Table 3.7: The double-digit percentages gradually creep downwards with each census, reflecting a rise in average age with each census. And, of course, the overall number of members decline. Though the decline is slower and the size of the group is much smaller, this is essentially the same pattern we saw in the case of New Zealand Anglicanism. Eckankar also appears in the UK census. In the 2001 census, 423 respondents self-identified as "Eckists" (which is how members of Eckankar refer to themselves). In the 2011 census, the figure was 379 Eckists, indicating the same gradual decline on the other side of the world.

Satanism presents a completely different pattern from any of the religions we have examined up to this point. The outstanding feature of Table 3.8 is how the core of self-identified Satanists cluster in the 15 to 29 age

Table 3.8 Census Data for Australian Satanists, 1996–2011

AU Satanists	1996	%	2001	%	2006	%	2011	%
0–4 Years	13	0.6	19	1.0	22	1.0	30	1.2
5–9 Years	11	0.5	15	0.8	26	1.2	26	1.1
10–14 Years	37	1.8	46	2.6	50	2.2	42	1.7
15–19 Years	372	**17.7**	356	**19.8**	349	**15.5**	347	**14.1**
20–24 Years	725	**34.6**	474	**26.4**	545	**24.2**	571	**23.3**
25–29 Years	425	**20.3**	358	**19.9**	389	**17.3**	396	**16.1**
30–34 Years	213	**10.2**	187	**10.4**	286	**12.7**	312	**12.7**
35–39 Years	128	7.5	117	6.5	231	**10.3**	253	**10.3**
40–44 Years	59	2.8	67	3.7	126	5.6	177	7.2
45–49 Years	32	1.5	49	2.7	71	3.2	148	6.0
50–54 Years	15	0.7	27	1.5	55	2.4	57	2.3
55–59 Years	18	0.9	17	0.9	30	1.3	35	1.4
60–64 Years	7	0.3	10	0.6	18	0.8	22	0.9
65–69 Years	13	0.6	16	0.9	13	0.6	17	0.7
70–74 Years	6	0.3	3	0.2	9	0.4	6	0.2
75–79 Years	6	0.3	6	0.3	6	0.3	7	0.3
80–84 Years	3	0.1	0	0.0	6	0.3	0	0.0
85–89 Years	3	0.1	3	0.2	6	0.3	4	0.2
90–94 Years	0	0.0	0	0.0	0	0.0	0	0.0
95+ Years	12	0.6	19	1.0	10	0.4	3	0.1
Male	1780	84.8	1409	78.5	1690	75.2	1788	72.9
Female	318	**15.2**	386	**21.5**	558	**24.8**	665	**27.1**
Total	2098		1795		2248		2453	
Average Age	26.87		29.11		29.02		29.64	

[Based on Australian Bureau of Statistics data.]

range in all four of the relevant censuses in Australia. This means that the great majority drop out at some point in their late 20s/early 30s and are replaced by an entirely new cohort of young Satanists. In a sense, then, Satanism is a true youth religion that presents an age profile congruent with the portrayal of new religions in NRM conversion literature from the 1980s (Barker 1984; Levine 1984; Melton and Moore 1982), namely young converts to a religion dominated by youthful members.

Though heavily dominated by young males, there appears to be a slightly increasing proportion of female involvement. Additionally, though core Satanists are youthful, one can also see a gradual increase in the number of older Satanists across the four censuses. Thus the core 15–29 age range in the 1996 census contained 72.6% of the total, whereas this core age range contained 53.5% of the total in 2011 (most of the balance are spread across the 30–49 years of age categories). So although Satanism will likely continue to be a youth religion into the foreseeable future, there does seem to be a tendency to retain a small percentage of Satanic "elders." And while the average is slightly younger, one can see exactly the same pattern among Satanists in the New Zealand census (refer to Table 7.1 in Chapter Seven).

In terms of their demographic profile, New Zealanders who indicated they were Rastafarians follow the same pattern as Satanists. Also like Satanism, Rastafarianism outside of the Caribbean appears to be more about self-identity than religion in the conventional sense. As indicated in Table 3.9, the great majority are young males in their late teens or 20s who drop out as they get older, though, again like Satanism, increasing numbers are staying into their 30s and 40s.

Where Rastafarianism differs markedly from Satanism is that more than half (e.g., 738 out of 1,383 in the 2006 census) identified themselves as Maori (the indigenous people of New Zealand) or as one of the other traditional peoples of the Pacific. This marks a sharp departure from the conventional wisdom about recruits to most contemporary new religions, which are said to overwhelmingly recruit individuals of European descent.

Druidry presents yet another pattern, a pattern I had originally anticipated finding in most of the NRMs in the censuses. Druidism is growing quite well, and appears to be "recruiting" new members from a variety of different age groups. If most new Druids were young, then we should see a heavy predominance of new numbers in the 15–24 age range as we did with Satanism. But instead what we see is that new Druids are "converting" at a wide range of ages, and that the overall age profile is getting older – as indicated by the pattern of double-digit percentages across four censuses (see Table 3.10).

Another pattern among the Druids we had anticipated seeing in all of the NRMs in the New Zealand census is the gradual balancing out of the gender

3 Increasing Complexity versus Prior Generalizations

Table 3.9 Census Data for New Zealand Rastafarianism, 1991–2006

NZ Rastafarians	1991		1996		2001		2006	
	N	%	N	%	N	%	N	%
0–4 Years	39	5.6	21	3.6	21	1.6	24	1.7
5–9 Years	21	3.0	33	5.7	27	2.1	27	1.9
10–14 Years	18	2.6	9	1.6	60	4.6	51	3.7
15–19 Years	126	**18.1**	108	**18.6**	294	**22.6**	261	**18.9**
20–24 Years	231	**33.2**	132	**22.7**	297	**22.9**	291	**21.0**
25–29 Years	153	**22.0**	114	**19.6**	204	**15.7**	189	**13.7**
30–34 Years	66	9.5	84	**14.4**	150	**11.6**	168	12.2
35–39 Years	27	3.9	42	7.2	132	**10.2**	147	**10.6**
40–44 Years	9	1.3	24	4.1	57	4.4	114	8.2
45–49 Years	3	0.4	9	1.6	27	2.1	60	4.3
50–54 Years	0	0.0	0	0.0	15	1.2	27	1.9
55–59 Years	3	0.4	3	0.5	9	0.7	15	1.1
60–64 Years	0	0.0	0	0.0	3	0.2	3	0.2
65 Years +	0	0.0	0	0.0	6	0.5	3	0.2
Male	573	**82.3**	468	**80.4**	1,092	**84.1**	1,161	**83.9**
Female	126	18.1	111	19.1	204	15.7	219	15.8
Total	**696**	100.0	**582**	100.0	**1,299**	100.0	**1,383**	100.0
Average Age	23.02		24.11		25.5		27.43	

[Courtesy of New Zealand Statistics.]

ratio, though the percentage of females in the 2011 census drops slightly from their percentage in the 2006 census. I believe, however, that this interruption in the pattern can be explained by the influence of the "Teen Witch" fad that I will discuss in greater detail in Chapter Six. During the period of this fad, a significant number of young women (predominantly) became self-identified Pagans. They then dropped out following the demise of the fad. The fad likely explains both the marked increase in numbers of self-identified Druids between the 2001 census and the 2006 census and the increasing percentage of women recorded in 2006. Many of the people (especially women) involved with the fad subsequently left, which explains both the slowing down of the rate of growth between 2006 and 2011, as well as the slight drop in the percentage of female participation.

The impact of the Teen Witch fad on Wicca – a form of Paganism particularly identified with women – is easier to see. The population of Wiccans jumped sharply between 1996 and 2001, from 1852 to 8754 (an increase of almost 500%), and then dropped to 8213 by 2006. Also in contrast with Druids, the average age dropped in 2006. Additionally, the predominance

Table 3.10 Census Data for Australian Druidry

Census Year	1996	%	2001	%	2006	%	2011	%
0–4 Years	11	2.0	6	0.9	13	1.3	12	1.2
5–9 Years	15	2.7	14	2.0	31	3.0	15	1.4
10–14 Years	12	2.2	15	2.2	31	3.0	16	1.5
15–19 Years	30	5.4	40	5.8	52	5.1	44	4.2
20–24 Years	81	**14.6**	61	8.8	92	9.0	57	5.4
25–29 Years	83	**15.0**	84	**12.2**	80	7.8	75	7.2
30–34 Years	71	**12.8**	89	**12.9**	94	9.2	63	6.0
35–39 Years	89	**16.0**	91	**13.2**	90	8.8	89	8.5
40–44 Years	66	**11.9**	85	**12.3**	116	**11.4**	99	9.5
45–49 Years	49	8.8	88	**12.7**	148	**14.5**	147	**14.0**
50–54 Years	19	3.4	56	5.8	110	**10.8**	176	**16.8**
55–59 Years	10	1.8	34	4.9	90	8.8	109	**10.4**
60–64 Years	8	1.4	15	2.2	27	2.6	69	6.6
65–69 Years	5	0.9	5	0.7	21	2.1	39	3.7
70–74 Years	0	0.0	3	0.4	9	0.9	19	1.8
75–79 Years	6	1.1	5	0.7	9	0.9	7	0.7
80–84 Years	0	0.0	0	0.0	6	0.6	5	0.5
85–89 Years	0	0.0	0	0.0	9	0.9	3	0.3
90–94 Years	0	0.0	0	0.0	3	0.3	3	0.3
95 + Years	0	0.0	0	0.0	0	0.0	0	0.0
Male	388	69.9	456	66.0	646	62.2	665	63.5
Female	167	**30.1**	235	**34.0**	376	**37.8**	382	**36.5**
Total	555		691		1022		1047	
Average Age	33.0		36.5		39.8		43.5	

[Based on Australian Bureau of Statistics data.]

of females over males gradually increases across all four censuses. What happened?

Because Druidry and Wicca are both part of the larger Pagan movement, I had expected to find roughly similar statistics for both of these two "sub-movements." However, Wicca was even more strongly impacted by the Teen Witch fad (a phenomenon discussed in, e.g., Johnston and Aloi 2007; Berger and Ezzy 2007) than Druidry. A significant number of adolescent women became involved in Wicca in those years, in large part because Wicca (which means something more generic outside of the UK than Gardnerian or Alexandrian Wicca) has been presented in popular publications as a particularly feminine form of Paganism. This is why the population of Wiccans "exploded" around the turn of the millennium (Lewis 2007). Subsequently, as the Teen Witch fad faded, Wicca not only stopped growing rapidly, but actually declined, at least in Australia and New Zealand.

Table 3.11 Census Data for Australian Wicca, 1996–2011

Census Year	1996	%	2001	%	2006	%	2011	%
0–4 Years	55	3.0	271	3.1	210	2.6	204	2.5
5–9 Years	32	1.7	217	2.5	228	2.8	238	2.9
10–14 Years	50	2.7	353	4.1	319	3.9	326	3.9
15–19 Years	233	**12.8**	1185	**13.5**	618	7.5	580	7.0
20–24 Years	440	**23.8**	1738	**19.9**	1065	**13.0**	807	9.7
25–29 Years	355	**19.2**	1675	**19.1**	1155	**14.1**	911	**11.0**
30–34 Years	247	**13.3**	1172	**13.4**	1119	**13.6**	1041	**12.5**
35–39 Years	164	8.9	823	9.4	878	**10.7**	1134	**13.6**
40–44 Years	116	6.3	604	6.9	620	7.6	1026	**12.3**
45–49 Years	77	4.2	344	3.9	347	4.2	851	**10.2**
50–54 Years	39	2.1	198	2.3	216	2.6	622	7.5
55–59 Years	19	1.0	87	1.0	87	1.1	351	4.2
60–64 Years	11	0.6	40	0.5	33	0.4	186	2.2
65–69 Years	8	0.4	24	0.3	15	0.2	75	0.9
70–74 Years	3	0.2	6	0.1	10	0.1	35	0.4
75–79 Years	3	0.2	3	0.04	4	0.05	13	0.2
80–84 Years	0	0.0	7	0.1	4	0.05	11	0.1
85–89 Years	0	0.0	3	0.04	0	0.0	3	0.04
90–94 Years	0	0.0	0	0.0	0	0.0	0	0.0
95+ Years	0	0.0	0	0.0	0	0.0	0	0.0
Male	611	**33.0**	2133	**24.5**	1975	**24.0**	2005	**22.9**
Female	1241	67.0	6621	75.5	6238	76.0	6409	77.1
Total	1852		8754		8213		8314	
Average Age	27.6		27.4		24.6		34.9	

[Based on Australian Bureau of Statistics data.]

When Westerners become involved in Asian religions, these religions are often – though certainly not always – somewhat modified forms of traditional religions directed specifically to a Western audience. Asian religious groups that recruit primarily Westerners (e.g., the Hare Krishna Movement) are usually regarded as new religions. With a few exceptions, the New Zealand Census has generally not separated these groups out from the larger body of Buddhism. The census bureau has, however, categorized census respondents into ethnic categories, meaning that people of European ancestry who self-identify as Buddhists can be separated from the larger population of New Zealand Buddhists. Across the four censuses from 1991 to 2006, "Euro-Buddhists" have constituted between a sixth to a quarter of all Buddhists.

Between 1991 and 1996, and then again between 1996 and 2001, the number of Euro-Buddhists more than doubled. In addition to this explosive growth, what is remarkable is that it attracted people from a wide range of

Table 3.12 Census Data for New Zealand Euro-Buddhists, 1991–2006

NZ Euro-Buddhists	1991		1996		2001		2006	
	No.	%	No.	%	No.	%	No.	%
0–4 Years	120	5.6	192	4.2	432	4.0	372	3.5
5–9 Years	75	3.5	159	3.4	438	4.0	396	3.7
10–14 Years	39	1.8	153	3.3	549	5.0	504	4.7
15–19 Years	153	7.1	372	8.0	987	**9.1**	912	8.5
20–24 Years	222	**10.3**	528	**11.4**	930	8.6	825	7.7
25–29 Years	255	**11.8**	477	**10.3**	921	7.6	678	6.3
30–34 Years	318	**14.7**	498	**10.8**	1,032	**9.5**	969	**9.0**
35–39 Years	348	**15.1**	561	**12.1**	1,098	**10.1**	1,023	**9.5**
40–44 Years	312	**14.4**	597	**12.9**	1,188	**10.9**	1,074	**10.0**
45–49 Years	135	6.2	483	**10.4**	1,155	**10.6**	1,119	**10.4**
50–54 Years	66	3.1	255	5.5	942	8.7	1,095	**10.2**
55–59 Years	36	1.7	120	2.6	498	4.6	843	7.8
60–64 Years	36	1.7	75	1.6	252	2.3	423	3.9
65 Years +	36	1.7	150	3.2	450	4.1	531	4.9
Male	1,329	**61.5**	2,982	**64.5**	6,240	**57.4**	5,892	**54.8**
Female	831	38.5	1,644	35.5	4,626	42.6	4,866	45.2
Total	**2,160**	100.0	**4,623**	100.0	**10,869**	100.0	**10,755**	100.0
Average Age	31.92		33.36		34.48		36.82	
All Buddhists:	12,756		28,131		41,634		52,362	

[Courtesy of New Zealand Statistics.]

age groups. If, alternately, a younger group of seekers were converting to Buddhism, then the large number of new young recruits would be reflected in an age drop from 1991 to 1996 and from 1996 to 2001.

Another feature of Table 3.12 is the sharp drop off in new Buddhists from European backgrounds between 2001 and 2006. New Zealand Buddhism in general continued to grow quite well in that five-year period (from 41,634 to a total of 52,362 members), but not Euro-Buddhism. It is difficult to say what factors are responsible for this retrenchment. Perhaps Buddhism only appeals to a certain segment of the population, and by 2001 that segment of the population among people with European ancestry had been tapped out. In any event, it will be interesting to see what the 2013 New Zealand census finds in this regard.

Conclusion

What can we conclude from this survey of census findings? The "problem" with these various statistics is that any attempt to make generalizations about the memberships of all NRMs fails miserably – and that is precisely the point. It is not difficult to perceive patterns within Spiritualism, Scientology, Satanism, Druidry et cetera. But the sum of their differences mostly defeats efforts to draw out commonalities, particularly with respect to a predominance of one gender over the other, and to the ages of members and of new recruits.

Lorne Dawson's overview of the characteristics of NRM members – originally an article (Dawson 1996) and later reproduced both in his textbook (Dawson 1998; 2nd edition 2006) and in his reader (Dawson 2003) – is a useful point of reference for discussions of the conventional wisdom about members of new religions. The very first characteristic on his list of traits is the youthfulness of converts: "members of most NRMs are disproportionately young" (1998, 86). The notion that people who join alternative religions are predominantly youthful was, as mentioned earlier, initially formulated in the 1970s when large numbers of former counter-culturists were joining alternative religions. This view about the youth of converts continues to be presented as state-of-the-art knowledge in overviews of research on conversion (e.g., Dawson 2003; Gooren 2010). What should be clear from the census data is that this characteristic fits Satanism, Rastafarianism and Wicca, but not Spiritualism, Scientology, Druidism and the other new religions we examined.

Such findings profoundly call into question the validity of the more general tendency of new religion researchers to extrapolate findings from the study of one or two NRMs to all NRMs. Back in the 1970s when recruits to alternative religions were predominantly former counter-culturalists, it might have been the case that the sociological profiles of members of different NRMs were quite similar. However, time has passed and the situation has changed.

It is now clear that the post-1960s period was an anomaly, at least for the purpose of understanding membership in alternative religions. This is especially evident with respect to the age of converts. With the exception of true youth religions like Satanism, the average convert to NRMs is typically in her or his 30s – though even this generalization is frustrated by alternative religions like Spiritualism which recruit, on average, people in their 40s, and other new religions that recruit people from a broader range of different age groups. The aging of new religions plus the emergence of the Internet has in turn produced increasing diversification, effectively defeating efforts to essentialize the characteristics of members of new religious movements.

4 Toward a Paradigm for Longitudinal Studies – The Order of Christ Sophia[1]

In Chapters One and Two, I utilized what I described as a quasi-longitudinal approach. In the present chapter, I bring together and compare the results of three demographic surveys of a specific new religion, the Order of Christ Sophia (OCS). I have already brought some of this data to bear in both of the first two chapters. In contrast to the set of MSIA studies that I will examine in Chapter Five, these were intentionally administered in three-year intervals. Though the span of time across which this data was collected is relatively brief (2005, 2008, and 2011), it is nevertheless hoped that this study will provide a useful paradigm for NRM researchers with an interest in conducting longitudinal research.

The Order of Christ Sophia

The Order of Christ Sophia (OCS) is a small new religion descended from the Holy Order of MANS (HOOM). An unusual synthesis of traditional Catholicism and esoteric cosmology, the HOOM was – and the OCS is – a fascinating religious movement. An excellent monograph on the Holy Order of MANS, Phil Lucas' *The Odyssey of a New Religion*, appeared in 1995.

Earl Blighton, who had been involved in alternative spirituality for much of his life, started the group during the heyday of the counter-culture. Blighton, known to HOOM members as Father Paul, wedded New Thought with an esoteric belief system that included elements from Indian yoga systems to traditional practices from Catholicism. Founded in 1968, the Holy Order of MANS grew rapidly until the mid-1970s, and then went into gradual decline. By the late 1980s, the HOOM had dropped its esoteric teachings and transformed into Christ the Savior Brotherhood, a branch of the Eastern Orthodox tradition.

---

1. All original human subject research reported in this chapter adheres to the guidelines drawn up by the Norwegian National Committee for Research Ethics in the Social Sciences and the Humanities (http://www.etikkom.no/).

Father Peter Bowes, who had been a minister in HOOM, founded the Brotherhood of Christ following HOOM's decline. Father Peter's Brotherhood was short-lived. But one of Bowes' students, Mother Clare Watts, subsequently founded an all-women's order, the Holy Order of Sophia, which later became the Order of Christ Sophia after Bowes and Watts joined forces. The Order of Christ Sophia situates itself firmly in the tradition of HOOM. This is evident in OCS's theological terminology, clerical attire, and day-to-day rituals. There have also been certain additions to the original HOOM synthesis.

Self-described Christian Mystics, the Order of Christ/Sophia, like the original HOOM, is a kind of "New Age mystery school" that trains its members in the doctrines and practices of esoteric Christianity (Lucas 2002: 400). Founded in 1999, the OCS acknowledges that it draws its teachings directly from the HOOM. The most significant difference between the two is that the OCS works intensively with its students' psychological issues (both of the co-leaders are trained therapists). Partly because of its small size, the OCS also focuses its energies on being an esoteric school, though a few years ago the Order opened its doors to lay participation. In the short span of a dozen years, the Order of Christ Sophia has experienced more than its fair share of controversy. From an accusatory media, to disenchanted ex-members, to direct assaults from the anti-cult Movement (ACM), the Order has matured in a hostile milieu.

I stumbled onto the OCS in early 2005, when I was teaching at the University of Wisconsin Milwaukee (one of the original Order centers was located in Milwaukee). In March 2005, I arranged with the Order to conduct a study of their organization. The results of the demographic aspect of this study were initially published as a research note the next year (Lewis 2006).

Then in May 2008, Barbara Johnson (an ex-member with a doctorate in sociology) and I re-administered the demographic portion of the questionnaire to the membership. Data from these two questionnaires formed the basis for a chapter in a book on the Order of Christ Sophia that I co-authored/co-edited with Nicolas Levine, *Children of Jesus and Mary* (Lewis and Levine 2010). In Chapter Three of that volume, Johnson and I examined the demographic characteristics of the membership, and discussed how people became members. Though some of the OCS data supported generally accepted conclusions that researchers had drawn from earlier studies of new religious movements (NRMs), on certain points the data called into question – sometimes dramatically – prior generalizations.

Finally, in early 2011, I re-contacted the leadership of the OCS and proposed to once again administer a questionnaire to the Order's membership as part of a long-term project to construct a longitudinal portrait of this dynamic organization. Father Peter and Mother Clare were agreeable. I hope to be able to continue to administer questionnaires to the OCS membership in three-year intervals.

In the following pages, I will be comparing data from the 2011 questionnaire with data from the 2005 and 2008 surveys. As in my earlier chapters, I will be referring to Lorne Dawson's 1996 overview of relevant NRM studies, "Who Joins New Religions and Why," as reproduced in the second edition of his *Cults and New Religions* (2003) as well as Chapter Four in his *Comprehending Cults* (2nd edition 2006). Dawson's systematic survey of new religion membership and conversion studies makes it a useful basis of comparison. In the first part of the present chapter, I have also liberally plagiarized my previous reports on findings from earlier OCS questionnaires.

Age and Affiliation

In early April of 2005, questionnaires were distributed to the full OCS membership. By late April, 77 useable questionnaires had been collected, which was a more-than-adequate sample, representing well over 50% of the Order's active membership. It should be noted that, given the questionnaire's length, this was an exceptionally good rate of return. In addition to standard demographic questions and a short set of open-ended items, respondents were also given essentially the same extensive questionnaire (slightly modified to reflect differences between The Family International and the OCS) that Bainbridge used as the basis for *The Endtime Family* (2002). Results from the attitude part of this first questionnaire were reported in Chapter Nine of *Children of Jesus and Mary*.

In 2008, the demographic section of the original questionnaire was re-administered to the Order's membership. By 2008, the Order had grown from slightly less than 100 active members to between 130 and 150 active members. Of these, 125 answered the questionnaire. In 2011, I posted an expanded OCS questionnaire on Survey Monkey. Between the 19th of July and the 21st of August, 154 members took the expanded survey. This once again represents an excellent rate of response, given that there were about 200–230 adult members (which does not count 50–65 children and teenagers) at the time.

The average age of the 2005 sample was 40. By 2008 the average had risen to 42 years-old. And by 2011 the average age was 44. In 2005, the mean length of membership was only two-and-a-half years; by 2008, this had increased to four years; and by 2011, to five years. For all three questionnaires, average age at recruitment was 37–38 years-old. I had originally suspected that the 40–44 years-old figure might be somewhat deceptive.

My impression had been that the OCS was a blend of baby boomers and a younger (relatively speaking) set of seekers. If this informal observation was accurate, I reasoned 40–44 represented a median figure between two different age groupings. And, in fact, when I broke the data down into five-year intervals, it revealed two groups – though the two were less dramatic than I had anticipated – instead of a bell curve (refer to Tables 4.1a-c).

The spikes in the 1950s/late 1940s can be explained as a function of members who are baby boomers. A number of the novices at the Milwaukee Center of Light (as the OCS refers to its local centers) with whom I spoke in 2005 were baby boomers who became self-identified spiritual seekers earlier in their lives. Their participation in the Order thus appeared to be the latest stage in a lifelong spiritual quest.

In contrast, the data for members born in the 1960s and 1970s (and, for the most recent questionnaire, the early 1980s) cannot really be called a "spike." Instead, what is striking about this group of members is the relatively even distribution of birth years across two decades. Also, this younger group is not really "young" compared with the youthfulness of recruits to the Unification Church and the Hare Krishna Movement in the 1970s and 1980s. Their average age works out to be mid-30s, meaning the average age at which they affiliated was in the early 30s range. These figures stand in sharp contrast to the age profile of the original HOOM, which drew its recruits almost exclusively from counter-cultural youth.

Education and Income

Another characteristic of NRM members often discussed by researchers is educational background. In the words of Lorne Dawson, "with few exceptions studies have found that recruits to NRMs are on average markedly better educated than the general public" (2003: 122). Despite its apparent importance, analysts' interpretation of this factor have been superficial. For example, Dawson cites Wilson and Dobbelaere, who suggest that, "To be properly understood, the teachings [of most NRMs] demand literate intelligence, a willingness to study, and lack of fear in the face of unfamiliar concepts and language" (2006: 85).

This conclusion, however, comes across as overly speculative, even ad hoc. Although the ideologies of many new religions are complex and sophisticated, members are not typically required to grasp their intricacies any more than average church-goers are required to master the nuances of Christian theology. For most new religions, a more likely explanation is the social class of recruits. Class is the third item of Dawson's survey, and he notes that members

Table 4.1a Age – 2005

Year of Birth	No.	%*
1980–85	2	2.6
1975–79	10	13.0
1970–74	12	15.6
1965–69	13	16.9
1960–64	11	14.3
1955–59	6	7.8
1950–54	13	15.6
1945–49	5	6.5
1940–44	4	5.2

Table 4.1b Age – 2008

Year of Birth	No.	%*
1980–85	12	9.6
1975–79	19	15.2
1970–74	26	20.8
1965–69	16	12.8
1960–64	20	16.0
1955–59	9	7.2
1950–54	8	6.4
1945–49	10	8.0
1940–44	5	3.2
< 1940	1	0.8

Table 4.1c Age – 2011

Year of Birth	No.	%*
1980–85	20	12.9
1975–79	30	19.5
1970–74	22	14.3
1965–69	17	11.0
1960–64	16	10.4
1955–59	20	12.9
1950–54	12	7.8
1945–49	6	3.9
1940–44	2	1.3
< 1940	4	2.6

[*Percentages in these and in subsequent tables do not total 100% because figures are rounded off to the nearest tenth of a percent.]

of NRMs are "disproportionately from middle- to upper-middle-class households, the advantaged segments of the population" (2003: 122). The relatively privileged position provided by their class background generally leads to a better education and the resulting opportunities to consider spiritual alternatives, as well as more freedom to experiment with these alternatives.

With respect to the Order of Christ/Sophia, a relevant questionnaire item requested gross annual income. Out of 71 responses (there were six non-responses) to the 2005 survey, the average was $46,000. This figure was for individual income. Some respondents explained that they were mothers working at part-time jobs, making anywhere from $4,000 to $15,000 per year. Had we requested annual *family* income, the figure would have been higher. Based on the relatively high average income of respondents, it is reasonable to infer that a substantial proportion were from middle- or upper-middle-class backgrounds. In 2008, the average annual income for Order participants increased to $53,754. By 2011, mean income had increased to $69,049 annually. Some but not all of this difference is due to inflation.

We should note in passing that the Order's economic structure is quite different from the economic structure of the original Holy Order of MANS. HOOM required full-time members to give all wages earned from outside jobs – often menial work – to the general fund of their home center (Lucas 1995: 79). OCS members, on the other hand, are often well-paid individuals who tithe 10% of their income to support the work of the Order.

If the average income of OCS members is surprising, their educational accomplishments are startling. In the 2005 survey, all but four respondents had attended college, and 62 – or slightly more than 80% – completed a bachelor's degree (refer to Tables 4.2a-c).

In terms of number of college graduates, OCS outpaces all other new religions for which we have data. The closest runner up is the Osho (Rajneesh) movement. In a study of Rajneeshpuram members, Latkin et al., (1987) report 64% held a college degree. In a further random sampling, they "uncovered 24% with a master's degree and 12% with a doctorate of some sort" (Dawson 2003: 122). In other words, Rajneeshpuram had a greater percentage of people with advanced degrees than OCS in 2005, but fewer members with advanced degrees than the Order in 2008 and 2011.

One factor explaining OCS members' greater attainment in this area is age. If a religion is recruiting middle- and upper-middle-class people in their late 30s, it is only natural that the group will have completed more education than a religion recruiting people in their late teens and early 20s. But it should also be said that a group which refers to its centers as "spiritual schools" (http://www.orderofchristsophia.org), and which offers "classes" as its primary vehicle for attracting new members, is likely to

Table 4.2a Highest Degree – 2005

Educational Level	No.	%
Advanced Degree	24	31
Bachelors	38	49
Some college	11	14
No college	4	5

Table 4.2b Highest Degree – 2008

Educational Level	No.	%
Advanced Degree	55	44
Bachelors	48	38
Some college	19	15
No college	3	2

Table 4.2c Highest Degree – 2011

Educational Level	No.	%
Advanced Degree	72	47
Bachelors	49	32
Associates/Tech Degree	9	6
Some college	18	12
No college	5	3

attract educationally-oriented individuals. Like the New Age/metaphysical subculture more generally (Lewis 2003: 134–38), the Order regards the spiritual path – indeed, the whole of one's life experience – as a "school" (Watts 2003: 43).

Gender Ratio

Yet another characteristic of NRMs examined in Dawson's survey is gender ratio. I discussed this in Chapter Three. The OCS is disproportionately female; in the 2005 sample, 56 (almost three-quarters) were women, and 21 were men. Part of this imbalance can be explained by the fact that the Order of Christ/Sophia grew out of an earlier, all-women's order, the Holy Order of Sophia. Had the OCS begun differently, perhaps the current Order would be closer to the two-thirds proportion of females to males I observed in MSIA (discussed in the next chapter). Dawson refers to a few studies which indicate sex imbalances may be adjusted over time. And though the proportion of women to men in the OCS will likely decrease, I anticipate women will continue to constitute a majority of the membership into the foreseeable future because of the women's spirituality issues addressed by the Order, and because of the opportunities for females assuming leadership positions in the organization (e.g., the great majority of OCS clergy are women). In 2008, the proportion of female to male was starting to change, with females making up 70% (87) of the membership and males 30% (38). This gradual shift continued to be evident in the 2011 survey, with 68% (105) females to 32% (49) males.

Religious Heritage

As with sex ratio, the religious backgrounds of people who join NRMs vary from group to group. Especially in the case of Eastern-oriented groups, new religions tend to draw disproportionately from people of Jewish heritage (e.g., one study found that 50% of the members of the San Francisco Zen Center were Jewish [Tipton 1982]). Catholic recruitment is roughly comparable to their percentage of the population. And Protestants are typically underrepresented, except in Protestant-type groups such as new religions arising out of the Jesus movement.

The Order of Christ/Sophia has a relatively minor over-representation of members from Jewish backgrounds – almost 8% in 2005, almost 5% in 2008 and over 7% in 2011, compared with less than 2% in the general US population. But in 2005, the Order had a markedly disproportionate percentage of former Catholics – close to 50% compared with 26% of the general population – though the percentage of people from the Catholic tradition dropped to 36.8% in 2008 and to 37.7% in 2011 (refer to Tables 4.3a-c).

Though the most obvious explanation is not always the correct one, in this case the explanation for the disproportionate number of ex-Catholics likely is that certain aspects of the OCS are reminiscent of Catholicism. As a consequence, people from Catholic backgrounds – and, to a lesser extent, people from Episcopalian and Lutheran backgrounds – are more likely to feel at home in the Order.

Interestingly, participation rates for Catholics and Protestants in OCS in 2005 corresponded almost exactly with participation rates for Catholics and Protestants in the Holy Order of MANS – 50% Roman Catholic and 35% Protestant. In his study of HOOM, Lucas postulates three factors that made the group 'particularly attractive to those reared as Catholics':

(1) its ceremonial and sacerdotal dimensions (which resonated with Catholic ritualism);
(2) its appropriation of Catholic religious garb and monastic practices;
(3) its hierarchical priesthood and governing structure (1995: 69).

Table 4.3a Religious Heritage – 2005

Religion	No.	%
Catholic	37	48.1
Protestant	27	35.1
Jewish	6	7.8
Muslim	1	1.3
None	6	7.8

Table 4.3b Religious Heritage – 2008

Religion	No.	%
Catholic	46	36.8
Protestant	52	41.6
Jewish	6	4.8
Muslim	2	1.6
None	19	15.2

Table 4.3c Religious Heritage – 2011

Religion	No.	%
Catholic	57	37.7
Protestant	57	37.7
Orthodox	2	1.3
Metaphysical Christian	7	4.6
Jewish	11	7.3
Muslim	0	0.0
Buddhist	4	2.6
Chinese Traditional	2	1.3
Pagan	2	1.3
Order of Christ Sophia	9	6.0
None	16	10.6

These observations can be extended to the Order of Christ/Sophia. Richardson and Stewart have pointed out that many of the recruits to the Jesus movement come from strict Protestant backgrounds – backgrounds they rebelled against as adolescents. Thus they are, in a sense, "returning fundamentalists" (1977: 819–38). If this is a fair characterization, then we might say that many of the people who join the OCS are, in some sense, "returning Catholics" (though it should immediately be said not all Order members from a Catholic background had "rebelled" against their Catholic upbringing before meeting the OCS).

78   Sects & Stats

This line of analysis seemed quite reasonable at the time of the first questionnaire in 2005. However, by 2008, the number of Catholics in the Order had declined by 11.3%, which tends to undermine my interpretation of the 2005 data. Nevertheless, ex-Catholics were on the rise again and the percentage of ex-Protestants falling by 2011. Also, as reflected in Table 4.3c, by 2011 the Order of Christ Sophia was recruiting people from a wider variety of backgrounds, including some individuals whose parents were members of the OCS.

Initial Point of Contact

As we have seen, researchers have been interested in how people become involved in alternative religions. The generalization that many members are recruited through family and friendship networks applies to the Order of Christ/Sophia, though the picture is a little more complicated than for other new religions (refer to Tables 4.4a-c).[2]

If we confine the OCS data to relatives and friends, the total percentage ends up being 42.9% in 2005, 37.6% in 2008, and 33.9% in 2011 – or

---

2. In the 2005 and 2008 surveys, the various 'Introduction to OCS' categories were composed retrospectively from responses to open-ended items. For the 2011 survey, respondents choose from a grid of preselected responses. The results from the latter, however, were less clear than anticipated. Almost 38% of the sample clicked the 'Other' category and wrote out their responses. I subsequently reclassified these discursive responses and placed them into the grid, though I found I also had to add a couple of new categories, such as 'Casual Meeting with a Member.' To provide some sample responses to the 'Other' option that were subsequently reclassified as 'Casual Meeting with a Member':

   One of the sisters spoke with me on the soccer sidelines and invited me to come.
   Met one of the Teachers.
   Mother Clare came to a dance class I was teaching.
   I met priests in the Order at a public festival
   A deacon came to volunteer at my work (a nursing home) and I started talking to her. She invited a co-worker and I to an Intro class.
   I sat next to Rev. Louise at a lecture and started a conversation before the lecture started and she invited me to her lecture the following weekend on the law of attraction.

   Table 4c thus represents a synthesis of responses to the original forced-choice grid of options with a condensation of responses to the open-ended 'Other' option.

less than half. Alternately, if we add co-workers and professional contacts to the "personal" category, the total percentage rises to 57.2% in 2005 and 52.8% in 2008 – or more than half – though the percentage in the most recent questionnaire rises only 8.3% (even adding the emergent category "Casual Meeting with a Member" still only brings the percentage up to 47.9%, though this is quite close to 50%). So the question of whether the Order fit the "majority" pattern in 2005/2008 that was noted by Dawson depends on how one interprets the data.

I was frankly surprised to find that so many respondents' (28.4% in 2005; 33.6% in 2008; 28% in 2011) first point of contact with the Order was via flyers, ads, publications, and public events like Body, Mind, Spirit Expos. (If we add the emergent category Websites, the 2011 figure rises to 43%).

Table 4.4a Introduction to OCS – 2005

Initial Point of Contact	No.	%
Relative or Partner	9	11.7
Friend	24	31.2
Co-worker	3	3.9
Professional Contact	8	10.4
Public Event	9	11.7
*Giving Birth to God**	5	6.5
Newspaper Ad	4	5.1
Flyer	4	5.1
Other	10	13.0
Non-Response	1	1.3

Table 4.4b Introduction to OCS – 2008

Initial Point of Contact	No.	%
Relative or Partner	11	8.8
Friend	36	28.8
Co-worker	1	0.8
Professional Contact	18	14.4
Public Event	18	14.4
*Giving Birth to God**	11	8.8
Newspaper Ad	6	4.8
Flyer	7	5.6
Other	15	12.0
Non-Response	2	1.6

[**Giving Birth to God* is a book by Mother Clare Watts, one of the Order's co-leaders.]

Table 4.4c Introduction to OCS – 2011

Answer Options	No.	%
Friend	31	20.1
Co-Worker	4	2.6
Professional Contact	8	5.7
Public Event	15	9.7
Partner/Spouse	14	9.3
Relative	7	4.5
Causal Meeting with a Member	8	5.7
Website	28	14.6
Book	3	2.0
Magazine	2	1.3
Newspaper/Newsletter Ad	3	2.0
TV or Movie	1	0.7
Flyer; Poster	13	8.4
Student group	1	0.7
Other	13	8.4
NR	3	2.0

By comparison, only 3.6% people who became involved in MSIA did so via impersonal media (Lewis 1997: 183). I should also point out that in questionnaire research on a sample of 500 current and former members of MSIA, only two respondents (or 0.4%) mentioned the movement's books (some of which had been on *The New York Times* best-seller list) as being primary factors attracting them to MSIA (Lewis 1997: 105). By comparison, the finding that five respondents (6.6%) in 2005 and 11 respondents (8.8%) in 2008 first became interested in the OCS via the book *Giving Birth to God* is quite remarkable (though this percentage falls to 2% for a "book" as the first point of contact in the 2011 survey).

Discussion

So what can we say about the development of the Order of Christ Sophia across the course of these three surveys? The most remarkable change is that the OCS has more than doubled in size since the first questionnaire in 2005. Some of the Order's other changing characteristics are a direct result of this expansion. Thus the gradually increasing age of its membership and the greater diversity in the religious backgrounds of members could probably have been anticipated.

The marked imbalance between male and female members appears to be gradually evening out, though the Order will likely remain dominated by females in the foreseeable future. Gender balance is a characteristic that bears watching if a fourth questionnaire is administered at some time in the future.

I was a little puzzled over the "Highest Degree" statistic. The overall educational level of the membership rose noticeably between 2005 and 2008, but seemed to level off or even decline slightly by 2011. This difference is too small to merit a closer examination at this juncture, but once again it bears watching in future questionnaires.

Finally, unlike certain European countries, it does not appear that the Order of Christ Sophia will go bankrupt anytime soon. The operating budget of the OCS is derived from a 10% tithe on the income of its active membership. And not only are the number of members of the Order increasing, but the average income of its membership also continues to rise. The result is a financially stable organization with the extra resources to fund its expansion.

Conclusion

While these findings are not particularly remarkable, it must be kept in mind that we are talking about changes that have taken place during only two three-year periods in the life of a young religion. Though it would have been more dramatic to have examined statistics for changes in an older religion across the course of, say, several ten-year periods, the NRM field currently has so few longitudinal studies that we should welcome any effort to fill the void. It should also be noted that shorter intervals of time between the administration of questionnaires to the same group is attractive because it allows one to chart the path of specific changes in ways that longer intervals do not.

Despite the widely-recognized lack of longitudinal studies in the new religions field, few if any NRM specialists are currently engaged in this kind of research. Part of the problem is that when we examine a long-range research project like the one reported in Gary Shepherd and Gordon Shepherd's *Talking with the Children of God* (2010), it is easy to feel intimidated by the time and effort that this kind of research requires. However, a basic longitudinal study does not require one to utilize the Shepherds' extensive project as their research paradigm. Particularly given the availability of online questionnaire services like Survey Monkey, it is comparatively painless to collect and calculate responses to a basic demographic survey. Hopefully, the research reported in this chapter will encourage future efforts in this direction.

5 The Movement of Spiritual Inner Awareness – Demographic Patterns, 1998–2011[1]

The study presented in this chapter was originally conceived as being part of my larger effort to fill the gap in quantitative and longitudinal data. However, instead of arising out of a project which aimed to construct a longitudinal study from the very beginning, the object of the present study was to take questionnaire data that had originally been reported in the late 1990s and construct a follow-up questionnaire that would constitute a two-term longitudinal study. The analysis will thus bring together and compare the results of two demographic surveys of the Movement of Spiritual Inner Awareness (MSIA, a NRM we met in Chapter One). The surveys were undertaken 13 years apart. The first, conducted by Constance Jones in 1998, was reported in two conference papers, one by Jones (1998) and the other by Michela M. Zonta (1998). The second surveyed MSIA's participants in late 2011.[2]

The Movement of Spiritual Inner Awareness

Briefly, the Movement of Spiritual Inner Awareness is a contemporary religious movement that was founded by John-Roger Hinkins in 1971. While MSIA has often been characterized as "New Age," and while it participates in the larger metaphysical subculture, MSIA's core spiritual practices lie

---

1. All original human subject research reported in this article adheres to the guidelines drawn up by the Norwegian National Committee for Research Ethics in the Social Sciences and the Humanities (available at: http://www.etikkom.no/).
2. I had conducted an earlier survey three years before Jones; those findings were reported in *Seeking the Light* (1997). I am not utilizing the 1995 data here, in part because I merged data from current and former members, which makes comparison problematic, and in part because the three year gap between 1995 and 1998 is too short to justify the complexity of juxtaposing data from all three surveys. I will, however, examine select items from the 1995 questionnaire in Chapter Ten.

squarely in the Sant Mat (Radhasoami) tradition. In 1963, while undergoing surgery for a kidney stone, Roger Hinkins fell into a nine-day coma. Upon awakening, he found himself aware of a new spiritual personality – "John" – who had superseded or merged with his old personality. After the operation, Hinkins began to refer to himself as "John-Roger," in recognition of his transformed self.

In common with Sant Mat groups, MSIA pictures the cosmos as composed of many different levels or "planes." At the point of creation, these levels sequentially emerged from God along a vibratory "stream" until creation reached its terminus in the physical plane. The Sant Mat tradition teaches that individuals can be linked to God's creative energy, and that this stream of energy will carry their consciousness back to God. The Mystical Traveler Consciousness – which formerly manifested through John-Roger (it has since been anchored in John Morton, his spiritual successor) – accomplished this link up during initiation, although the individual still had to appropriate and utilize the link through the practice of special meditation techniques (referred to as spiritual exercises), particularly meditation on the mantra "Hu."

Approach

The first questionnaire consisted of a set of simple demographic questions that was mailed to a sample of 1,300 MSIA participants in the spring of 1998. The sample was drawn from North American Discourse subscribers (meaning people who receive monthly lessons from the organization, the only way MSIA keeps track of its broader pool of participants). At the time, approximately 5,000 people were subscribing, the largest number of whom were US residents. Five hundred and sixty-six people (44%) responded. The second questionnaire was quite lengthy, containing a total of 76 items (both open and forced choice), that collected a wide variety of demographic and attitude data. It was posted online via Survey Monkey. The MSIA organization very generously sent letters to 2662 US discourse subscribers notifying them about the research project.

The questionnaire was open from the second week of November until New Year's Eve 2011. By midnight December 31st, the survey had received 531 responses. Respondents were given the option of printing out and mailing in their questionnaires rather than saving them in Survey Monkey, and I received another 46 by mail for a total of 577. This represents a response rate of approximately 22%, which is not bad considering that a 72–item survey requires hours to time to complete properly. Because of the time that would be involved tabulating data from pen-and-paper surveys, I will only look at the figures from the online respondents to the 2011 questionnaire in the present article.

Sex Ratio

MSIA's sex ratio has remained steady, namely twice as many female (67% in 1998; 66% in 2011) as male (33% in 1998; 34% in 2011) respondents to both surveys. Though the evidence may not favor a predominance of women in new religions as a general pattern, my participant-observer experience at New Age events over the years has been that roughly two-thirds of participants are female. Thus, one might reasonably expect to find a predominance of women in New Age-type NRMs. This was, in fact, the case with the Order of Christ Sophia, which had almost three times as many female as male participants (Lewis 2006: 95–96).

Table 5.1 Gender

	1998		2011	
	%	No.	%	No.
Male	33	183	34	177
Female	67	380	66	347

Unlike the first survey, the 2011 survey also asked about sexual orientation. The larger majority responded heterosexual (87%), then lesbians (4%), gay (4%), bisexual (3%) and other (2%).

Age

In the 1998 survey, birth data was collected in terms of decade of birth, ending in 1983 – presumably the birth year for the youngest person/people to respond to the questionnaire. The 2011 survey collected data in terms of year of birth, ending in 1994 – the birth year of the youngest respondent. Zonta identifies everyone born in the 1940s and 1950s as baby boomers (1998: 2), which means that 72% – or almost three-fourths – of respondents were baby boomers, with the balance split about equally before (12%) and after (15%) that generation.

If we use the same criterion for data from the 2011 survey, then baby boomers still predominate, though the percentage works out to more like two-thirds (66%) of the sample. However, the US Census Bureau delimits the baby boom as those born between 1946 and 1965. By this criterion, somewhat fewer 2011 questionnaire respondents were baby boomers (62%). Looking at the columns of figures for each survey side by side in Table 5.2, it appears not much has changed in the 13 years between 1998 and 2011. Some of the older participants have died and a handful (relatively speaking) of younger people have joined, leaving the folks born in the 1940s and 1950s pretty much as they were. There is, however, more dynamism among MSIA participants than these figures seem to suggest.

Table 5.2 Decade of Birth

	1998		2011	
	%	No.	%	No.
1900–39	12	70	7	36
1940–49	32	181	32	170
1950–59	40	227	34	180
1960–69	12	70	15	80
1970–83	3	15	9	49
1984–94	0	0	1	5

Part of the problem, as discussed in prior chapters, is that we tend to assume that new recruits to alternative religions are youthful. This makes it appear that only a handful of people came on board between 1998 and 2011. However, the 2011 questionnaire asked respondents both when they became participants as well as how old they were at the time. When these figures are laid out in a table of five-year periods, it can be seen that recruitment age has steadily risen over time until, in the past couple of years, the "average convert" is now topping 45 years of age (refer to Table 1.5 in Chapter One).

Marital Status

Almost half (47%) of respondents to the 1998 survey were married, a bit more than a fifth (21%) were single, about the same number divorced or separated (32%), and a handful widowed (3%). The 2011 survey provided twice as many categories, making straightforward comparison difficult. I have therefore separated the data into two tables.

If we add "divorced and remarried" and "widowed and remarried" to the legally married category, then half (50%) of respondents were married. Depending on how one wishes to treat the "live with life partner" and "committed relationship" categories, then there were fewer or more single respondents than in 1998. And if we add figures for divorced and separated categories from the 2011 survey, we get a figure comparable to 1998. Overall, these are very similar profiles.

Table 5.3 Marital Status

	1998	
	%	No.
Single	21	120
Married	47	268
Separated/Divorced	21	121
Widowed	3	19

	2011	
	%	No.
Single; Never Married	14	78
Live with life partner	5	27
Committed Relationship	5	30
Married Legally	42	225
Divorced	20	107
Separated	2	12
Widowed	4	24
Divorced and Remarried	7	41
Widowed and Remarried	1	4

Children

Given the similarity in marital patterns, it is perhaps unsurprising that that numbers of offspring and percentages of respondents having children were quite similar between the two surveys. Both in 1998 and 2011, 43%-45% of participants had no children, with similar percentages of respondents reporting one, two, and three or more. One difference is that the 2011 questionnaire found that 116 respondents (22%) had grandchildren. This statistic was not recorded in 1998.

Table 5.4 Number of Children

	1998		2011	
	%	No.	%	No.
None	43	246	45	239
One	17	98	17	90
Two	19	109	23	121
Three+	17	99	15	81

Education

I have referred to Lorne Dawson's work earlier, in the discussion of the age of recruits. After age, the second characteristic of NRM members examined by Dawson is educational background. In his words, "with few exceptions studies have found that recruits to NRMs are on average markedly better educated than the general public" (2003: 122).

Both the 1998 and the 2011 surveys included an item asking respondents about their highest degree. Using the four categories from the 1998 study, we get Table 5.5.

Table 5.5 Highest Degree

	1998		2011	
	%	No.	%	No.
Graduate Degree	43	242	64	337
Bachelor's Degree	28	159	18	97
Some College	20	115	14	81
High School or Less	8	47	4	24

Unlike the findings on marriage and children patterns, here we see a significant difference between the two surveys. We should also note that 87 respondents to the 2011 questionnaire were working on a Bachelor's or on a graduate degree at the time, which would raise MSIA's current educational level even higher.

In terms of percentage of college graduates, MSIA is in the same league as the Order of Christ Sophia (OCS), 83% of whose members had Bachelor's degrees in 2008 (Lewis and Levine 2010: 72) – compared with MSIA's 82%. MSIA, however, has a higher percentage of graduate degrees, 64% in contrast with OCS's 44%. Like the OCS, a major factor explaining MSIA participants' greater attainment in this area is age. If a religion is recruiting mostly middle-class people in their 40s, it is only natural that group members will have completed more education than a religion recruiting people in their early 20s. But it should also be said that a group which refers to its meetings as "seminars," and which offers "classes," "trainings," and spiritual science "degrees," is likely to attract educationally-oriented individuals.

Occupation and Income

In the United States, the most important factor determining class status is one's occupation. The 1998 survey indicated a heavy predominance of in the

Table 5.6 Occupation

	1998	
	%	No.
Professional/technical	46	259
Administrative/self-employed	30	168
Sales/clerical	11	60
Skilled labor	2	13
Unskilled labor	0	0
Farming	1	4
Unemployed	1	3
Not in labor force	9	54

	2011	
	%	No.
Student	4	14
Computer Science Professional	4	16
Editor/Writer	2	7
Homemaker	6	22
Teacher/Professor	11	38
Artist	4	15
Graphic Artist/Designer	2	7
Counselor/Therapist/Psychologist	11	38
Medical Doctor	1	4
Registered Nurse	3	10
Other Health Professional	5	17
Administrator/Manager	9	34
Administrative Assistant/Secretary	2	7
Sales Personnel	3	12
Cook/Chef	0.3	1
Self-Employed Business Owner	21	75
Librarian/Archivist	0	0
Accountant	2	8
Social Worker	1	5
Engineer	2	7
Technician	2	7
Legislator or Elected Government Official	0	0
Lawyer or Other Legal Professional	2	8
Military	0	0
Statistician; Other Mathematics Professional	0	0
Architect	0	0
Cashier/Teller	1	2
Travel Attendant	0	0
Housekeeping or Restaurant Service Worker	1	5
Personal Care Worker	0.3	1

"professional/technical" and the "administrative/self-employed" category. In Zonta's discussion of these findings, she implies that they indicate higher socio-economic status. Though this attribution is reinforced by observations in the field, the categories are too ill-defined to reach definitive conclusions in this regard.

Findings from the 2011 survey are simultaneously more satisfying and less satisfying. They are more satisfying in the sense that 28 job categories gives one a better "map" of MSIA occupations; less satisfying in that 116 respondents skipped the item while another 171 respondents checked "other," which means that only 344 people placed themselves into the grid of occupation options. The responses clicked most frequently were "Self-Employed Business Owner" (21%), "Teacher/Professor" (11%), "Counselor/Therapist/Psychologist" (11%), and "Administrator/Manager" (9%) – together totaling a little over half (52%). If we add these figures together with the other professional categories, we reach the same provisional conclusion as implied by Zonta's analysis, namely that MSIA participants are predominantly middle class/upper-middle class.

The other indicator of class is one's level of income. The income levels reflected in the survey findings from 1998 are good. Median income appears to have been in the $35,000 to $40,000 range. Given that the average national wage in 1998 was $28,861, this places MSIA participants significantly above average. By 2011, the income picture had changed significantly. In fact, so many respondents now fall into the $65,000+ category, that Zonta's four levels needed to be stretched out into six income levels to adequately represent them. Median income now appears to be in the $55,000 range. By 2010 (2011 figures were not available at the time of this writing), the national wage average had risen to $41,674, meaning MSIA participants continue to outpace the general population, and by an increasingly wide margin.

MSIA's occupational and income patterns indicate a membership that has been highly successful in our society's economic arena. These findings

Table 5.7 Income

	1998		2011	
	%	No.	%	No.
Less than $25,000	28	156	18	83
$25,000-45,000	29	166	21	95
$45,000-65,000	16	93	15	70
More than $65,000	22	126		
$65,000-85,000			13	60
$85,000-105,000			10	47
More than $105,000			21	97

fly in the face of the popular stereotype of "cults"— a stereotype that portrays members of minority religions as financially exploited drones who toil long hours at demeaning, low-skilled jobs for the sole purpose of enlarging the leader's bank account.

Political Affiliation

In terms of political orientation, we once again face a problem with commensurate scales of measurement. This is because rather than modeling the 2011 survey after the 1998 survey, we utilized a questionnaire that – with a few variations – has been administered internationally to a dozen different spiritual groups. This will make the template used for the 2011 MSIA survey useful for future comparisons, but for present purposes it is rather awkward.

The 1998 survey used two different approaches, a liberal to conservative scale and a party scale. Because it is more useful for making comparisons with the 2011 survey, we will examine the former. As Zonta notes, MSIA participants tend to be at the liberal end of the scale (41%), with less than 10% self-identifying as conservatives – though a significant percentage (21%) responded that they were not political. As with the earlier survey, in the 2011 survey the largest group of respondents place themselves in the

Table 5.8 Political Orientation

	1998 Survey	
	%	No.
Conservative	8	45
Moderate	27	151
Liberal	41	232
Non-political	21	119

	2011 Survey	
	%	No.
Non-Political	17	87
Libertarian	5	25
Green	5	24
Socialist	2	8
Left-Liberal	37	193
Independent	24	125
Right-Conservative	6	31
Far Right	0.2	1
Other	14	71

liberal category (37%), though adding "green" and "socialist" to the "liberal" respondents makes the liberal category even larger. Both the "non-political" and the "conservative" categories shrunk slightly.

While the generally liberal political orientation of MSIA participants is not a surprising finding, it contrasts sharply with the conservative political inclinations of certain other, comparable minority religions. The Unification Church and the Church Universal and Triumphant, for example, are socially conservative, and the majority of their US members are Republicans.

As far as voting frequency is concerned, 432 (76%) respondents to the 1998 survey said that they voted in the last election. The balance, or 121 (21%) respondents, said they did not. This fits together nicely with the 119 respondents to the political orientation question who said that they were non-political. In the 2011 survey, 92% (483) said they were registered to vote, 67% (347) said they voted in the last local election, and 90% (468) said they voted in the last national election. In all cases, these are high percentages, though one has to wonder about how the 17% of respondents who placed themselves in the non-political category and yet who must have voted if 90% of the sample voted in the last national election. Based on field observations, however, I suspect that what many of the people who responded that they were "non-political" actually meant to communicate was that they were independent, "non-partisan" voters. This would explain the apparent contradiction in the 2011 figures.

Religious Heritage

Both the 1998 survey and the 2011 survey contained an item asking about religious heritage. In terms of percentages from the major US religious traditions – Protestantism, Catholicism, and Judaism – the two samples are comparable in a general way. Relative to its percentage of the national population, Protestantism was underrepresented in both. Consistent with previous research on new religions, a disproportionate number – when compared with the general population – of MSIA respondents were from Jewish households, though many families were clearly non-practicing. Also consistent with previous research, a disproportionate number of respondents were raised Catholic. The proportion of people from Catholic backgrounds would obviously have been substantially larger had Latin American and Spanish members been surveyed.

The "other" category in the 2011 survey was meant to allow people whose religious backgrounds may have been missed to supply this information. Instead, many respondents used it to amplify their responses. This

5 The Movement of Spiritual Inner Awareness 93

Table 5.9 Religious Heritage

	1998		2011	
	%	No.	%	No.
Catholic	28	158	30	158
Protestant	44	252	37	192
Jewish	13	72	14	75
Eastern	0	2	2	11
Occult/Metaphysical	1	5	2	11
Other	1	5	11	57
MSIA			14	74
None			7	36

explains, in part, why the percentages for the 2011 survey add up to more than 100%. Also, a significant number of respondents to the most recent survey were raised in the movement. And finally, some respondents noted they were not raised in any religious tradition.

Length of Membership

The questionnaire contained a number of items designed to measure the length and depth of respondents' membership. As one might anticipate, there were significant differences between the 1998 and the 2011 surveys in these respects. The simplest measure was years of membership. Zonta reported this statistic rather oddly. Her table presented numbers on people who came into the movement during the last ten years in two 5-year intervals, and then people involved between 10 and 20 years prior as a single 10-year interval. What makes this odd grid even odder is that, just to look at the table, it appears that splitting the 11–20 year interval into 11–15 and 16–20 intervals would probably have made the data appear more proportionate in the sense that each interval would have been in the neighborhood of 20% for around 100 respondents. For the 2011 questionnaire, the length-of-involvement data was split into 5-year intervals.

Initiatory Level

Beyond the number of years one has spent in MSIA, there are other criteria for determining the depth of one's involvement. Chief among these is level of initiation. As discussed in *Seeking the Light* (Lewis 1997: 70), there are four formal initiations. Sequentially, these are the Causal, Mental,

Table 5.10 Length of Membership

	1998 Survey	
	%	No.
0–5 years	20	115
6–10 years	17	95
11–20 years	42	240
Over 20 years	18	104

	2011 Survey	
	%	No.
1–5 years	12	63
6–10 years	9	46
11–15 years	11	58
16–20 years	9	47
21–25 years	13	66
26–30 years	14	74
31–35 years	14	73
36–40 years	12	60
41–45 years	6	33

Etheric, and Soul initiations. As one might anticipate, proportionally more 2011 respondents had received the higher initiations than 1998 respondents.

These figures indicate either that the majority of participants in MSIA have reached the soul level, or that the majority of respondents attracted to taking the survey were long-term participants. Likely both factors are at work. However, if the age ranges of the sample reflect the age ranges of the population, then the majority have been involved for 20 years or more, meaning it is likely that the majority have simply gone through all of the initiatory levels.

Table 5.11 Initiatory Level

	1998		2011	
	%	No.	%	No.
Non-initiate	12	70	8	40
Causal	13	74	10	49
Mental	10	56	9	44
Etheric	20	115	12	62
Soul	38	218	62	323

Concluding Remarks

As I indicated earlier, the purpose of this chapter was not to demonstrate any particular point about the Movement of Inner Spiritual Awareness. Rather my primary goal was simply to gather and to make available new empirical data – especially retrospective longitudinal data – in a field of study hobbled by the general lack of such data.

Along certain parameters, MSIA participants have remained essentially the same across 13 years. As one might well have predicted, they are older and a greater percentage have passed through all of MSIA's initiatory grades. What an outside observer might not have anticipated, however, is that the movement as a whole seems to have excelled in terms of the classic indicators of achievement – education, income and profession – so that the average participant has become considerably better off by 2011 than she or he was in 1998.

This appears to be, on the one hand, a testament to the class backgrounds of converts who, like the early converts to any number of NRMs one could think of, tend to be from middle- to upper-middle class backgrounds. (Though my overall task in the present work is to critique the conventional wisdom about members, for MSIA the conventional wisdom about NRM participants' middle class background bears out.) On the other hand – and in contrast to certain other NRMs – MSIA encourages members to cultivate an attitude that attracts abundance. Though John-Roger's teachings on wealth are placed in a larger context of well-being (e.g., as presented in the book *Wealth 101*), they nevertheless encourage members to seek a level of healthy prosperity. Though we lack the hard data to be able to make a definitive statement in this regard, it appears that these teachings have helped to make MSIA participants higher achievers than members of many other NRMs.

Part III

Mixed Method Approaches

6   Demise of the Teen Witch Fad

Some years ago I wrote a paper on the startling growth of Paganism that became the basis for several different conference presentations. It was eventually published as the opening chapter in Hannah E. Johnston and Peg Aloi's *New Generation Witches* (2007) under the title "The Pagan Explosion" (Lewis 2007). Though I offered a partial analysis of the emergent phenomenon of the youthful Paganism that was the book's focus, my primary interest was in census and other data indicating an extraordinarily rapid expansion in the number of people self-identifying with some form of Paganism – an explosive growth fuelled largely by the Teen Witch fad. What I have recently concluded, however, is that the long-range impact of this fad has been nil. Furthermore, the demise of this phenomenon has led some observers to conclude that the Pagan movement is currently going through a period of retrenchment. Available census and other statistical data provide, at best, a mixed picture. And while some sources appear to indicate that Paganism continues to expand quite rapidly, others indicate that growth has come to a complete standstill, barely keeping up with the growth of the overall population.

Because of the statistical slowdown, I have had in mind writing the present follow up for some time now, but never got around to it, in part because I have been waiting for data from new censuses. For instance, the religion data report from the 2011 UK census was not issued until December 2012, and, even then, only raw numbers. This particular report is especially important for the purpose of measuring growth using census statistics because it is only the second British census to include religion data – meaning this is the first time we actually have comparative data from which we can measure growth using the UK censuses. The new report does not contain exactly the same set of categories as the 2001 UK census, but there are enough of the same major Pagan categories to be able to contrast the two census years and measure growth. Additionally, Australia released religion figures from its 2011 census in the summer of 2012 – figures which appear to indicate that, *measured as a percentage of the total population*, the growth of Paganism has ground to a complete halt.

Because contemporary Paganism is a decentralized subculture rather than an organized religion, any effort to construct a general profile of participants – and, especially, to quantify participation – necessarily involves some degree of speculation. Since the late 1960s, there have been widely varying estimates of the total population of practicing Pagans.[1] To focus on turn-of-the-millennium estimates, in a 1999 article Jorgensen and Russell (1999) presented a figure of 200,000 practitioners in the US (though the authors also indicated that "estimates of twice that number are not implausible"). This was an important statistical study which indicated that Pagans tended to be successful, educated and involved rather than the marginal individuals they had been portrayed in certain earlier studies. Although published in 1999, the empirical data for the Jorgensen-Russell study was collected in 1996. Other scholarly studies from the same period also placed the Pagan population at around 200,000 (e.g., Berger 1999; Pike 2001).

In contrast, figures put forward by other contemporaneous observers and insiders were much larger. For example, in 1999–2000, then First Officer Kathryn Fuller of the Covenant of the Goddess (COG) – a large networking organization and umbrella group that promotes official recognition of Paganism as a religion in North America – initiated an internet poll in response to public attacks on Pagans in the military. Based on 32,854 responses (30,735 of whom were Americans, 1,219 Canadians, and 900 Others) Fuller estimated that there were 768,400 Witches and Pagans in the United States. This was an extrapolation based on an estimated total return of 4%.

An important though neglected source of information bearing on the question of numbers of adherents to alternative religions is national census data. My 2007 paper mentioned above was based on census reports and on the American Religious Identification Survey (ARIS). As discussed in Chapter Three, the censuses of four Anglophone countries – New Zealand, Australia, Canada and the United Kingdom – collect information on religious membership. There was also a series of major religion surveys conducted in the US in the years 1990, 2001 and 2008, the American Religious Identification Surveys (ARIS)[2] that, in addition to mainstream religions, collected data on a handful of alternative religions. By the 2008 report, the survey-takers were lumping all alternative religions into a "NRMs and Other Religions" category, primarily because the samples of respondents from which overall size was calculated were too small to produce accurate statistics. Academic researchers could, nevertheless, request a breakdown of this category from the ARIS. The breakdown contains data on three categories of Pagans – Druids, Pagans and Wiccans.

---

1. For a comprehensive overview, refer to Bruce A. Robinson, "How many Wiccans are there in the US?" http://www.religioustolerance.org/wic_nbr3.htm
2. The first survey in this series was called the National Survey of Religious Identity (the NSRI) rather than ARIS.

6 *Demise of the Teen Witch Fad* 101

Though a few scholars and observers of Paganism have referred to one or more of these censuses (e.g., Hughes and Bond 2003; Reid 2001), no one before the publication of "The Pagan Explosion" attempted a general survey. In the current chapter I will survey updated census data, updated data from the ARIS survey and PCR data for the light these various sources of data shed on the growth of Paganism.

Canadian Census

The 2001 Canadian census recorded 21,085 Pagans. Canada fit all varieties of Pagans into a single generic category (various relevant census reports from Canada include a footnote mentioning that the Pagan category also contains Wiccans). The 1991 census recorded 5,530 Pagans. Canadian Pagan scholars with whom I have communicated have said that these figures are inaccurately low, and speculate that many people were cautious about identifying themselves as Pagans. As a consequence, they did not report their religious affiliation to census takers. This consideration was likely a major factor explaining the apparent four-fold growth Canadian Paganism appeared to experience in a decade. The religion part of the 2011 census was collected in a somewhat different way from prior censuses, which might or might not result in a more adequate final report. Data from this census was recently released, providing a figure of 25,495 self-identified Pagans (including, for the first time, a subcategory for Wiccans, who numbered 10,225). This obviously represents a significant slowdown in the rate of growth of Canadian Paganism. Instead of fourfold growth, Paganism grew by just under 21% – about twice the national growth rate, but nowhere near what one would call explosive growth.

United Kingdom Census

The 2001 and 2011 United Kingdom censuses recorded a reasonably good spread of different Pagan groups, and is the best national census in this regard. Regrettably, religious participation was not measured in censuses prior to 2001. Figures for the English and Welsh parts of the two censuses for Pagans are as follows:

While the total population of England and Wales rose by 7.8%, in the ten years between the two censuses, the Pagan population rose by 85.6%. I would label this growth quite remarkable, bordering on explosive, but nothing like the threefold and fourfold expansion Paganism appeared to be

Table 6.1 Pagan Statistics for England and Wales from the 2001 and 2011 British Censuses

Tradition	2001	2011
Pagan	30569	56,620
Wicca	7227	11,766
Druidism	1657	4189
Pantheism	1603	2216
Animism	401	541
Heathen	278	1958
Asatru	93*	
Celtic Pagan	508*	
Witchcraft		1276*
Total	42,336	78,566

*The Asatru and Celtic Pagan categories were discontinued in the 2011 census whereas the Witchcraft category was added.

[Source: Office for National Statistics © Crown Copyright 2013.]

experiencing around the turn of the century. Projecting from the Australian and New Zealand censuses, I also strongly suspect that, had census data been taken in 2006, it would indicate that most of this growth took place between 2001 and 2006, followed by a slowdown between 2006 and 2011.

Religion Survey Data for the United States

Unfortunately, the United States census does not collect religion membership data. However, in 1990 the Graduate Center of the City University of New York conducted a National Survey of Religious Identification (NSRI) via randomly dialed phone numbers (113,723 people were surveyed). Eleven years later in 2001, the Center carried out the American Religious Identification Survey (ARIS) in the same manner (over 50,000 people responded), though callers probed for more information than the earlier NSRI. A second (or third, depending on how you look at it) ARIS survey was carried out in 2008. Categories were developed post-facto. The results were quite interesting with respect to the Pagan population:

Although it would have been much more useful had researchers broken down their data into more subcategories, the results are nevertheless striking. In the initial period of 11 years, the Pagan population (counting Wiccans, Druids, and Pagans together as Pagans) increased remarkably, even considering that 8,000 Wiccans clearly represents a significant underestimate (like the Canadian census, the low number is likely the result of respondents' reluctance to self-identify as Pagan). The increase in the Pagan

Table 6.2 Pagan Data from NSRI, ARIS 2001 and ARIS 2008

	1990	2001	2008
Wicca	8,000*	134,000	342,000
Druid**		33,000	29,000
Pagan**		140,000	340,000
Totals	8,000	307,000	711,000

*Numbers have been rounded off to the nearest 1,000. Unlike a census, which attempts to reach the entire population, these figures represent statistical extrapolations.

**The Druid and Pagan categories did not emerge as significant in the 1990 NSRI survey.

[Source: Kosmin and Keysar (2001); Kosmin and Keysar (2004); and Barry A. Kosmin, personal communication (February 2, 2012). Adapted table used with permission.]

population in the seven-year period between 2001 and 2008 was 131.6%. This is a striking pattern of growth, though nowhere near the "explosion" that seemed to occur between 1990 and 2001 when I originally wrote "The Pagan Explosion." Totals for 1990, 2001 and 2008 are all almost certainly underestimates. Hypothetically, if we could depend on these figures and a continued 131.6% growth rate, then the current population of adult Pagans in the USA would be approaching a million.

New Zealand Census

In 1991, the New Zealand national census contained only a single, generic category for Pagans, which was "Nature and Earth Based Religions." The censuses of 1996–2006 subsequently broke down Paganism into a number of subcategories, but continued to use the label "Nature and Earth Based Religions" as a larger category to cover the total of all forms of Paganism. In Table 6.3, I have provided figures for the generic category, plus I have picked out Druidism and Wicca for separate examination.

What we can see from the total figures is a rapid expansion between 1991 and 1996, and again between 1996 and 2001. Growth between 2001 and 2006 is still quite impressive, but less so than in preceding 5-year periods. I have included separate figures for Druids and Wiccans because the growth rate for Druidism seems relatively constant, whereas Wicca explodes between 1996 and 2001, but then falls off between 2001 and 2006. What happened?

Table 6.3 Growth in Paganism from 1991 to 2006 in New Zealand

Census Year	1991*	1996	2001	2006
Nature & Earth Based Religions**	318	1,722	5,862	7,122
Druids		123	153	192
Wiccans		792	2,196	2,082

*As mentioned, the New Zealand census did not start identifying and recording Pagan subcategories until the 1996 census.

**There were other categories in the New Zealand census, such as "Animism" and "Pantheism," that contributed to these totals.

[Source: Statistics New Zealand.]

In contrast with Druids, whose average age steadily grew from 35 to 38 to 42 in 1996, 2001 and 2006, the average age of Wiccans as recorded by the census fell from 30 in 1996 to 27 in 2001, though it was up again to 32 by 2006. Additionally, while the male-dominated Druids were gradually moving toward gender balance across these three census years, the proportion of females to males in female-dominated Wicca actually went up slightly between 1996 and 2001, only to fall back again, though only slightly, in 2006. This is quite evident when we place the relevant census data into a frequency table (Table 6.4).

What appears to have happened is that Wicca was heavily impacted by the Teen Witch fad of the late 1990s and early twenty-first century – a phenomenon discussed in the aforementioned Johnston and Aloi collection in which my "The Pagan Explosion" appeared. A significant number of adolescent and young women became involved in Wicca in those years, in large part because Wicca has been presented in popular publications as a particularly feminine form of Paganism (thus distinguishing it from Druidry, which had been viewed as male oriented). This is the primary reason why the population of Wiccans "exploded" around the turn of the millennium. Subsequently, as the Teen Witch fad faded, Wicca not only stopped growing, but actually declined slightly, at least in New Zealand. A better sense of the growth in numbers of "serious" Pagans in New Zealand between 1996 and 2006 can probably be gained by examining the growth rate of Druidism, which seems to have been little-affected by the Teen Witch fad.

Australia National Census Data

The Australian census contains information similar to the New Zealand census, except no relevant data was gathered in 1991. The pattern of

Table 6.4 Census Data for New Zealand Wicca, 1996–2006

	1996		2001		2006	
	No.	%	No.	%	No.	%
0–4 Years	18	2.3	42	1.9	36	1.7
5–9 Years	24	3.0	48	2.2	36	1.7
10–14 Years	15	1.9	129	5.9	93	4.5
15–19 Years	78	9.8	432	**19.7**	261	**12.5**
20–24 Years	144	**18.2**	411	**18.7**	294	**14.1**
25–29 Years	120	**15.2**	309	**14.1**	282	**13.5**
30–34 Years	117	**14.8**	249	**11.3**	255	**12.2**
35–39 Years	87	**11.0**	216	9.8	228	**10.9**
40–44 Years	84	**10.6**	144	6.6	201	9.6
45–49 Years	48	6.1	93	4.2	189	9.1
50–54 Years	33	4.2	72	3.3	90	4.3
55–59 Years	12	1.5	24	1.1	66	3.2
60–64 Years	6	0.8	9	0.4	33	1.6
65 Years +	6	0.8	18	0.8	18	0.9
Male	186	23.5	477	21.7	462	22.2
Female	603	**76.1**	1,719	**78.3**	1,617	**77.7**
Total	**792**		**2,196**		**2,082**	
Average Age	30.23		27.31		31.52	

[Courtesy of New Zealand Statistics.]

explosive growth and then slowdown is clear enough from the figures for the 1996, 2001, 2006 and 2011 censuses (Table 6.5).

As with the New Zealand census, we can once again see that after a period of explosive growth between 1996 and 2001, Wicca actually lost participants between 2001 and 2006 – again reflecting the collapse of the Teen Witch fad.

In the most recent census the total figure for all Pagans was 32,083 and for Wiccans/Witches was 8413. What these numbers indicate is that, on the one hand, Wicca has started to grow again, though it has not yet recovered to its 2001 level. On the other hand, Paganism's growth has continued to slow. In fact, the rate of growth from the 2006 census total of 29,391 to the 2011 total of 32,083 is 9%, which is only slightly better than the national average of 8.3% between 2006 and 2011. In other words, in terms of net growth as a percentage of the national population, Australian Paganism is doing little better than treading water.

What I argued in my 2007 paper was that two important factors (not to exclude the possibility of others) contributing to Paganism's rapid

Table 6.5 Pagan Statistics from the 1996–2011 Australian Censuses

Tradition	1996	2001	2006	2011
Animism*	727	763	870	780
Nature Religions	1734	2225	2745	3599
Druidism	555	691	1022	1049
Paganism	4353	10,632	15,514	16,851
Pantheism*	835	1085	1031	1391
Wiccan/Witchcraft	1849	8755	8213	8413
Total	10,053	24,151	29,395	32,083

*Animism and Pantheism are common categories in both the Australian and the New Zealand censuses, and both are grouped together with Pagan categories. Neither of these refer to members of indigenous religions, which are covered by other categories.

[Based on Australian Bureau of Statistics data.]

expansion were the Internet and the emergence of youthful Paganism of the Teen Witch variety. The Internet was exploding in the latter 1990s, and the Pagan community, in part because of its decentralized (perhaps I should say anarchistic) authority structure, quickly became involved in this medium.[3] I also discussed the role played by the emergent phenomenon of adolescent and youthful Paganism in fueling the "Pagan explosion," but I had anticipated that more of these new adherents would hang around after it was no longer a fad. However, as indicated by Australian and New Zealand census data, I was incorrect. It is difficult to say with absolute certainly what would have happened to Wiccan numbers in the UK had Britain taken religion censuses in 1996 and 2006, but I suspect the results would have been roughly similar to the Australian and New Zealand patterns – a sharp rise followed by a fall. It is more difficult to decide how to interpret the ARIS data, which makes it appear that US Paganism was not impacted by the demise of the Teen Witch fad. The ARIS surveys, however, have been criticized for their sampling methods, especially calling into question their estimates for smaller groups that were ultimately based on a relative handful of respondents. In other words, we cannot really generalize from these survey findings unless we have confirming data from other sources.

A somewhat different take on the demise of the Teen Witch fad is offered by data from Pagan Census Revisited (PCR) study I conducted with Helen Berger in 2009–2010 which I have already discussed in earlier chapters.

---

3. Refer for example, to tables measuring Internet expansion at Hobbes Internet Timeline at http://www.zakon.org/robert/internet/timeline

Table 6.6 Average Age at which People become "Practicing Pagans"

2009 Sample: Five-year Periods

Time Period	Mean Age	No.
2005–2009	30.51	1049
2000–2004	27.35	1235
1995–99	24.32	1339
1990–94	23.06	917
1985–89	21.97	773
1980–84	19.85	484
1975–79	18.27	301

For reasons explained earlier, the figures in Table 6.6 (which is a replication of Table 1.1) are drawn from 2009 data.

In addition to the E-correlation which I discussed in Chapter One, the data also describes a bell curve in terms of rate of growth. Numbers of new Pagans grow each five-year period, and then begin falling off by 2000–2004. Whatever the causal factors, the growth of Paganism had slowed early in the new millennium. In a recent article, Douglas Ezzy and Helen Berger examine data from a variety of different Internet sources which "suggests that growth is slowing, and interaction appears to be less intensive, at least in some types of internet communities. We suggest that this indicates that Witchcraft is now entering a new phase of slowing growth, and consolidation of community" (Ezzy and Berger 2009: 166). As we have seen, Ezzy's and Berger's conclusions about slowing growth are confirmed by data from the 2006 Australian Census and the 2006 New Zealand Census, as well as from the PCR.

I also wondered if recent Pagans were, like converts to the Order of Christ Sophia, composed of two cohorts, namely a set of baby boomers plus a younger group (Lewis and Levine 2010). However, examining the birth years for people who most recently became practicing Pagans (within one year of responding to the questionnaire), we get Table 6.7.

So although one can say that the cluster of new Pagans in the 15–25 year-old group are being counterbalanced by older recruits, these new elders are not members of any specific generation.

It also struck me that there might be a difference between the North American situation (more than 80% of respondents to the PCR were residents of the United States) and other nations – an important issue, given that the relevant census data is all from other countries. Besides the US and Canada, the two nations with the most PCR respondents were Australia and the United Kingdom. Because these two subsamples were relatively small, the data showed more variability, but the overall patterns were nevertheless

Table 6.7 Birth Years of Most Recent Self-Identified Pagans

Birth Year	No. of New Pagans
1995–1999	5
1990–1994	57
1985–1989	63
1980–1984	40
1975–1979	38
1970–1974	38
1965–1969	36
1960–1964	30
1955–1959	20
1950–1954	23
1945–1949	6
1944–earlier	8

congruent with the E-correlation. Collapsing the data into 10-year periods rather than 5-year periods, we get Tables 6.8a and 6.8b.

When I first examined the PCR data, I concluded that I must have been mistaken about the importance of the Teen Witch phenomenon. Had I been correct, I thought, then the mean age of new Pagans would have taken a sharp drop over the course of the last decade, and obviously it had not. Also, total numbers of new participants in Paganism should have increased during the early part of the new millennium, whereas the data indicates that the numbers were starting to fall off.

However, after juxtaposing the PCR figures with the Wiccan census figures from Australia and New Zealand, it finally dawned on me that most of

Table 6.8a Australia Subsample (Ten-year Periods)

Time Period	Average Age	Number of Respondents
2005–2009	28.06	27
1995–2004	23.21	65
1985–1994	18.65	34
1975–1984	16.07	14

Table 6.8b United Kingdom Subsample (Ten-year Periods)

Time Period	Average Age	Number of Respondents
2005–2009	28.69	54
1995–2004	25.10	88
1985–1994	21.47	39
1980–1984	17.19	16

the young Witches recorded in the 2001 censuses had simply dropped out by 2006 – as reflected by the drop in total numbers of Wiccans between the two census years. In contrast, the PCR did not record the explosion of Silver Ravenwolf-type Witches, who had, for the most part, left the movement by the time Berger and I began gathering data in 2009. Had we posted the PCR in 2001 or 2002, the results would likely have been markedly different.

What we are left with, then, are figures indicating that the most rapid increase in the numbers of new Pagans who maintained their commitment took place in the late nineties – an increase due, in part, to the advent of the Internet. In other words, in terms of understanding Paganism as a serious religious movement, it turns out that the period of apparent explosive growth in the early part of the new millennium was a noisy side act featuring an ephemeral fad that did little more than distract attention from the real story of contemporary Paganism's emergence as a maturing religious tradition.

Conclusion

No one likes to be mistaken, and I was frankly surprised when the most recent census figures were published. However, even at the time I was writing "The Pagan Explosion" article, I was aware that Paganism's rapid expansion was being fueled by the Teen Witch fad. In fact, I anticipated a slowdown, and said as much in the penultimate paragraph of my original paper. However, I did not anticipate that the fad would burst so suddenly and that the numbers would fall off so dramatically. One lesson the reader should hopefully walk away with is that s/he should be ready to offer an analysis of her or his failed predictions, especially when, as in the present case, my original paper was built around an analysis of dramatic growth that later dropped off so radically.

Another lesson here is the virtue of juxtaposing multiple sources of data. In the present case, it is only when the relevant census data is examined alongside the "Pagan Census Revisited" data that it becomes clear what happened. The problem, of course, is that one only rarely has access to data sets drawn from such contrasting sources. And unless future New Religion scholars are hired by – or at least consulted by – census bureaus, we will never have specific census data on smaller groups like the Movement of Spiritual Inner Awareness or the Order of Christ Sophia.

7 Who Serves Satan?

> I studied different religions and philosophies, and eventually found LaVeyan Satanism to be attractive – I already believed most everything in *The Satanic Bible*, so it fit like a glove.
> – Respondent to SS-2

As I have previously noted, when new religious movements (NRMs) first became the subject of serious social-scientific inquiry in Western countries in the 1960s and 1970s, researchers initially focused on trying to understand how and why members became involved. It is not difficult to understand why this issue should have become a focal point for scholarly attention: in the less-than-objective words of one anti-cult psychiatrist, the question motivating this work was: "What kind of nutty people get into these crazy groups?" (Cited in Bromley and Richardson 1983: 5) Though the topic of conversion was gradually displaced from the center stage of NRM studies, it never completely disappeared as a topic of research. In fact, conversion is still the single most discussed subject in the field.

The present chapter explores the question of how and why individuals convert to Satanism[1] – a process that might better be described as how individuals come to self-identify as Satanists. In order to answer this question, I will bring together data from census findings and questionnaire research with discussions of conversion to other alternative religions – particularly to contemporary Paganism – as lenses through which to interpret conversion to Satanism. Additionally, I raise the question of whether declaring oneself to be a member of an anarchistic Internet religion should properly be considered "conversion" or whether it would be more appropriate to regard the adoption of the label "Satanist" as being a form of identity construction.

Studies of conversion to alternative religions have typically focused on conversion to high-demand groups such as the Family Federation (formerly the Unification Church), the Family International (formerly the Children of

---

1. Within the past dozen years, however, so-called "religious" Satanism has finally attracted the serious attention of academic researchers, resulting in a modest-but-expanding body of studies (e.g., Lewis 2001; Petersen 2002; Lewis 2002; Petersen 2005; Dyrendal 2008; Lewis and Petersen 2008; Bobineau 2008; Lewis 2009; Petersen 2009a; Petersen 2009b; Fügmann 2009; Partridge and Christianson 2009; Hjelm 2009).

God), and the Hare Krishna Movement. Earlier studies portrayed conversion as something that happened to a passive self. This approach appears to be a residue of Christian discussions of conversion that took Paul's road to Damascus experience as the paradigm for all conversions. Later studies have stressed that converts are active agents, "the prototype for which is the 'seeker'" (Reid 2009: 173).[2]

As we have seen, social scientists studying conversion to non-traditional religions have also reached certain conclusions regarding the question of "Who Joins New Religions and Why" (Dawson 2003). Among other characteristics, involvement in NRMs "seems to be strongly correlated with having fewer and weaker ideological alignments" (Dawson 2003: 120). However, in Eileen Barker's oft-cited study of the Unification Church, Barker makes the infrequently-noted, but extremely important point that recruits who end up staying with that organization are often individuals for whom Unification teachings and the lifestyle of Church members address issues they were concerned with before ever coming into contact with the Unification Church.

For example, Barker relates the story of a Sunday-school teacher who had been having problems understanding certain parts of the Bible. He was also experiencing frustration at not finding the ideal romantic relationship. After he came in touch with the Unification Church, he read Revd Moon's *The Divine Principle*, which "cleared everything up" about scripture. This individual was also struck by the Unification solution to relationship issues, which corresponded with his own conclusions:

> [T]he idea of perfect marriage, where it's God who brings people together: that really struck me because that [was the] sort of conclusion I'd reached after a lot of struggle. I'd reached the stage where I'd say, 'OK, God, it's up to you.' ... So the idea of the perfect marriage really excited me (Cited in Barker 1984: 256–57).

I have come to refer to this affiliation factor as "fit." (I derived "fit" from some of the questionnaire respondents' own affiliation accounts; I was also partly inspired by Barker's phrase "non-conscious fit" [1984: 258], though the "fit" I am analyzing here is mostly *conscious*.) Susan Palmer makes a similar point about women who joined the Rajneesh movement when she observes that "...women choose to participate in this particular NRM... because it offers an alternative philosophy of sexuality which is consistent with their previous lifestyle, and which validates their life choices" (1993:

---

2. James Richardson has been influential in promoting a more active view of conversion (Richardson & Kilbourne 1988).

7 *Who Serves Satan?* 113

105). "Fit," as we shall see, was also a central theme in the narratives of the Satan Survey respondents.

The Satan Surveys

Over a dozen years ago, I began collecting basic demographic data on contemporary Satanists via an Internet survey. When conducted properly, research has shown that Internet surveys can be highly representative (Stenbjerre & Laugesen 2005). To this end, I constructed a simple, 20-item questionnaire – which for my purposes here I will refer to as "Satan Survey One" (SS-1) – that could be answered in a relatively short period of time. Through e-mail addresses posted on Satanist websites, I began sending out questionnaires in early August 2000. Also, a number of Satanists posted the questionnaire on their websites. By the end of February 2001, I had received 140 responses, which I felt was adequate to use as the basis for constructing a preliminary profile. I also sent a short follow-up questionnaire to a few dozen respondents who had expressed a willingness to be contacted a second time.

I subsequently utilized this questionnaire data as the basis for my initial article on Satanism, "Who Serves Satan? A Demographic and Ideological Profile," which first appeared online in the *Marburg Journal of Religion* (2001a). Constructing a statistical caricature, at the time I stated that the "average" Satanist was:

> [A]n unmarried, white male in his mid-twenties with a few years of college. He became involved in Satanism through something he read in high school, and has been a self-identified Satanist for seven years. Raised Christian, he explored one non-Satanist religious group beyond the one in which he was raised before settling into Satanism. His view of Satan is some variety of non-theistic humanism and he practices magic. His primary interaction with his co-religionists is via e-mail and Internet chat rooms (Lewis 2001a).

I was aware, of course, that there were significant problems making generalizations from this sample, and, early in the article, I discussed these problems along with other critical feedback I had received from my Satanist contacts. However, the bottom line was that, because of the decentralized, anarchistic nature of the "Satanic milieu" (to use Jesper Petersen's handy designation), it was simply impossible to gather a statistically random sample of Satanists. So for better or for worse, I found myself forced to work with whatever data I was able to collect.

The good news is that over the years I received positive feedback from Satanists, who mostly confirmed the general picture I had presented in "Who

Serves Satan?" Additionally, much more recently, using Alexa's *Web Information Database* (www.alexa.com) to research profiles of search engine users who access Satanist websites, Jesper Petersen has written that, "as a whole, the tendencies of the demographic data do seem to confirm James R. Lewis' conclusions about average age, education, geography and online activity" (Petersen 2013).

Between 2002 and 2009, I did not write anything new on Satanism. Then in 2009, I was invited to the first international scholarly conference on "religious" Satanism, held November 19–20 in Trondheim, Norway. In response to that invitation, I conducted a second survey of Satanists to use as the basis for my presentation. So, in late June of 2009, I began to gather new data on contemporary Satanists using a more ambitious, 40-item survey – which I will refer to here as "Satan Survey Two" (SS-2) – using Survey Monkey (http://www.surveymonkey.com). My goal was to determine if and how the Satanic milieu had changed since 2001, as well as to gather other kinds of information. By the 4th of November, the questionnaire had received 260 responses. I continued to collect responses until the end of 2009, but I tabulated the data at that juncture in preparation for the conference (Lewis 2009b). I closed SS-2 in late 2009 after collecting a total of 300 responses. Not long after launching SS-2, I became quite dissatisfied with the way I had worded some of the items, and with the fact that I had inadvertently left out certain important questions. So in early 2011, I initiated a third questionnaire, "Satan Survey Three" (SS-3). The third questionnaire was closed at the end of that year after collecting over 400 responses.

Though members of samples from all of the surveys were predominantly white males raised in Christian households, the average age of respondents rose from 25 to 30 between 2001 and 2011. Partly as a consequence of higher average age, the SS-2 and SS-3 samples exhibited more diversity – in terms of having a broader range of educational backgrounds, an increased likelihood of being a parent, and so forth. Similarly, while the majority of respondents to SS-2 and SS-3 were still broadly in the LaVeyan tradition, a far greater percentage than respondents to the SS-1 professed some variety of Theistic Satanism. When contrasted with the first questionnaire, the picture that emerges from the latter questionnaires could be summarized as "Little Nicky grows up."

Census Profiles of Satanism and Paganism

As part of the present analysis, I will be examining analyses of "conversion" to contemporary Paganism that throw light on "conversion" to modern Satanism (both the Satanic community and the Pagan community are adverse to the term *conversion*, which is why I sometimes place it in quote marks). Though Satanism and Paganism are comparable in terms of conversion motifs and in terms of their utilization of the Internet, their sociological profiles differ in certain significant ways. It will be useful to briefly examine some of these differences using census data from New Zealand.

Table 7.1 presents age and gender data on Satanism in the New Zealand census. The pattern is almost exactly the same as we saw with Australian Satanists, though the Australians were, on average, a little older. The outstanding feature of this data is how the core of self-identified Satanists clusters in the 15 to 24 age range in all four censuses. This means that the great majority drop out at some point in their mid-20s and are replaced by an entirely new cohort of young Satanists. In a sense, then, Satanism is a true youth religion that presents an age profile congruent with the portrayal of new religions in NRM conversion literature from the 1980s (Barker 1984; Levine 1984; Melton and Moore 1982), namely young converts to a religion dominated by youthful members.

Though heavily dominated by young males, there appears to be a tendency toward an increasing proportion of female involvement. Additionally, though core Satanists are youthful, one can also see a gradual increase

Table 7.1 Census Data for New Zealand Satanists, 1991–2006

Census Year	1991		1996		2001		2006	
	No.	%	No.	%	No.	%	No.	%
0–4 Years	9	1.4	3	.3	3	.3	6	.5
5–9 Years	3	.5	0	.0	3	.3	3	.3
10–14 Years	9	1.4	27	3.0	45	5.2	54	4.6
15–19 Years	**258**	**40.2**	**315**	**34.7**	**288**	**32.3**	**390**	**33.4**
20–24 Years	**210**	**32.7**	**315**	**34.7**	**228**	**25.6**	**300**	**25.7**
25–29 Years	75	11.7	141	15.5	156	17.5	141	12.1
30–34 Years	33	5.1	69	7.6	75	8.4	114	9.8
35–39 Years	12	1.9	21	2.3	54	6.1	66	5.7
40–44 Years	9	1.4	15	1.7	18	2.0	39	3.3
45–49 Years	6	.9	3	.3	6	.7	30	2.6
50–54 Years	3	.5	0	.0	3	.3	6	.5
55–59 Years	3	.5	3	.3	3	.3	6	.5
60–64 Years	0	.0	0	.0	6	.7	3	.3
65 Years+	0	.0	3	.3	6	.7	6	.5
Male	549	85.5	792	87.1	741	83.2	930	79.7
Female	93	14.5	117	12.9	150	16.8	240	20.6
Total	**642**	100.0	**909**	100.0	**891**	100.0	**1,167**	100.0
Average Age	21.69		22.47		23.77		24.17	

[Courtesy of New Zealand Statistics.]

in the number of older Satanists across the four censuses. Thus the core 15–24 age range in the 1991 census contained 72.9% of the total, whereas this core age range contained 59.1% of the total in 2006 – the balance were spread across the 25–49 years of age categories. So although Satanism will likely continue to be a youth religion into the foreseeable future, there does seem to be a tendency to retain a small percentage of Satanic "elders." (We saw similar patterns in Australian Satanism.)

Druidry, which I chose for comparison with Satanism because of the predominance of males (other forms of Paganism primarily attract women), presents a contrasting pattern. Druidism is growing in New Zealand, and appears to be "recruiting" new members from a variety of different age groups. If most new Druids were young, then we would see a heavy predominance of new numbers in the 15–24 age range as we did with Satanism. But instead what we see is that new Druids are "converting" at a wide range of ages, and that the overall age profile is getting older – as indicated by the pattern of double-digit percentages across three censuses (see Table 7.2).

Another pattern among Druids that contrasts markedly with Satanists in the New Zealand census is the gradual balancing out of the gender ratio. In

Table 7.2 Census Data for New Zealand Druidry, 1996–2006

Census Year	1996		2001		2006	
	No.	%	No.	%	No.	%
0–4 Years	3	2.4	3	2.0	0	0.0
5–9 Years	3	2.4	3	2.0	0	0.0
10–14 Years	0	0.0	3	2.0	3	1.6
15–19 Years	12	9.8	9	5.9	15	7.8
20–24 Years	12	9.8	15	9.8	15	7.8
25–29 Years	21	**17.1**	12	7.8	12	6.3
30–34 Years	21	**17.1**	24	**15.7**	18	9.4
35–39 Years	9	7.3	15	9.8	24	**12.5**
40–44 Years	15	**12.2**	15	9.8	21	**10.9**
45–49 Years	9	7.3	18	**11.8**	21	**10.9**
50–54 Years	6	4.9	12	7.8	21	**10.9**
55–59 Years	6	4.9	9	5.9	21	**10.9**
60–64 Years	6	4.9	6	3.9	9	4.7
65 Years+	3	2.4	9	5.9	12	6.3
Male	102	**82.9**	111	72.6	129	67.2
Female	24	19.5	39	25.5	63	32.8
Total	**123**	100.0	**153**	100.0	**192**	100.0
Average Age	34.57		37.96		41.48	

[Courtesy of New Zealand Statistics.]

1996, almost 83% were male. By 2006, this had fallen to somewhat more than 67%. These census findings provide a context for understanding certain characteristics of "conversion" to these kinds of decentralized religious movements.

"Coming Home" to Paganism

Modern Satanism became a decentralized movement following Anton LaVey's dismantling of the Church of Satan as a religious body in 1975. Similarly, contemporary Paganism became increasingly decentralized in the decades following its founding. In particular, well before the Internet took off in the 1990s, Paganism had been experiencing increasing fragmentation due to the growing numbers of solitaries – individuals who, for the most part, practiced their religion alone (though they might occasionally participate in group rituals, particularly at festivals). Also parallel to Satanism, the Pagan subculture was substantially impacted by the Internet. The Internet did more than simply bring new people into the movement; it also dramatically altered the overall social organization of the Pagan subculture via the emergence of Internet Paganism. The Internet allows Pagans – and Satanists as well – to participate actively in a lively online community without ever getting together in the non-Internet realm.

The widespread availability of how-to Pagan books – and, later, information readily available on the Internet – meant that new, solitary witches had abundant sources of information for hand-crafting their own individualized forms of Paganism (Ezzy and Berger 2007b: 42). They could also choose to undertake, or not to undertake, certain rituals and celebrations, such as the rites associated with the Wheel of the Year. There were no authorities above them dictating what was and what was not "proper" Paganism, and no enforceable criteria for determining who was and who was not a "real" Pagan. Given this movement's lack of hierarchical authorities and its lack of sharp boundaries, how do we understand "conversion" to Paganism?

In her influential book, *Drawing Down the Moon*, Margot Adler rejects the idea that most participants "convert" to Paganism. Rather, people discover Paganism, and feel that it merely confirms:

> ... some original private experience, so that the most common feeling of those who have named themselves Paganism is something like 'I finally found a group that has the same religious perceptions I always had.' A common phrase you hear is 'I've come home,' or as one woman told me excitedly after a lecture, 'I always knew I had a religion, I just never knew it had a name' (1979: 14).

Expressing a similar perception, Graham Harvey has asserted that Paganism contains no conversion narratives (1999: 234).

This portrayal of Paganism as being "a religion without converts" has been criticized by a number of different scholars (e.g., Gallagher 1994; Berger and Ezzy 2007a; Ezzy and Berger 2007b; Reid 2009). In their study of teenage Paganism, Helen Berger and Douglas Ezzy offer a compelling analysis of why so many new Pagans can seriously assert "that they did not so much convert to a new set of beliefs as find a name for the beliefs they always had" (2007a: 56). Though these individuals feel that they have been led to Paganism by "some internal compass that has not been influenced by the larger culture," in fact, the larger, non-Pagan culture holds many ideas in common with Paganism – ideas about ecology, the paranormal, and individualistic discovery.[3]

The mass culture also contains many positive representations of Witches, as in the television program *Charmed*. "These broad cultural factors on their own do not result in conversion to Witchcraft, but they do provide a cultural context in which seekers can feel as though they have 'come home' to Witchcraft" (2007a: 58). One of the virtues of Ezzy's and Berger's analysis is that, while analyzing the "coming home" experience in terms of a shared cultural orientation, they go further and emphasize that conversion to Paganism also involves the active agency of the individual seeker (2007b: 42).

In an important anthology on the phenomenon of Teen Witches (Johnston & Aloi 2007), several contributors emphasize that the attraction of Paganism for adolescent girls is often the sense of empowerment they receive from self-identifying as Witches; for example:

> Calling themselves Witches and practicing spells seemed to give the girls a sense of identity, made them feel special, was part of their group friendship, helped them deal with their problems, was fun, and most of all gave them a sense of control over, and meaning in their lives (Cush 2007: 148).

These observations can be extended to Pagans more generally, and to Satanists as well.

---

3. In Chapter Six of his influential study of the New Age subculture/cultic milieu (which he refers to as "occulture"), Christopher Partridge describes the process by which producers of popular culture are influenced by occult/New Age ideas, which subsequently influences popular culture to become the bearer of occulture, which in turn spreads these ideas to consumers of popular culture (2004: 119–42).

Natural Born Satanists

Like many Pagans who claim to be "born Pagans," a significant percentage of respondents to the Satan Surveys expressed the opinion that they were "born Satanists" – that they were already Satanists before they knew anything about the religion. To quote from a handful of representative responses:

> Read the 'Satanic Bible' about 19 years ago, and found that I have shared the ideals of the book all of my life, without having been able to put a label on my belief system. It was as if I could have written the book myself....

> On some level I think I always knew what I was. It took me years to accept it because of all the Christian propaganda about Satan being evil. I still felt drawn to it, somehow, and when I found other people who felt the same as I, I felt that I had come home.

> I have always identified with the imagery of the 'gentlemanly devil' the cunning but polite, powerful but controlled creature who delights in personal gain and improvement. It's an appealing archetype. ... [So]by the time I found *The Satanic Bible* at age 17, it only reaffirmed what I already felt, but had never been able to put a name to.

> Here is the bottom line, when you have to change to be part of a religion it is the wrong religion. When you feel your religion swarming around you as if it comes directly from you, then it's the right one. Either one will cause changes in you, but only one will cause the changes effortlessly.

Respondents to the Satan Surveys often articulated the idea that they became Satanists because Satanic philosophy fit with the conclusions they had already reached. This was stated explicitly by 40 members (15%) of the SS-2 sample. Eight people even used the word "fit" in their responses;[4] to quote a selection of examples:

---

4. At least one of the respondents in Ezzy's and Berger's study explicitly uses the term "fit," where she says that when she "picked up that RavenWolf book, everything fit" (2007b: 49). Similarly, at least one respondent to the OCS questionnaire used the term "fit" in his account of how and why he joined the Order of Christ Sophia: "OCS was a natural fit for my spiritual searching. I had come home to a place where I could begin to 'practice' all of the theory that I had wrestled with for most of my life" (Lewis & Levine 2010: 78).

> I read a website briefly describing the ideals put forward by Anton LaVey and found that they mirrored my own, almost in their entirety. I looked into Satanism in more depth, read some books, discussed it with some people and realised I was already living as a Satanist and had arrived at my mindset independently. The label simply fits.
>
> My friend's dad accused her mom of turning her into a Satanist because she didn't want to visit him, and she told me about it. I had heard it mentioned negatively before, and started wondering what was so bad about it, so I did my research. Everything seemed to fit me.
>
> I was looking for something deeper, and darker, however, what I found was not that for which I sought. It did 'fit' correctly enough, though.
>
> It just fit. When I became acquainted with the philosophy, it wasn't a matter of conversion, it was a reflection of what I am.

This view of conversion – that Satanism is simply a label for what one already is – resonates with the academic analysis of Satanism as a variety of "self-religion" (Petersen 2005; Petersen 2009a; Harvey 2009; Dyrendal 2009). In his discussion of New Age spirituality, Paul Heelas describes what he terms Life Spirituality or Self-religion:

> In sum, New Age spiritualities of life are all about realizing one's inner, true life. Such spiritualities are (albeit to varying degrees) *detraditionalized*.... Ultimately, life can only be experienced through one's own inner-directed life. One has to be able to live one's life, express one's own life, experience the wisdom inherent in one's life. Traditions, with their supra-self, externally sustained frames of reference and injunction, can have little or no role to play (Heelas 202: 362).

Though Satanism has little in common with the New Age, both describe the individual's "true" self as having been subverted and obscured by socialization at the hands of the dominant culture (as well as at the hands of *traditional* religions). Satanism and the New Age (in large part) also share the idea that the individual should throw off these external influences and seek to realize her or his real nature. The Pagan view of the human condition replicates this pattern. Like Satanism, a goal of Paganism is to throw off one's (by implication artificial and harmful) socialization, and "come home to" and revive one's natural self. Satanism's and Paganism's views of the natural self are, of course, quite different, but at a broad level, their otherwise divergent portrayals of the human condition are strikingly similar – which may account, in part, for other parallels.

Berger and Ezzy analyzed Pagan expressions of "coming home" in terms of the cultural orientation shared by contemporary Paganism and the individuals who found in Paganism everything they had already believed. One can make a comparable argument for the parallel experiences of individuals who convert to Satanism. Some of the points of the shared cultural orientation between the "philosophy" of Satanism and converts to Satanism are not, of course, shared with modern Paganism. In the case of the Church of Satan, LaVey drew much of his inspiration from social Darwinism and the iconoclastic philosophy of Ayn Rand. Though often explicitly rejected in official cultural discourses, these kinds of ideas nevertheless constitute significant strands within contemporary society, and are particularly appealing to rebellious adolescents. One could also point to the often attractive images of the Devil as a clever, powerful being in horror films, certain types of music, and other entertainment media as a factor in the attraction of Satanism. As Asbjørn Dyrendal has observed in a recent article, "satanic identity does seem to be mediated and partly learned through popular culture" (Dyrendal 2008: 80).

Gateways to Involvement

One of the ways in which decentralized movements like Satanism and Paganism differ from more centralized religious bodies is that conversion to structured religious groups tend to happen primarily through social networks – though this is beginning to change, as I noted in Chapter Three. With regard to the paradigm of social network conversion, Berger and Ezzy note that, "Witches do not fit this model" (2007a: 85). Neither do Satanists. Pagans and Satanists overwhelmingly become involved in their respective movements through something they read, either in books or on websites:

> Most do not come to the religion through friendship networks, but to the contrary find out about Witchcraft primarily through books and secondarily through the Internet. Young Witches do not join because of growing affective ties with other Witches, and they typically maintain their friendships outside the religion (2007a: 84).

Berger's and Ezzy's findings about the conversion patterns of young Witches apply equally well to Satanists. The contrast between high-demand groups and decentralized movements like Paganism and Satanism on this particular point is easy to demonstrate.

As we discussed in Chapter Three, one of the generally accepted items of conventional wisdom about conversion to NRMs is that new members most often become involved through family and friends.[5] The pattern found in the Satan Surveys was significantly different. If we combine book and website readings, well over half of the respondents indicated that they were introduced to Satanism by something they read. I also found that these figures changed in significant ways over time. Taking the data from the first seven items in question 38 in SS-3 ("How did you initially become involved? Specifically, what was your initial point of contact?") and subdividing responses into 3-year periods according to how long they had been self-identifying as Satanists (question 37. "How many years have you been a self-identified Satanist?"), gives us Table 7.4.

Though only three of the respondents to SS-3 reside in New Zealand, it appears that the age pattern of the sample parallels New Zealand Satanists (as reflected Table 7.1) in that the great majority of the sample are younger, new Satanists. Thus the majority of respondents to SS-3 have been Satanists for three years or less. As we examine the data on Satanists who have been involved longer, the numbers fall off rapidly in the succeeding three-year periods. Nevertheless, the data clearly indicates (1) that something they read (either a book or a website) initially prompted most Satanists to become involved; (2) that as the Internet has grown, the key role originally played by books has declined; and (3) though the figures for the "Friend" category are highly variable, overall it appears that the importance of something potential Satanists read grows over time as the influence of friends decline.

The Pagan Census Revisited questionnaire contained a grid similar to the grid in SS-3 asking respondents how they first came into contact with Paganism, which allows us to construct a table for Paganism comparable to the "Introduction to Satanism" table. However, because Paganism tends to attract participants who stay with the program longer than participants in Satanism (as reflected in the contrast between Table 7.1 and Table 7.2), it is possible to construct a Pagan Table comparable to Table 4 that extends backwards in time more than 18 years. (For the sake of convenience, I am here reproducing the same Table 3.5 that I used in Chapter Three). Using only the first seven items in the "first contact" grid and arranging the data into 5-year periods (instead of 3-year periods) produces Table 7.5.

---

5. Though note James Coleman's finding that the majority of American converts to Buddhism report that they were initially attracted to Buddhism because of its teachings (Coleman 2001).

Table 7.4 Introduction to Satanism in Three-Year Time Periods

Years*	1–3		4–6		7–9		10–12		13–15		16–18	
	%	No.	%	No.	%	No.	%	No.	%	No.	%	No.
Friend	**16.9****	27	**15.5**	9	**31.7**	13	**20.8**	5	**20.0**	4	**44.4**	4
Co-worker	0.6	1	0.0	0	0.0	0	0.0	0	0.0	0	0.0	0
Partner/Spouse	1.9	3	0.0	0	4.9	2	4.2	1	0.0	0	0.0	0
Relative	0.6	1	5.2	3	0.0	0	0.0	0	10.0	2	0.0	0
Website	**57.5**	92	**43.1**	25	**39.0**	16	**29.2**	7	**15.0**	3	**11.1**	1
Book	**43.1**	69	**46.6**	27	**48.8**	20	**50.0**	12	**65.0**	13	**66.7**	6
TV or Movie	8.1	13	6.9	4	2.4	1	4.2	1	10.0	2	0.0	0

*Represent the number of years since respondents began self-identifying as Satanists.

**Percentages add up to more than 100% because respondents were allowed to check more than one option.

Table 7.5 Introduction to Paganism*

No. of Years Involved	45+		40–44		35–39		30–34		25–29	
	%	No.	%	No.	%	No.	%	No.	%	No.
Friend	12.1	16	18.4	27	23.9	49	23.9	70	28.6	137
Relative	31.8	42	19.0	28	13.7	28	11.3	33	9.4	45
Co-Worker	0.8	1	0.7	1	2.0	4	1.7	5	2.9	14
Partner/Spouse	3.0	4	1.4	2	0.5	1	2.0	6	4.8	23
TV or Movie	0.8	1	0.0	0	1.0	2	1.4	4	1.3	6
Book	21.2	28	34.0	50	40.0	82	32.1	94	38.2	183

No. of Years Involved	20–24		15–19		10–14		5–9		4–0	
	%	No.	%	No.	%	No.	%	No.	%	No.
Friend	31.3	238	31.8	286	33.3	437	33.9	409	28.2	289
Relative	7.6	58	6.5	58	6.9	91	5.2	63	4.8	49
Co-Worker	1.7	13	2.0	18	2.3	30	2.6	31	2.0	20
Partner/Spouse	3.7	28	4.8	43	4.6	61	5.5	66	6.5	67
TV or Movie	2.0	15	1.7	15	3.6	47	3.0	36	4.8	49
Book	39.9	304	41.5	373	36.5	479	35.5	429	33.2	340
Website			8.2	74	19.5	256	26.1	315	31.5	323

For respondents who had been self-identified Pagans for 45 or more years, 43.9% indicated relatives and friends had originally introduced them to Paganism. Adding co-worker and partner/spouse categories brings the social networks total up to 47.7%. For more recent converts, relatives and friends declined to 33.0%, though an interesting development within the social network category was how relatives became progressively less important and friends became more important across time. Adding co-worker and partner/spouse categories brings the social networks total up to 41.5% for the most recent recruits. The primary non-personal introduction to Paganism has been books, a factor that is more significant than friends in all periods. And though the influence of partners/spouses and the entertainment media show steady growth, the real rising star is the Internet, which appears to be on the edge of out-influencing every other single factor.

Though the pattern of responses is less marked than responses to the parallel item in SS-3, significantly more than half of the Pagan sample indicated that book and website readings played a central role in introducing them to Paganism during the most recent four 5-year periods – periods that roughly correspond to the six 3-year periods in Table 7.4. Hence, despite their many differences, both Satanism and Paganism have been increasingly impacted by the Internet.

In SS-2, I also asked how frequently and by what means respondents communicated with other Satanists. The pattern of responses supports the observation that Satanism is predominantly an Internet religion (Petersen 2008; Pettersen 2013) (refer to Table 7.6). The heavily web-oriented nature of the Satanic subculture at least partially explains why the initial point of entry for new "converts" is *in*frequently a face-to-face contact. This same item appears in the Pagan questionnaire. Pagans engage in much more face-to-face interaction than Satanists, though Pagans also tend to do a significant amount of communications via electronic means (refer to Table 7.7).

Additionally, respondents to SS-2 were asked if they ever gathered with co-religionists for religious or ritual purposes. The great majority (78.6%) replied "Never or almost never" (refer to Table 7.8). The parallel item in the Pagan questionnaire received a much greater diversity of responses. Nevertheless, a full third of the sample (33.5%) never or almost never met with co-religionists for religious or ritual purposes, while another 14.7% responded that they met with other Pagans only once per year (refer to Table 7.9). The former would in all probability self-indentify as solitaries, while the latter are likely solitary practitioners who occasionally attend Pagan festivals. Taken together, these two groups of respondents add up to almost half (48.2%) of the sample.

Table 7.6 How Often Do You Communicate with Other Satanists? (SS-2):

	Daily	Weekly	Monthly	Yearly	Never
In Person:	12.8% (31)	13.6% (33)	13.2% (32)	14.9% (36)	45.5% (110)
By Telephone:	9.2% (22)	11.3% (27)	13.0% (31)	10.9% (26)	55.5% (132)
Public Internet – Blogs, Message Boards, etc.:	39.6% (99)	4.4% (61)	5.6% (39)	6.8% (17)	13.6% (34)
Private Internet – E-mails, Private Messages, etc.:	31.6% (79)	26.0% (65)	14.8% (37)	6.4% (16)	21.2% (53)

Table 7.7 How Often Do You Communicate with Other Pagans?

	Daily	Weekly	Monthly	Yearly	Never
In Person:	20.0% (1,313)	30.3% (1,989)	23.4% (1,535)	11.3% (739)	5.0% (987)
By Telephone:	18.4% (1,196)	28.8% (1,874)	19.3% (1,254)	7.0% (457)	26.5% (1,720)
Public Internet-Blogs, Message Boards, etc.:	51.7% (3,416)	22.6% (1,493)	12.0% (792)	3.7% (243)	10.0% (661)
Private Internet-E-mails, Private Messages, etc.:	46.5% (3,087)	26.2% (1,738)	13.4% (886)	4.0% (263)	10.0% (661)

Table 7.8 How Often Do You Meet with Other Satanists for "Religious" or Ritual Purposes?

Frequency	%	No.
Daily or almost daily	3.1	9
Weekly	3.4	10
Monthly	6.5	19
Yearly	8.5	25
Never or almost never	78.6	231

Table 7.9 How Often Do You Meet with Other Pagans for Religious/Spiritual/Ritual Purposes?

Frequency	%	No.
Daily or almost daily	3.6	242
Weekly	15.4	1,037
Monthly	32.9	2,219
Yearly	14.7	990
Never or almost never	33.5	2,261

What we end up with for Satanism, then, is a movement whose members rarely if ever meet face to face, and who almost never engage in group religious activities. The primary activity of contemporary Satanists appears to be emailing or otherwise engaging in online discussions with other Satanists.[6] Though a much larger percentage of contemporary Pagans gather together with co-religionists for festivals and the like, there is still a significant percentage whose Paganism consists primarily of email communications and other web-based interactions (Cowan 2005).

Conversion or Identity Construction?

In 2003, I recruited Pagan students from some of my courses at the University of Wisconsin for several group independent studies on Paganism. Six students eventually signed up in the spring of 2003. In the subsequent term, I organized a second independent study with seven students. We met once a week for two hours and discussed assigned readings. What I sought to gain from these classes was a clearer sense of what might be referred to as "new generation" Pagans. The students not only provided me with feedback and constructive criticism, but just coming to know them as people and observing them in the context of our discussions was enlightening.

---

6. In his *The Re-Enchantment of the West*, Partridge notes in passing that some emergent groups within the cultic milieu meet "only in the chat rooms of cyberspace" (2004: 43).

All were self-taught solitaries. I had assumed, based on my familiarity with the growing body of literature directed to Teen Witches, that magic would be a major component of their practice – but it was not. When asked questions about "spells" and such, all of these students stated that they hardly ever worked magic. What seemed to be most important for my students were not the practices associated with Paganism, but rather that Paganism confirmed their personal attitudes toward life and their beliefs about the nature of reality. Thus when we read *Drawing Down the Moon*, they completely concurred with Adler's notion that people who become Pagan experience a sense of "coming home" rather than a traditional conversion experience.

My students also identified with the pre-Christian peoples and religions of ancient Europe – a self-identity which gave them the sense that they were not participating in a marginal movement. Thus, for example, during a discussion in which we talked about the discrimination that some modern Pagans had experienced at the hands of Christians, one of my students commented that, "Well, back in the days of the Roman Empire, we persecuted them!" This was a striking remark, reflecting a strong sense of solidarity with ancient Paganism – a solidarity this student felt despite the fact that earlier in the semester we often critiqued the notion that modern Paganism was a lineal descendant of the pre-Christian religions of Europe.

It is obvious that what these youthful students gain from Paganism – and what other individuals gain from Satanism – is a sense of identity. The drive to forge a self-identity is particularly acute in adolescence and young adulthood, but constructing and reconstructing "the story or stories by means of which self-identity is reflexively understood" (Giddens 1991: 244) is peculiarly characteristic of the modern world, and is by no means confined to adolescents.[7] However, if adopting a Pagan self-identity or a Satanic self-identity involves neither ritual practices nor non-Internet communities of co-religionists, is it really valid to say that one has *become a member of* a particular religion?[8]

Let us consider as a contrasting example someone who happens to come across information about Zoroastrianism on the Internet, decides Zoroastrian ideas align almost perfectly with what she/he already believes, and decides that she/he is a Zoroastrian. If this hypothetical individual subsequently never

---

7. There is a useful discussion of Pagan identity construction in terms of Anthony Giddens' analysis of identity construction in Reid's article (2009).
8. The ambiguity between 'joining' Paganism, creating one's own version of Paganism, and constructing a Pagan self-identity is evident in Magliocco's discussion in the second chapter of her *Witching Culture* (2004: 57–92).

engages in Zoroastrian rituals nor communicates with any other Zoroastrians except via Internet chat rooms, would she/he legitimately be regarded as a convert to Zoroastrianism? Or would she/he be regarded as someone who had simply adopted the label, and who was not "really" a Zoroastrian?

My purpose in raising this question is not to dismiss either Internet Paganism or Internet Satanism (or, for that matter, Internet Zoroastrianism) as inauthentic. Rather, this line of questioning arises from, on the one hand, how fundamentally the virtual environment has problematized what we traditionally regard as religious communities and religious conversion. On the other hand, the idea of conversion to online Paganism and to Satanism as a project of identity construction prompts me to consider how conversion to "traditional" religions is also a form of identity construction. Given that identity construction has become such a significant topic within the social sciences in recent decades (e.g., Cerulo 1997; Magliocco 2004: 9; Turner 2006: 277–78; McLean 2008:1–18), this should be a fruitful direction for future research and theorizing.[9]

---

9. There are some discussions in which researchers have explored this connection, though in a somewhat different manner than I am indicating (e.g., Chue 2008; Engberg-Pedersen 2000).

8 New Religious Movements and Gender – The Case of Scientology

With Inga Bårdsen Tøllefsen

With the exception of all-male bodies like monastic orders, women are in the majority in every Christian organization, conservative or liberal, and are generally more religious than men on any scale by which religiousness can be measured. Why this should be the case has sometimes been presented in terms of sexual stereotypes that are little more than sophisticated versions of the compatibility of women's imputed greater emotionality with religion. Alternately, some have argued that women are more physically vulnerable or that they have a lower social status than men, which makes them more susceptible to the appeal of religion. Yet other writers have pointed out that women are socialized to be more religious than men. And the list of explanations goes on, with no definitive agreement among observers (Walter and Davie 1998; Trzebiatowska and Bruce 2012).

People writing on the topic of the greater religiousness of women seem to have ignored data from national censuses, perhaps because such data adds nothing new to what we already know. Another consideration is that ticking a box about religious identification on a census form often does not say much about one's religious life – in many cases, it likely means only that one was raised in a particular tradition and that one continues to identify as Catholic or Presbyterian or something else, but otherwise one has not actively participated in Church life for decades. For our purposes here, however, it is worth glancing at select census statistics on religious self-identification among members of conventional religions to serve as a backdrop for an examination of data on members of alternative religions.

Out of the censuses of four Anglophone countries that we have been considering, the only year during which all four of these countries gathered religion data was 2001, which makes 2001 a good year from which to draw comparative data. Table 8.1 brings together religion identification data from New Zealand, Australia and Canada – for Catholics; for two "mainstream" (to use conventional nomenclature) denominations, Anglicans and Presbyterians; and for two "sectarian" denominations, the Latter-day Saints (popularly called Mormons) and the Jehovah's Witnesses.

Table 8.1 Sex X Religion Figures from the 2001 Census for Select Denominations: Three-Nation Comparison

		New Zealand	Australia	Canada
Catholic:	M	225,996	2,395,878	6,263,540
	F	258,822	2,563,402	6,657,745
Anglican:	M	258,918	1,847,828	954,840
	F	325,875	2,033,334	1,080,665
Presbyterian:	M	198,270	302,709	189,270
	F	232,869	322,183	220,560
Latter-day Saints	M	18,186	22,954	49,165
	F	21,729	25,821	54,035
Jehovah's Witnesses	M	7,617	35,683	68,255
	F	10,209	45,385	86,490

[Courtesy: Statistics New Zealand, Statistics Canada and Australian Bureau of Statistics.]

This pattern of female dominance was characteristic of all Christian denominations in the census figures for all three countries. Similarly, in the 2001 Census for England and Wales, the figures for the generic Christian category were 17,442,248 males and 19,895,270 females (as I mentioned earlier, the UK does not collect data on individual Christian denominations). No surprises.

We have been discussing the gender issue with respect to the memberships of New Religious Movements (NRMs). Regarding the New Age movement, Gilhus and Mikaelsson (2005) note that there are quite a few quantitative studies on practitioners in this field. Referring to Rose (1998), they say that although New Age practitioners come from all walks of life, they tend to share three defining characteristics – namely, at least half are middle aged, they are overwhelmingly middle class and almost three-quarters are women (also refer to Rose [2001] in this regard). The demographics of Norwegian participants in the Art of Living Foundation (AoL), a large schism from Transcendental Meditation that has been appropriated by the New Age subculture in Western countries (Tøllefsen 2011), fit well with Gilhus and Mikaelsson's observations. In a recent survey, participants were approaching middle age and the ratio of men to women was 29.6% male to 70.4% female (Tøllefsen 2012).

However, not all contemporary NRMs fall into the New Age category. In fact, an examination of relevant census data from the four nations reflects a surprising variety of different New Religions as well as a wide variation in sex ratios for these groups. The different national censuses were also surprisingly diverse in the comprehensiveness of their reporting of NRM memberships.

Only a relative handful of NRMs made it into all four censuses. Everyone seemed to be concerned about the progress of Scientology and Satanism, so all four nations included a category for these two movements. Rastafarianism, which mainly consists of young males, was also a surprisingly popular category. Wicca was an option in three censuses, but not in Canada. However, a note to the Pagan category in the 1991 and 2001 Canadian censuses indicates that it "includes Wicca." Finally, unlike other nineteenth century new religions, Spiritualism has enjoyed renewed popularity in the last four or five decades and was recorded in all four censuses, so we decided to include it in Table 8.2.

As one might anticipate, the pattern of more females than males can be found in Wicca and Spiritualism. There was a similar predominance of women in groups that fell into the New Age category. Thus in New Zealand, there were 138 males and 282 females who were simply labeled "New Age." Similarly, in England and Wales 338 males and 568 females fell into the same sort of generic New Age category. Druidism is a male-oriented form of contemporary Neo-Paganism, and this is reflected in the data from New Zealand (111 males; 39 females), Australia (456 males; 235 females) and from England and Wales (1155 males; 502 females).

Table 8.2 Sex X Religion Figures from the 2001 Census for Select Movements: Four-Nation Comparison

		New Zealand	Australia	Canada	United Kingdom*
Spiritualism:	M	1562	2769	1060	10,502
	F	4293	6510	2235	21,902
Wicca/	M	477	2133	7830**	2392
Witchcraft:	F	1719	6621	13,225**	4837
Rastafarian:	M	1092	898	865	3309
	F	204	167	270	1383
Satanism:	M	741	1409	715	1233
	F	150	386	140	290
Scientology:	M	174	1166	875	1076
	F	108	868	650	705

* Figures for England and Wales

** Figures are for "Pagan"

[Figures Courtesy: Statistics New Zealand, Statistics Canada, Australian Bureau of Statistics and the UK Office for National Statistics © Crown Copyright 2013.]

Both Satanism and Rastafarianism strongly appeal to young males (as discussed in Chapter Three). In a study of the demographics of self-identified Satanists, 101 males responded to an online questionnaire out of a total sample of 140 (Lewis 2001: 6). Subsequent studies (e.g., Lewis 2011; Lewis 2014; Lewis and Bauman 2011) have largely confirmed that the core of contemporary Satanism is constituted by youthful males. Though we do not have comparable questionnaire data on Rastafarians, the youthfulness of census respondents (e.g., average age 25.5 years in the 2001 New Zealand census) indicates that a similar pattern of young male rebelliousness is likely at work among self-identified Rastafarians.

The predominance of males in Scientology, however, has no apparent explanation. In many ways, Scientology fits the New Age category (Gruenschloss 2009), and there are no apparent barriers to females rising to positions of authority within the Church of Scientology (Anderson 2012). We considered the possibility that there might have been some sort of anomaly within this organization that made 2001 an idiosyncratic year for census data on Scientology, but an examination of New Zealand figures for four consecutive censuses indicated an ongoing demographic pattern in favour of males. Instead of a tendency toward gender balance, the data indicates a slight variation back and forth between greater or lesser male dominance (refer to Table 8.3).

Comparatively, the prior (1996) Australian Census recorded 843 males and 647 females, while the subsequent (2006) Census recorded 1522 males and 985 females (refer to Table 3.5 in the third chapter). Similarly, the 2011 UK Census showed a predominance of male (1510) to female (908) Scientologists, while the 2011 Canadian Census recorded 995 male to 745 female Scientologists. The single exception to the preponderance of males in any of the four Anglophone census nations was the 1991 Canadian census, which recorded 575 males and 645 females. However, the Canadian census asks only one-fifth of its population to answer the religious identification

Table 8.3 Census Data for New Zealand Scientologists, 1991–2006

Census Year:	1991		1996		2001		2006	
	N	%	N	%	N	%	N	%
Male	126	60.0	144	66.7	174	61.7	246	68.9
Female	81	38.6	72	33.3	108	38.3	114	31.9
Total	210	100.0	216	100.0	282	100.0	357	100.0
Average Age	34.75		34.51		34.15		35.40	

[Courtesy: New Zealand Statistics.]

question, and then multiplies the result by five (note that all figures from Canada in Table 8.1 and in Table 8.2 are divisible by five). This means that the 575 and 645 figures were derived, respectively, from 115 and 129 Scientologists (a difference of only 14 people). Hence, while there might have been more female than male Scientologists in Canada in 1991, the larger proportion of females might also have been a function of Canada's approach to collecting religion affiliation data.

In his overview of "Who Joins New Religious Movements and Why?" Lorne Dawson refers to a few studies which indicate that gender imbalances may be adjusted over time. In this regard he notes that "Krishna Consciousness began life in America as a largely male phenomenon, but this imbalance in sexual representation has been corrected as the movement has become an order of 'householders' and not strictly priestly ascetics" (Dawson 2003: 123). This assertion is not, however, borne out by figures from the two censuses that explicitly mention the Krishnas, New Zealand (198 male; 162 female) and the United Kingdom (392 male; 245 female).

The third "classic cult" to appear in the same two censuses was the Unification Church. Once again, we were surprised to find a predominance of males in figures from the New Zealand census (432 males; 309 females) and from England and Wales (134 males; 114 females). We assume, however, that the low total numbers for the UK are the result of the majority of British Unificationists ticking the generic Christian box, rather than ticking "Other" and writing in "Unification Church." To once again refer to his discussion of sex ratio differences, Dawson observes that, "In Korea and Japan, prior to its emergence in America, the Unification Church actually appealed more to women," though he also notes that Eileen Barker found a "two-to-one ratio in favor of men for the Moonies in Britain" in her well-known 1984 study (Dawson 2003, 123).

Total numbers for both the Hare Krishna Movement and the Unification Church are quite small, and the peculiarities of the UK census mean that the 2001 census figure for the Unification Church in that country constitutes at best a non-randomized sample. Further research on these two groups might yield statistically significant figures that reinforce the impression of male dominance, or demonstrate that the preponderance of males in the above census data is anomalous. The same cannot be said for the Church of Scientology (CoS), which is disproportionately male in all four 2001 censuses and across four consecutive New Zealand censuses.

In 1976, in the earliest systematic study of the Church of Scientology, *The Road to Total Freedom*, Roy Wallis put forward the figure of 59% male and 41% female Scientologists, based on the first names of people listed as "clears" (people who had achieved a certain level in their Scientology processing) in available issues of *The Auditor*, a CoS publication. More recently, a number of researchers associated with the University of Copenhagen have been studying members of the Church of Scientology in Copenhagen (where the first center for promulgating Scientology to continental Europe was established) for the past three decades. In 1988, Merete Sundby-Sørensen constructed a statistical stereotype of a "typical" participant in the Church of Scientology in Copenhagen, which included the observation that the statistically average participant was a 35-year-old man (Sundby-Sørensen 1988).

Sundby-Sørensen and several other researchers at the University of Copenhagen such as Peter B. Anderson have administered three questionnaires to Scientologists in the Copenhagen area since 1982.[1] Andreas Baumann, a graduate student at the Department for Cross-Cultural and Regional Studies at the University of Copenhagen, graciously calculated the relevant figures to produce Table 8.4.

These figures are not huge, and the differences between the sexes are not large, but they provide non-census evidence supporting the contention that more men than women become members of the Church of Scientology.[2]

---

1. Figures courtesy of Andreas Bauman. Based on data materials filed at the Dansk Data Arkiv: http://www.sa.dk/dda/
   DDA 01494: Scientology som identitet og institution: kernemedlemmer, 1986–1987, primary investigator Merethe Sundby-Sørensen.
   DDA 01605: Scientology som identitet og institution II: Opfølgning, 1991–1992, primary investigators Merethe Sundby-Sørensen and Jesper Demian Korsgaard.
   DDA 05680: Scientology som identitet III, 1999, primary investigator Peter B. Andersen.
   DDA 13095: Scientology som identitet I, II og III, 1986–1999.
   For a summary description of the series of surveys that were administered to members of the Church of Scientology in Denmark on file at the Dansk Data Arkiv, refer to Andersen and Wellendorf 2002; Andersen and Wellendorf 2009.
2. One of our Church of Scientology informants in the United States supplied us with findings from a March 2010 survey of Sea Org members. (The Sea Org's position in the Church of Scientology is roughly parallel to that of the Jesuits in traditional Catholicism). Out of a worldwide total of 5514 respondents (representing more than 90% of all Sea Org members), the questionnaire recorded 2448 men and 3066 women – 44.4% males and 65.6% females (Farny 2013). We have no reason to doubt the accuracy of these figures, but they cannot be extrapolated to the gender ratio of CoS as a whole. However, perhaps within the framework of the Church of Scientology's larger subculture, it is in the greater attraction of women to the Sea Org that we see

Table 8.4 University of Copenhagen Data for Danish Scientologists, 1982–1999

Survey Year:	1982		1992		1999	
	No.	%	No.	%	No.	%
Male Staff	93	62	96	59	74	58
Female Staff	56	38	68	41	54	42
Male Parishioner	101	55	112	50	184	55
Female Parishioner	81	45	110	50	150	45
Male Unidentified*	10	71	6	50	6	75
Female Unidentified*	4	29	6	50	2	25
Total Male	204	59	214	54	264	56
Total Female	141	41	184	46	206	44

Average gender ratio for the three surveys: M – 56%; F – 44%

* Indicates respondents who did not identify as Staff or Parishioner

A similar pattern can be found among samples of former members. Thus in a recently published study of former members of CoS, Lisbeth Tuxen Rubin's convenience sample of ex-members consisted of 24 men and 19 women (Rubin 2011). And in a current PhD project focused on former members of the Church of Scientology and former members of the Jehovah's Witnesses, Sean Currie's sample of ex-CoS members is 65% male and 35% female (Currie 2013).

Among studies of members of the Church of Scientology, the only exception to the pattern of male dominance was a 1988 Australian study which used a sample consisting of 24 men and 24 women (Ross 1988). As far as we can determine, there is no source of data beyond the 1991 Canadian census which indicates that there might be more women than men in the Church of Scientology. Why should this be the case?

We floated the census data past a number of former members of the Church of Scientology. Some of our contacts flatly denied the compelling evidence that more men than women were attracted to Scientology. Additionally, more than one or two other people responded with the *non sequitur* that gender didn't matter, because Scientology teaches that we are not ultimately either male or female. Finally, we received gender-stereotypical style responses about how women are more emotional, which leads them into "feminine" religions like Christianity, whereas men are more intellectual, and thus more attracted to "masculine" religious systems like Scientology. None of these provided the insight we were looking for.

---

evidence for the imputed greater religiousness of the female gender.

There was, however, one ex-member informant we asked who suggested a possible connection with science fiction fandom: "Science fiction has a higher male to female ratio, and there were many science fiction devotees amongst Dianetics followers and early Scientology followers – that might have some connection" (Beatty 2013). As many critics like to emphasize, the founder of CoS, L. Ron Hubbard, originally gained fame as the author of popular fiction and was especially successful in the science fiction genre. The negative inference critics draw from this is that the creation of Scientology was the same as – and thus no more real than – the invention of a fantastic alternative world by a talented science fiction writer.

Academic observers have also noted that "it is understandable that some people think that science fiction has been a factor in the formation of this group" (Possamai and Possamai-Inesedy 2012: 588). Efforts to reduce Scientology to "just" science fiction, however, typically ignore the preexisting connection between science fiction and occult spirituality in American culture – a connection explored in some depth in Harriet Whitehead's insightful essay on these interconnections (1974). William Sims Bainbridge, yet another academician deeply familiar with Scientology, even regards Scientology's roots in "the popular science fiction subculture" to be one of its "strengths" (1987: 59).

These considerations aside, the more salient connection between Scientology and science fiction might be sociological rather than ideological. The original piece announcing Hubbard's Dianetics (the Dianetics movement was the precursor to the Church of Scientology) appeared in *Astounding Science Fiction* magazine. It has further been observed that during its developmental phase, Dianetics was tested out on science fiction fans recruited by Hubbard's early collaborator, John W. Campbell, who was also Hubbard's publisher (Miller 1987: 150). Furthermore, science fiction fans were the first converts to Dianetics (Gardner 1957: 265).

Many science fiction fans, from Hubbard's contemporaries when he was a productive Sci-Fi author in the 1940s to the Trekkies of more recent decades, are what have been referred to as "geeks." Geek is an old word with a variety of different meanings, from fool or freak to crazy or clever. In contemporary usage, it tends to refer to young people, frequently individuals with low social skills, who are often adept at working with hi-tech electronics – particularly with computers ("computer geeks") – and who are skilled at pursuits like online gaming. Although there are also "girl geeks," geeks are predominantly male (Beynon 1993; Christensen 2006; Dunbar-Hester 2008). With the exception of those who claim to have been abducted by aliens, people with serious, ongoing interests in UFOs participate in a subculture that also tends to be predominantly male (Denzler 2003; Dewan

2006). And while UFO buffs are not necessarily geeks, there is some degree of overlap between the UFO milieu and Sci-Fi fandom, and, in turn, with the online gaming milieu.

In other words, there are a number of different overlapping male-majority milieus which, when taken together, might constitute a substantial source of male recruits to Scientology. To restate this in a more general way, there are several subcultures that attract a similar type of person – perhaps we should say similar types of people – who tend to be predominantly male. It seems reasonable to hypothesize that this same personality type constitutes a significant enough percentage of members to push Scientology's gender ratio in the direction of more men than women. Thus explanations for the predominance of males among science fiction fans or the predominance of male ufologists should also be extended to Scientologists. And while not all participants are geeks, it might not be unfair to conclude by characterizing Scientology as a geek-friendly religion.

Conclusion

Here once again we have a case where it was possible to juxtapose survey and census data, the results of which neatly dovetail with each other. As noted earlier, being able to compare data from two independent sources is not always – perhaps we should say rarely – possible. Furthermore, the idiosyncrasies of the four censuses meant that we found tantalizing data on male predominance in the Unification Church and the Hare Krishna Movement that we did not pursue, primarily because only two censuses tracked data on these two movements. Instead, we followed up on the Church of Scientology because the data for that particular group was both strong and consistent across all of censuses as well as the independent survey data collected by researchers at the University of Copenhagen.

Part IV

Ex-Members

9 Post-Involvement Attitudes

My interest in quantitative approaches to New Religions began in the early 1980s when I was a graduate student. The heyday of the "cult" controversy had been the 1970s, but the conflict was still quite lively during my graduate years. The specific incident that prompted my interest in the controversy was a public forum sponsored by the university law school at which people were debating the issue. As it turned out, more than a few people in attendance were former members of New Religious Movements who had been kidnapped and "deprogrammed" until they renounced their faith. Whenever any of these particular audience members spoke, I couldn't help but notice that they were sitting right next to older people who I assumed to be their parents. It was a little weird. I was also struck by the uniformly negative picture they painted of the time they spent in their new religion.

As someone who had been involved in an NRM in his youth, I eventually spoke up and tried to provide a more balanced view, basing what I said on my own personal experience. Subsequently, no one responded to me. And during the break, I actually received dirty looks from some of the other members of the audience. It was disconcerting. People were clearly passionate about their opposition to alternative religious groups. It was also clear to me that, despite claims to the contrary, deprogramming was simply a form of re-socialization that attacked the religious beliefs of "deprogrammees" and forced them to accept a reinterpretation of their NRM experience in terms of entrapment and "cultic mind control" (i.e., brainwashing).

It should also be noted that, at the time, media attention given to this conflict often revolved around the negative testimony of former members of controversial NRMs. It made good copy: Heroic parents "rescue" their adult children from the clutches of an evil "cult" – offspring who then turn around and testify to all the "horrors" about which outsiders could only fantasize. It was also "smoking gun" evidence for the people who wanted to destroy minority religious groups.

The unacceptably prejudiced nature of the testimony provided by deprogrammed former NRM members had been demonstrated in an important study by social psychologist Trudy Solomon. Specifically, Solomon found that the negative attitude of ex-Moonies toward the Unification Church (at the time, the paradigm of the "evil cult") was a direct function of "method of exit and degree of contact with the anticult movement" (1981: 281). In other words, as one might anticipate, former Moonies who were forcibly deprogrammed and who continued to associate with the anti-cult movement were far more negative toward the Church – and were far more likely to repeat anti-cult rhetoric about mind control and the like – than were ex-Moonies who left voluntarily and had little or no contact with anti-cult groups.

My experience at the public forum mentioned above eventually led me to undertake a research project similar to Solomon's, though I sought out ex-members of other controversial religions as well (not just Moonies, though Moonies were included).[1] I was also interested in other issues that I will discuss directly. Though the basic findings in this chapter have been published before (e.g., in Lewis 2003), it seemed worthwhile to republish them in the differing context of the present volume.

Methodology

This was before the days of online questionnaire services, so data were gathered by means of a mail survey conducted in 1984. The sample consisted of 154 ex-members of groups often labeled cults: the Unification Church (26%), Yogi Bhajan's 3HO (23%), the Hare Krishna Movement (20%), the Way International (16%), the Divine Light Mission (8%), the Church of Scientology (1%), and miscellaneous groups (5%). Anti-cult groups put me in touch with 72 ex-members, 72% of whom responded, plus 37 snowballs (people who were contacted on the basis of being referred by other respondents). I was directly or indirectly acquainted with 25 ex-members, 68% of whom responded (plus 4 snowballs). The Unification Church gave me a list of 16 former Unificationists, 62% of whom responded. The lists of former followers which the Way International and the Hare Krishna Movement passed on to me contained many partial and out-of-date addresses, so it is difficult to estimate response rates for these sample sources.

As far as could be determined, there was no evidence of intentional bias in the lists of ex-members that the anti-cult groups and the new religions passed on to me. The strongest evidence for non-bias was the similarity of the two subsamples. For example, 21% of the former members in the sample from the new religions were coercively deprogrammed; while 26% of the ex-members in the anti-cult sample were coercively deprogrammed.

---

1. This research was supported by modest grants from the Society for the Scientific Study of Religion and Syracuse University. Data from the survey formed the basis for three papers published in the 1980s (Lewis 1986; Lewis and Bromley 1987; Lewis 1989).

Of greater importance for indicating the non-presence of intentional bias, the patterns of responses relative to mode of exit were comparable.

Forty-five percent of the respondents were females and 55% were males. Median age at recruitment was 21, with a broad range of 14 to 55. Average length of involvement was 4–1/4 years with a range of several weeks to 13 years. Consistent with previous studies (e.g., Solomon 1981; Wright 1984), the great majority of respondents were caucasian. In terms of religious upbringing there were, again consistent with previous research, a disproportionately greater number of subjects from Jewish and Catholic backgrounds: 18% Jewish, 34% Catholic, 39% Protestant, and 10% who either had no religious affiliation or who did not respond to the item. At the time they joined, 4% had some kind of advanced degree, 26% had completed college, 41% had at least some college, 23% had completed high school, and 6% had not completed high school. Fifty-eight percent of the respondents left their groups voluntarily and were not exposed to any form of anti-cult counseling, 19% voluntarily experienced some form of anti-cult counseling, and 23% were coercively deprogrammed.

I found essentially the same pattern among these 154 former members of different controversial religious movements (Lewis 1986; Lewis 1989) as Solomon found in her sample of former Unificationists. Solomon divided her sample into eight subgroups across which post-involvement attitudes varied (1981: 281). For a number of reasons (explained in Lewis 1986), I utilized a much simpler typology:

(1) No Exit Counseling (NEC): Voluntary defection and no counseling connected with the anti-cult movement (N = 89)
(2) Voluntary Exit Counseling (VEC): Some form of voluntary counseling at the hands of the anti-cult movement – e.g., exit counseling, re-entry counseling, etc. (N = 29)
(3) Involuntary Exit Counseling (IEC): Coercive deprogramming with or without other forms of treatment following their deprogramming (N = 36)

While there are, of course, other factors involved in anti-cult socialization, the intensity of the counseling process appeared to be the primary operant factor.

Four questionnaire items measured respondents' attitudes toward their former movements. These items asked respondents to evaluate the extent to which they felt that (1) they had been recruited deceptively, (2) they had been "brainwashed," (3) their leader was insincere, and (4) the group's beliefs were spurious. The fourth item, for example, was:

Evaluate the doctrine/ideas/world view of your former group:

1. Completely true
2. More true than false
3. More false than true
4. Completely false

The responses to each of these measures were treated as interval data for the purpose of analysis. All four attitude measures were found to be highly correlated with the degree of one's exposure to anti-cult counseling, which was also treated as a variable by assigning values to each of the treatment groups (NEC = 1, VEC = 2, and IEC = 3). The correlation coefficient (r) for deceptive recruitment was .392, for brainwashing .587, for leadership insincerity .407, and for spurious world view .551 – all significant at the .001 level.

Three other variables that might possibly have been factors in shaping attitudes were computed as controls: (1) length of membership, (2) age at recruitment, and (3) time between exit and the point at which they completed the questionnaire. None of these calculations yielded significant correlations.

The four forced-choice items were replicated elsewhere in the survey instrument by open-ended questions that requested essentially the same information. For example, the open-ended question corresponding to the multiple-choice item cited above was:

How would you describe and/or evaluate the doctrine/ideas/world view of your former group?

Consistent with the quantitative data, qualitative expressions of post-involvement attitudes were found to vary according to the extent of one's anti-cult socialization: Ex-members who had experienced coercive deprogramming tended to express negative, stereotyped attitudes; voluntary defectors who had no links with anti-cultists tended to feel ambivalent or positive about their former movements; and the attitudes of respondents who were not kidnapped but who had experienced some form of voluntary counseling at the hands of anti-cultists tended to lie somewhere in between.

What follows is a qualitative analysis of some exemplary sample responses, which have been selected according to treatment group and according to the four cult-stereotypical attitudes for which I collected quantitative data. The pattern of responses to each of the four attitudes will be discussed in turn.

1. Recruitment

IEC: At the time of recruitment there were unethical techniques of coercion being utilized against me.

VEC: I was not lied to. However, I didn't really know what I was getting into.
NEC: The people were very sincere.

These three responses reflect the overall pattern of post-involvement attitudes with respect to the three categories of ex-member. Voluntary apostates tended to discount the idea of deceptive recruitment unless they had joined the Unification Church via the Oakland Family's well-known (but now defunct) recruiting operation. Many deprogrammees tended to draw on mind control type explanations to explain their recruitment, but others made use of less exotic notions of deception, such as, "I was lied to."

2. Brainwashing

IEC: I was hypnotized, also performed self-hypnosis to block out my old self, any doubts.
VEC: I was exposed to only one doctrine, and not encouraged to question or doubt.
NEC: Someone who says "I was brainwashed" has little self-esteem and/or sense of who they are.

As predicted, the IEC group supported the brainwashing notion, the NEC group rejected it, and the opinion of the VEC group fell somewhere in between. Individuals in the intermediate VEC group who said they had been brainwashed tended to describe "brainwashing" more in terms of indoctrination into a rigid, narrow belief-system than as some type of hypnosis.

3. Leader

IEC: He has psychologically "raped" or taken advantage of thousands of people. I would like to see him dead.
VEC: I think he's sincere, but his sincerity gives him an excuse to use people and manipulate them because he believes in himself.
NEC: A spiritual teacher of considerable merit and great sincerity, somewhat limited by his own culture, and especially by many of his close disciples.

This item elicited a more complex range of responses than the recruitment and brainwashing questions. A number of individuals, for example, evaluated their former leader as "sincere but deluded." Also, the evaluation of the leadership by voluntary defectors tended to be far more ambivalent than their evaluation of mind control claims because difficulties or disenchantment with leaders often contributed to apostates' decisions to leave their movements. Voluntary defectors often made such remarks as, "I think he started out sincere, but became corrupted."

4. World View

> IEC: The doctrine states that the world is a miserable prison and people are simply pigs, dogs, camels, asses in human form. They must be converted or killed.
> VEC: There is much truth in the philosophy which I still believe in. There is also much I don't believe in.
> NEC: Pure, just not represented in a perfectly pure way.

Deprogrammees described their former group's ideology as being fanatical, twisted, fabricated by the founder, and the like. Individuals in the VEC group, although they sometimes resorted to the same kind of stereotyped, anti-cult evaluations, often perceived that at least some portion of their former belief-system overlapped their present belief-system, and thus tended to be less harsh in their criticisms. Voluntary defectors tended to express positive or ambivalent attitudes toward their former group's belief-system. Like their attitude toward the movement's leadership, voluntary defectors' evaluation of the ideology tended to be critical at certain points. More often than not, voluntary defectors retained large portions of their former groups beliefs.

The questionnaire also contained forced-choice and open-ended items which solicited ex-members' evaluations of the anti-cult movement. To an open-ended question about the anti-cult movement, I received the following kinds of responses:

5. Anti-cult Movement

> IEC: It warns people of the dynamics of cults and how they use unethical tactics.
> VEC: The educational part is good. I think the deprogramming part has gotten out of hand.
> NEC: Ignorant, closed-minded people who are unable to accept any ideas except their own.

The pattern was, as one could have predicted, an inverted mirror image of ex-member's attitudes toward their former movements, in that respondents at either end of the spectrum tended to express strong negative or positive evaluations, whereas subjects in the intermediate group tended to have mixed opinions (r. = .499). There were also a number of people in each treatment group (though proportionately more in the NEC group) who described the anti-cult movement as an "anti-cult cult"; to cite an example:

> The anti-cult movement appears to me to be a group of self-righteous do-gooders who have their own cult going on. They appear to have just as much, if not more so, of a 'savoir complex' as Moon, Wierwille, or any other charismatic religious leader.

As reflected in this particular response, ex-members sometimes held negative attitudes toward both the anti-cult movement and their former religious group.

In terms of the influential line of thought initiated by one of the founders of sociology, Emile Durkheim (1960), the labeling and persecution of minorities is usually more of a response to doubts and anxieties about norms and values within the dominant culture than a response to tangible threats from minority groups. In other words, in a society confronted with unsettling tensions such as arise in the wake of rapid social change (particularly in a society without pressing external threats), a sub-community will be found that can be perceived as the larger community's "criminal opposite," and then persecuted "as a means of ritually reaffirming the group's problematical values and collective purposes" (Bergesen 1984: vii). The deviant group is thus forced to play a self-clarifying role for the dominant society by serving as a screen onto which the dominant society projects an inverted image of itself.

Because the image of the minority group is more of a projected "otherness" than an empirical "otherness," one would expect to find a marked tendency on the part of "projectors" to blur the distinctions between various groups of "projectees." In other words, the empirical diversity should be obscured beneath a unitary projection (Gilman 1985: 21). Thus, for example, archdeprogrammer Ted Patrick asserted, regarding the diversity among the movements he attacked, that,

> You name 'em. Hare Krishna. The Divine light Mission. Guru Maharaj Ji. Brother Julius. Love Israel. The Children of God. Not a brown penny's worth of difference between any one of 'em (Patrick & Dulack 1977: 11).

One of the results of this tendency to blur distinctions is that common sets of accusations are leveled against various groups which are empirically quite different. The four accusations leveled against contemporary religious movements that were reflected in the attitudes of deprogrammed ex-members – deceptive recruitment, brainwashing, insincere leadership, and bogus belief-system – are examples of such common themes. If we turn back in time, it is not difficult to find parallel themes in anti-Catholicism and anti-Mormonism: Joseph Smith was often accused of fabricating the Mormon religion for the purpose of personal gain (for example, Belisle 1855); the Catholic confessional was frequently described as a mind control device (for example, Monk 1977 [1836]); both Mormons and Catholics were accused of deceptively recruiting or kidnapping young Gentile/Protestant women; and so forth. Such themes seem to constitute part of a common "deep structure" through which the dominant social group perceives all forms of religious otherness (Cox 1978). Why, one might ask, should the same themes resurface time and again?

When a minority group forced to play the role of deviant is a religious movement, one of the first points of contrast with the dominant society is in the area of competing belief systems. Non-mainstream beliefs are "obviously" untrue to individuals securely enmeshed in the perspective of the dominant culture. But this obvious spuriousness presents certain problems, such as, where did such weird ideas come from in the first place? The easiest solution to this quandary is to accuse the cult leader of having cynically concocted a false belief-system. This approach also enables one to explain the genesis of the movement: The entire thing was dreamed up by the leader for the purpose of gaining wealth and power. The other two accusations arise naturally out of this picture: Why would anyone ever become part of such a nutty movement? It must be because they were recruited deceptively. And why, once they were actually inside the group and could see what it really was, did they not leave immediately? It must be because they were brainwashed. These four themes thus fit together into a neat package that de-legitimates alternative religious movements and saves us from the trouble of having to take them seriously. Conveniently and not coincidently, these themes also serve to legitimate the persecution of such groups.

The apostate fits into this structure as the chief source of evidence for its truth. In other words, the testimony of ex-members who have actually been there, and who have supposedly witnessed all of the horrors about which outsiders can only fantasize, provide the stereotype with its most important source of empirical evidence. What the above data indicates, however, is that the apostates who are paraded before the public by the anti-cult movement have been carefully selected. Though few if any apostates are ever completely objective about their former religion, ex-members who have been intensively "counseled" – especially those who were kidnapped – should be especially suspect as being less than neutral witnesses.

By relying upon this subset of ex-members, the anti-cult movement involves itself in a hermeneutic circle: Instead of forming generalizations based on a broad range of data, the anti-cult movement generates its own data by imposing an *a priori* ideology on a select number of individual cases (deprogrammees), and then "discovers" evidence for its ideology in the testimony of these same individuals. Anti-cultists depend upon this subset of former members for the ultimate proof of their accusations.

Without the legitimating umbrella of brainwashing ideology, deprogramming – the practice of kidnapping members of non-traditional religions and destroying their religious faith – cannot be justified, either legally or morally. Though advocates claim that deprogramming does nothing more than reawaken cult members' capacity for rational thought, any actual examination of the process reveals that deprogramming is little more than a heavy-handed assault upon a person's belief system. The vast majority of deprogrammers have little or no background in psychological counseling. They are, rather, "hired gun" vigilantes whose only qualifications, more often than not, are that they are physically large or that they are themselves deprogrammed ex-cult members.

To understand how deprogramming actually works, Stuart Wright's study of voluntary defectors – originally his dissertation (1983); later published in book form under the title *Leaving Cults: The Dynamics of Defection* – is a useful point of reference. Making use of the notion of socialization, Wright described defection as a process of "desocialization," and found that the first step in the deconversion process was a disruption of one's sense of the group's plausibility, which could be brought about by one of four situations:

I. A breakdown in members' insulation from the outside world.
II. The development of romantic relationships within the group that were expressly forbidden by the group.
III. Perceived lack of success in achieving the group's goals, particularly the goal of transforming the outer world.
IV. Inconsistencies between the actions of the leadership and the ideals and values they claimed to represent.

Wright also found that, once the plausibility of the group had been disrupted in the follower's mind, certain secondary factors could come into play that would further increase the likelihood of apostasy. The secondary "defection factors" indicated by Wright were:

V. The pull of family ties.
VI. Conventional careers.
VII. Alternative religious belief systems.

This general framework can be adapted for the purpose of understanding what happens during deprogramming. At least four of Wright's "defection factors" are clearly present in deprogramming:

(1) A breakdown in insulation from the outside world (accomplished by physically removing the member from her or his group).
(2) A highlighting of the inconsistencies between group ideals and the actions of leaders.
(3) The pull of family ties. (Deprogrammings are almost invariably paid for by other family members who then participate in the sessions).
(4) The presentation of an alternative belief system. (Though Wright's analysis of voluntary defection discussed this as the *discovery* of alternate *religious* belief systems, in deprogramming, the alternate belief system usually presented is some highly secular system of beliefs and values).

In addition to these four factors, deprogramming seeks to shatter one's faith by:

(5) Pointing out internal inconsistencies *within* the group's belief system (as differentiated from inconsistencies between ideals and practices).
(6) By offering an alternative explanation for the individual's recruitment and membership – the familiar deception/mind control ideology.

These six factors effectively disrupt the plausibility of the deprogrammee's religious beliefs. Success is not, however, necessarily guaranteed, as the high failure rate of deprogramming – between a third and a half return to their respective movements – demonstrates.

The additional two factors explain certain systematic differences that exist between the attitudes of deprogrammees and the attitudes of voluntary defectors: Voluntary defectors tend to retain more aspects of the world view and the ideals of their former movement than do deprogrammees. Also, as has already been demonstrated, voluntary defectors rarely rely upon notions of mind control to interpret their former group or their membership in that group.

These two special tactics of deprogramming are not difficult to document. One of the respondents to my survey, for example, said that his deprogrammers demonstrated to him that, "The *Divine Principle* [a Unification

Church scripture] was flawed, had contradictions and thus could not be absolute truth."

Indoctrination in brainwashing ideology is an essential component of deprogramming. Another deprogrammed respondent related, for instance, that,

> After three days of dialogue I had a basic understanding of thought reform and how it had been applied to me.

The attractiveness of this ideology was reflected in yet another deprogrammee's response:

> It still makes me cringe to think of the 'witnessing' I did to co-workers during free times. But my deprogrammer made sure I knew it wasn't my fault.

This last statement clearly indicates how anti-cult ideology's provision for a face-saving "absolution from blame" makes it attractive to ex-members.

Deprogramming is much more effective at destroying beliefs than in providing deprogrammees with new systems of meaning. The deprogrammees among questionnaire respondents who did not become crusading anti-cultists after their faith was broken reported experiencing a very bleak psychological landscape during the time period immediately following their exit; for example:

> I felt as if my whole world had caved in.

> I didn't know who I was, where I was going, why I should try. I just wanted to crawl into a dark corner and be put out of my misery.

> I was kidnapped and deprogrammed, so my whole world was suddenly ripped out from under me...before, every single action had cosmic importance, but, afterwards, I felt small and unimportant. Life had no meaning.

Not unsurprisingly, deprogrammees frequently reported experiencing suicidal tendencies after their exits, and at least one of my deprogrammed contacts killed herself before the questionnaire reached her.

The one other characteristic of deprogramming that sets it apart from voluntary defection is its comparative rapidity. Voluntary apostates characteristically take a long time to reach a decision to leave, and, after leaving, they continue to reflect on their membership period in what Stuart Wright describes as a "sifting process in which favorable events or experiences are separated out from what is later perceived as wrong, immoral or theologically adrift" (Wright 1984: 180). As a result of this lengthy process of deliberation, their attitude toward their former movement is usually complex and ambivalent. Deprogrammees, on the other hand, frequently experience a sudden shift of perspective that resembles a classic conversion experience in its rapidity, totality, and one-sidedness. The motivation for making this sudden shift in perspective can be explained as a reaction to the intensity of the assault carried out by deprogrammers. If the attacks on their faith have a real impact on kidnapped cult members, they can resolve the conflict they feel by completely adopting the point of view of the deprogrammer.

Without claiming to be exhaustive, this description provides an outline of how deprogramming "works." In addition to avoiding pseudo-scientific notions of brainwashing, this account is able to explain why deprogrammees' understanding of their cult experience is so different from voluntary defectors.

Beyond shaping public opinion by recounting stereotyped atrocity tales, deprogrammees feed into the cult controversy in a number of other ways: At the level of basic research, these former members are interviewed in pseudo-scientific surveys designed to substantiate such claims as that cultic brainwashing techniques induce mental illness in their members (for e.g., Conway & Siegelman 1982), and that child abuse is widespread in alternative religious groups (for example, Gaines *et al.* 1984). In a variety of different court battles, ex-members recruited by anti-cultists provide negative testimony against their former movements, such as in child custody cases where one of the parents is a cult member (for example, Driscoll 1983), and in cases where governmental agencies need evidence for cult violations of various governmental regulations (for example, *Cult Observer* 1986). The testimony of a deprogrammed Branch Davidian was, for example, part of the evidence used to obtain a search warrant before the assault on the Davidian community (Lewis 1994).

The Post-Involvement Syndrome

A useful example of how deprogrammees feed into research that supports certain critics of NRMs is research on the so-called post-involvement syndrome. Because members of NRMs test normal on measures of intelligence and psychological health, it was standard practice back in the 1980s to focus on the "syndrome" that former members experience following forced removal from their religious community. This syndrome was described in various ways, depending on the source, and usually includes such symptoms as poor attention span, "floating" in and out of altered states, amnesia, hallucinations, suicidal tendencies, guilt, fear, violent outbursts, and lack of a sense of directedness. Anti-cult researchers asserted or implied that this psychological disorder was specifically the result of exotic mind control techniques, parading under the guise of ordinary religious practices – praying, meditating, and Bible-reading – to which cult members were subjected. Concentration on the post-involvement period characterized the empirical work of such anti-cultists as Flo Conway and Jim Siegelman (1982), Margaret Singer (1979), and John Clark (Clark et al. 1981).

Of these studies, the one that conveyed the most substantial appearance to casual readers was Conway and Siegelman's survey of 400 ex-members of controversial religions that was reported in a 1982 article entitled "Information Disease: Have Cults Created a New Mental Illness?" Conway and Siegelman presented data on seven symptoms – floating/altered states, nightmares, amnesia, hallucinations/delusions, "inability to break mental rhythms of chanting," violent outbursts, and suicidal/self-destructive tendencies – for which respondents reported long term mental and emotional effects. More particularly, Conway and Siegelman claimed that, "The psychological trauma cults inflict upon their members is directly related to the amount of time spent in indoctrination and mind control rituals" (1982).

Although one could critique many aspects of this study, the decisive weakness of the information disease notion – and it should be noted that Singer and Clark never used the *term* "information disease," although the same basic *notion* of a "cult withdrawal syndrome" is implicit in their work – is that this supposedly new and unique syndrome is actually nothing more exotic than a traumatic stress response.

There are, in fact, a number of different syndromes with which information disease can be compared. Sociologist Brock Kilbourne, for example, has pointed out that a wide variety of psychological disturbances – from bereavement to the mourning symptoms which follow divorce – parallel the symptomatology of the post-cult involvement syndrome (1983: 35 36). Although any of these disorders could be used to point out the parallels between information disease and responses to traumatic stress, it is easiest to make a case for the connection between the cult withdrawal syndrome and what the *Diagnostic and Statistical Manual of Mental Disorders (DSM)* calls the "Post-Traumatic Stress Disorder." The *DSM* describes the cause of the Post-Traumatic Stress Disorder (PTSD) as any "psychologically traumatic event that is generally outside the range of usual human experience," such as assault, military combat, natural disaster, or an accident (American Psychiatric Association 1980: 236). The trauma of deprogramming, particularly a deprogramming of the classic "snatch" type (Patrick and Dulack 1976), clearly fits the category of a stressful event outside the range of normal human experience. And, because two-thirds to three-fourths of the samples used by anti-cult researchers were deprogrammed (71% in Conway and Siegelman's 1982 "Information Disease" study and 75% in Singer's 1979 "Coming out of the Cults" study), it is reasonable to hypothesize that the difficulties which these individuals experienced would be partially – if not entirely – a response to traumatic stress.

Most of the overlap between the cult withdrawal syndrome and the Post-Traumatic Stress Disorder is quite straightforward: Simply compare the symptomatology of the PTSD – nightmares, guilt, memory impairment, difficulty concentrating, phobic response, explosive outbursts, suicidal tendencies, and so on – with the symptomatology (mentioned earlier) reported in anti-cult studies of ex-members. In addition to these obvious parallels, some of the more bizarre symptoms of the post-involvement syndrome, such as hallucinations and the tendency to slip into dissociated states, express another essential component of PTSD symptomatology.

The *DSM* describes this other symptom as "recurrent and intrusive recollections," and as the "sudden acting or feeling as if the traumatic event were reoccurring" which in some instances is experienced as "dissociativelike states, lasting from a few minutes to several hours or even days" (American Psychiatric Association 1980: 238). This intrusive recalling of the traumatic event – which can be experienced either as waking "flashbacks" or as unpleasant dreams – is the more central symptom of the Post-Traumatic Stress Disorder. This symptom is probably also related to the experience of "floating" described by former "cult" members.

The problem with the term "floating," however, is that it is a "technical" term coined by deprogrammers to refer to ex-members' alternation between the values and belief-system of their former group, and the values and beliefs of mainstream society. Thus when an individual "drifts" back into the perspective of her or his former faith, it appears to parents and deprogrammers that she or he has lost touch with the real world. Because a person who has gone through deprogramming has been indoctrinated to interpret her or his experience in terms of this perspective, I suspect that many former members of non-traditional religions who report experiencing this symptom are actually thinking about their alternation back and forth between their religious group's perspective and the perspective of mainstream culture, rather than any sort of actual trance or altered state of consciousness.

Similarly, the symptom described by Conway and Siegelman as the "inability to break mental rhythms of chanting" might also be an expression of what the *DSM* describes as "recurrent and intrusive recollections." Here once again, however, we have to reckon with the factor of indoctrination at the hands of deprogrammers, relatives, and other people in the anti-cult movement. As is commonly known in anti-cult circles, individuals being tormented by deprogrammers frequently respond to heavy-handed interrogation by breaking off the dialogue and attempting to enter a contemplative, prayerful, or meditative state. If these individuals' deprogrammings are later successful, they will subsequently reinterpret such strategies as part of their indoctrinated mental state (i.e., they were "unable" to prevent themselves from "trancing out"). Hence with this symptom, I am similarly persuaded that many of the individuals reporting an "inability to stop mental rhythms of chanting" are responding out of the interpretive framework of their counter-indoctrination.

Finally, the other characteristics of the post-involvement syndrome reported by anti-cult researchers – indecisiveness, a sense of meaninglessness, blurred mental acuity, and so forth – are symptomatic of a major Depressive Disorder which the *DSM* notes regularly accompanies the Post-Traumatic Stress Disorder (American Psychiatric Association 1980: 237). This analysis demonstrates that information disease symptoms are either exact parallels to the Post-Traumatic Stress Disorder or, where the parallel is weak, can be explained in terms of the influence of anti-cult indoctrination. We are thus fully justified in hypothesizing that information disease is the direct result of the traumatic transition out of a non-traditional religion rather than the result of anything experienced while in such a group.

If this line of reasoning is correct, it suggests that there should be a high correlation between the post-involvement syndrome and the experience of deprogramming. Though not all traumatic exits occur under the circumstances of forcible abduction and intensive counter-indoctrination, it seems reasonable to assume that the majority of exit traumas would be experienced by deprogrammed ex-members. In my research on former members of controversial religious groups, I found this to be the case.

My ex-member questionnaire, which was partially discussed earlier in this chapter, contained a section that asked subjects to compare their pre-involvement period (before joining their religious group) with their post-involvement period in terms of the various symptoms described in anti-cult literature. Using for the sake of simplicity only the seven symptoms for which Conway and Siegelman presented quantified data in their "Information Disease" article, and dividing the sample into the three treatment groups I described above, a distribution of information disease can be charted out which, as anticipated, clearly links the post-involvement syndrome with deprogramming/exit counseling (refer to Table 9.1).

It might be possible to argue – as Derks and van der Lans appear to argue (1983) – that negative indoctrination at the hands of anti-cultists accounts

Table 9.1 Relationship between Mode of Exit and Incidence of Information Disease Symptoms

Symptom	Percent of Respondents Reporting Symptom			
	No/ Counseling	Voluntary Counseling	Involuntary Counseling	Correlation Coefficient*
Floating	11	41	61	.414
Nightmares	11	41	47	.358
Amnesia	8	41	58	.482
Hallucinations	4	24	36	.337
Chanting	3	55	56	.530
Violence	9	31	42	.301
Suicidal	9	34	41	.270

*All correlations significant at the .001 level.

almost entirely for the post-involvement syndrome. However, though such indoctrination undoubtedly accounts for a portion of the syndrome, it is difficult to imagine that the experience of being snatched off the street and held against one's will until after one's religious beliefs were destroyed would *not* induce traumatic stress. Also, the many parallels observed between information disease and the Post-Traumatic Stress Disorder are too striking to be easily passed over.

Conclusion

An important point I did not mention at the beginning of this chapter is that – in the material I was reading back then – several writers called attention to the fact that, at the time, there was little data on voluntary defectors. So part of my attraction to this topic was the opportunity to address a recognized gap in the literature. This turned out to be a wise decision in the sense that the articles I authored and co-authored on this topic became standard references for later writers.

10 Member versus Ex-member Profiles

Back in the mid-1990s when I was studying the Movement of Spiritual Inner Awareness, I collected the same sort of demographic data we examined in Chapter Five. At the same time, I was also able to collect comparable data on 53 former participants. This fit so perfectly with the 447 questionnaires I received from current members that I felt irresistibly drawn to the idea of combining the two subsamples into a single sample – and so I calculated a joint profile. There were, however, a number of different characteristics on which the two subsamples differed in statistically-significant ways. So for those specific items, I presented calculations for both subsamples. The differences seemed to fit into a pattern I will discuss after surveying the items where the two subsamples differed.

Marital Status

Marital status is one of the statistics for which there was a significant difference between current and ex-members of MSIA. Almost half (47%) of all Discourse subscribers were married at the time (this was 1995) in contrast to less than a third (28%) of all former subscribers (see Tables 10.1a and 10.1b).

What does this difference between the two subsamples indicate? Because there is no significant difference age-wise, the difference in percentage of single people cannot be explained away as a function of age. Another hypothesis might be that the greater number of divorced respondents among ex-members can be explained in terms of marital disputes resulting from the exit of one spouse from MSIA while the other spouse remained. This hypothesis was, however, not substantiated by other answers on the questionnaires, which requested former members to describe their exit from MSIA. Furthermore, this type of explanation fails to explain the larger percentage of people who had never been married in the ex-member subsample.

This leaves two alternatives: Either (1) the kind of person who sticks with a commitment to a religious group also tends to be the kind of person who can commit to a marriage, or (2) there is something about belonging to MSIA that promotes and/or reinforces the married state. Initially, I favoured the first explanation. MSIA's teachings, while not unfavorable toward marriage, simultaneously do not exalt the married state as an ideal.

Table 10.1a Currently Involved: Marital Status

Status	Count	Percent
Single	102	22.8
Married	210	47.0
Divorced/Separated	127	28.4
Widow	6	1.3
No response	2	0.4
TOTAL	447	100.0

Table 10.1b. Formerly Involved: Marital Status

Status	Count	Percent
Single	18	34.0
Married	15	28.3
Divorced/Separated	19	35.8
Widow	1	1.9
TOTAL	53	100.0

Also, John-Roger's status as a person who has never been married does not provide a model for married life, although John Morton, the spiritual director of MSIA and the current Mystical Traveler, is married.

However, as I became more familiar with MSIA's teachings, I realized that J-R has consistently taught that difficulties – including marital difficulties – should be regarded as opportunities for growth rather than as evils to be escaped and that it is important to take responsibility for one's own life, rather than blaming circumstances or other people. Discourse subscribers are regularly brought into contact with this type of thinking through their monthly Discourses, if not through MSIA tapes, lectures, and other readings. Thus serious members trying to put what they are being taught into action would be prompted to keep working on their marriages in ways that non-members might not. As a consequence, it now appears to me that this second explanation is at least as significant – if not more so – for understanding the correlation between membership and marriage as the first explanation.

Education

Another point on which the two subsamples differed was education. Specifically, a significantly higher percentage of current Discourse subscribers had completed a master's degree than former subscribers. The ex-member subsample compensated for its lower percentage of master's degrees by a

Table 10.2a Currently Involved: Highest Degree

Schooling	Count	Percent
High School	49	11.0
Some College	60	13.4
Bachelor's	146	32.7
Master's	166	37.1
Ph.D.	21	4.7
Other	2	0.4
No Response	3	0.7
TOTAL	447	100.0

Table 10.2b Formerly Involved: Highest Degree

Schooling	Count	Percent
High School	5	9.4
Some College	11	20.8
Bachelor's	18	34.0
Master's	14	26.4
Ph.D.	4	7.5
No Response	3	0.7
TOTAL	53	100.0

correspondingly higher number of respondents who had attended college but who had not received a bachelor's degree (see Tables 10.2a and 10.2b).

A significant factor shaping this educational pattern is that over a decade ago John-Roger, the founder of MSIA, helped to give birth to the University of Santa Monica (USM), a graduate school offering master's degrees in psychology. Particularly in the early years of its institutional life, MSIA members were the mainstay of USM. As a consequence, many current members hold USM master's degrees. In a separate questionnaire item, respondents were asked whether they had ever attended USM. Almost 37% of current Discourse subscribers responded "Yes," in contrast to only 17% of former subscribers. This difference easily accounts for the difference in number of master's degrees between the two subsamples.

Occupation

In the United States, the most important factor determining class status is one's occupation. On this item, there was once again a significant difference between current and former members, with more current members pursuing higher-status careers than ex-members (see Tables 10.3a and 10.3b).

Table 10.3a Currently Involved: Occupation

Occupation	Count	Percent
Professional	100	22.4
Business, Manager	92	20.6
Technical, Skilled	64	14.3
Teacher, Research	40	8.9
Artist	32	7.2
Clerical, Manual	59	13.2
Unemp, Stud, Home, Ret.	56	12.5
No Response	4	0.9
TOTAL	447	100.0

Table 10.3b Formerly Involved: Occupation

Occupation	Count	Percent
Professional	9	17.0
Business, Manager	8	15.1
Technical, Skilled	8	15.1
Teacher, Research	3	5.7
Artist	5	9.4
Clerical, Manual	10	18.9
Unemp, Stud, Home, Ret.	10	18.9
TOTAL	53	100.0

Income

The difference in occupation was, unsurprisingly, reflected as a difference in income between current and former MSIA Discourse subscribers (see Tables 10.4a and 10.4b).

MSIA's occupational and income patterns indicate a membership that has been comparatively successful in our society's economic arena. The income differences between current and former members indicate either (1) that, as a group, ex-member respondents had less financial potential to begin with, or (2) that remaining a member of MSIA tends to promote financial success. Like the marriage item, my first inclination for this item was to attribute the difference to the different personal tendencies of respondents. In other words, the same personality type that strives for economic success also tends to stay with their chosen spiritual path, and vice versa.

However, as discussed in Chapter Five, MSIA also encourages members to cultivate an attitude that attracts abundance. Although John-Roger's teachings on wealth are placed in a larger context of well-being (e.g., as

Table 10.4a Currently Involved: Income

Yearly Income	Count	Percent
< $10,000	26	5.8
10-20,000	43	9.6
20-40,000	138	30.9
40-60,000	105	23.5
60-100,000	59	13.2
> 100,000	39	8.7
No Response	37	8.3
TOTAL	447	100.0

Table 10.4b Formerly Involved: Income

Yearly Income	Count	Percent
< $10,000	5	9.4
10-20,000	11	20.8
20-40,000	14	26.4
40-60,000	10	18.9
60-100,000	2	3.8
> 100,000	6	11.3
No Response	5	9.4
TOTAL	53	100.0

presented in the book *Wealth 101*), they nevertheless encourage members to seek a state of healthy prosperity. People who remain in MSIA are regularly brought into contact with J-R's low-key prosperity teachings through tapes, lectures, and other readings, and they would thus be encouraged to become financially successful. As a consequence, it now appears to me that this influence is at least as significant for understanding the correlation between membership and career success as one's personality type. Interestingly, the three areas of difference between the 1998 and the 2011 demographic profiles of MSIA participants we found in Chapter Five – education, profession and income – show up again in this chapter as areas of difference between current and former members.

Length of Membership

The questionnaire contained a number of items designed to measure the length and depth of respondents' membership. As one might anticipate, there were significant differences between current and former members on

Table 10.5a Currently Involved: Years of Membership

Years	Count	Percent
0–5 years	94	21.0
6–10 years	103	23.0
11–15 years	87	19.5
16–20 years	79	17.7
21–25 years	76	17.0
No Response	8	1.8
TOTAL	447	100.0

Table 10.5b. Formerly Involved: Years of Membership

Years	Count	Percent
0–5 years	25	47.2
6–10 years	13	24.5
11–15 years	3	5.7
16–20 years	7	13.2
21–25 years	1	1.9
No Response	4	7.5
TOTAL	53	100.0

these items. The simplest measure was years of membership (see Tables 10.5a and 10.5b).

While I was not surprised to find substantially shorter membership periods for ex-members, I did not expect to find that over half of those who had left MSIA did so after being involved for more than five years. Previous longitudinal studies, such as Saul Levine's work (reported in his book *Radical Departures*), have indicated that more than 90% of those who join an intensive religious group drop out after only two years or less of membership.

I believe that this unanticipated finding can best be explained in terms of the contrast between the nature of participation in MSIA and participation in most of the groups studied by Levine. Unlike such "high-demand" groups as the Hare Krishnas, membership in MSIA does not involve leaving mainstream society and taking up residence in a new, highly defined world strictly segregated from the mainstream. While one may participate in a wide range of MSIA activities that can, if one so desires, fill up most of one's free time, one may also simply read MSIA Discourses and practice one's spiritual exercises and still be regarded as a member in good standing. In other words, MSIA is not a high-demand group in the same sense as Levine's sample of movements were high-demand groups.

At this point we can ask if the differences in these five characteristics add up to anything like a coherent pattern. Greater success with the institution of marriage plus staying with MSIA suggest a characteristic that we might refer to as *persistence*. On the other hand, greater educational and economic success suggests *ambition*, among other talents. Taken together, these two personal traits indicate that the people who stay with MSIA are in no way inferior to the people who disaffiliate – in sharp contrast to critics who would portray NRM members as defective or in some manner "damaged goods."

Post-Involvement Attitudes

In addition to demographic items, I also requested ex-members to respond to a brief set of questions about their current attitude toward the Movement of Spiritual Inner Awareness. (The reader will notice that some of these were inspired by the questionnaire items discussed in Chapter Nine). The fact that former participants do not generally think in terms of MSIA being a "cult" is reflected in ex-members' general lack of awareness of the anti-cult movement (ACM), an ignorance measured by two questionnaire items that requested (1) how one evaluated the ACM and (2) the extent of one's contact with the ACM. The first question asked was:

How would you evaluate "anti-cult" groups like the Cult Awareness Network?

1. Very Negative
2. More Negative than Positive
3. More Positive than Negative
4. Very Positive

More than anything else, the pattern of responses – such as they were – indicated a general lack of knowledge about anti-cult organizations (see Table 10.6). Before examining the results, a couple of things should be pointed out about the following table:

First, a half-dozen people answered certain questionnaire items by simultaneously marking two adjacent responses (e.g., "1–2" instead of "1" or "2"), indicating that their attitude was somewhere between the two alternatives. Rather than deleting these respondents from the batch, my relatively small sample of completed Former Member Questionnaires (53) persuaded me to utilize such responses by assigning a half-point to each of the adjacent alternatives (an assignment that produced the ".5" values recorded in Table 10.6).

Table 10.6 Attitude Toward Anti-cult Movement

	Count	Percent
1	8	15.1
2	17.5	33.0
3	2.5	4.7
4	3	5.7
N/R	22	41.5

Second, note that percentage points have been rounded off to the nearest tenth of a percentage. As a consequence, the percentages in each table will not always add up to exactly 100%. Finally, note that "N/R" means "Non-Response."

The most striking aspect of responses to this item was the large number of people (more than two-fifths of the respondents) who chose to leave it blank. Eighteen of the 22 wrote something on the questionnaire beside the item like, "I have no information about it," "Don't know them," or "I'm not even aware of the Cult Awareness Network." In a couple of cases, respondents simply put a question mark in the blank provided for the answer.

My impression that most former MSIA members were largely uninformed about the "cult" controversy was reinforced by the item that measured the extent of one's contact with the ACM:

How would you describe the extent of your contact with "anti-cult" groups?

1. None
2. Minimal
3. Moderate
4. Extensive

Responses to this questionnaire item are tabulated in Table 10.7 – Contact with Anti-cult Movement.

Over four-fifths (81.1%) of respondents had never been in direct contact with the anti-cult movement, and, of those who had, not a single respondent

Table 10.7 Contact with Anti-cult Movement

	Count	Percent
1	43	81.1
2	7	13.2
3	1	1.9
4	0	0.0
N/R	2	3.8

10 *Member versus Ex-member Profiles* 167

described her or his contact as "extensive." From answers to this item and to the first item, it is clear that few ex-members feel motivated to seek out the anti-cult movement after leaving MSIA.

As stated earlier, we can isolate four key assertions that capture the essence of the negative stereotype through which minority religions are perceived: they recruit people by deceptive means; once recruited, they brainwash their members; their leadership is insincere; and their belief systems are bogus concoctions of the leader/founder. Four items on the former-member questionnaire measured these attitudes. The first of these asked respondents how frequently they had described their socialization into MSIA as "brainwashing":

Do you ever use the term "brainwashed" to describe your involvement in MSIA?

1. Never
2. Rarely
3. Sometimes
4. Frequently or Always

Responses to this questionnaire item are tabulated in Table 10.8 – "Brainwashed."

This exaggerated pattern of response – over four-fifths of the sample asserting that they never described their MSIA indoctrination as "brainwashing" – is not surprising, given the general non-exposure of ex-members to anti-cult ideology. While almost everyone has come into contact with the "cult" stereotype via the mass media, the great majority of these respondents obviously did not feel that the stereotype fit their experience of MSIA. In other words, while many of these former members might believe that there are evil cults in society that attempt to snare innocent people and "brainwash" them, they clearly did not feel that they had been members of such a "cult."

A closely related aspect of the negative stereotype of minority religions is that they deceptively recruit their members. The relevant item on the

Table 10.8 "Brainwashed"

	Count	*Percent*
1	43	81.1
2	4	7.5
3	4	7.5
4	1	1.9
N/R	1	1.9

Table 10.9 Deceptive Recruitment

	Count	Percent
1	47	88.7
2	2	3.8
3	1	1.9
4	1	1.9
N/R	2	3.8

ex-member questionnaire requested respondents to describe the degree of deception/insincerity involved in their recruitment:

The people/events/literature that led you to become involved in MSIA was/were:

1. Mostly honest and sincere
2. Somewhat misleading
3. Very misleading
4. Completely deceptive and insincere

Responses to this questionnaire item are tabulated in Table 10.9 – Deceptive Recruitment.

Like the "brainwashing" item, the pattern of response to this item presents us with a clear pattern, indicating that the great majority of these respondents do not feel that this aspect of the "awful cult" stereotype applies to their experience of MSIA anymore than do sensationalistic notions of "cultic brainwashing."

What, then, one might ask, caused these ex-members to leave MSIA in the first place? Clearly their disaffiliation from MSIA rests on a significantly different basis than is expressed in the shallow categories of anti-cult ideology. We might thus well anticipate a less exaggerated pattern of responses on such items as a question asking respondents to evaluate the truth of MSIA's teachings. The relevant questionnaire item put the issue in terms of truth and falsity:

Which of the following best describes the teachings of MSIA?

1. Completely True
2. More True than False
3. More False than True
4. Completely False

Responses to this questionnaire item are tabulated in Table 10.10 – Evaluation of MSIA Teachings.

Table 10.10   Evaluation of MSIA Teachings

	Count	Percent
1	8	15.1
2	38.5	72.6
3	3.5	6.6
4	2	3.8
N/R	1	1.9

Here we finally get something that begins to look like a statistical curve, though more than 70% of the respondents marked the "More True than False" item. After carefully reading over the completed Former Member surveys, I came away feeling that I overstated responses One and Four. In other words, instead of wording the first and fourth choices "Completely True" and "Completely False," I should have worded them so as to read "Mostly or Completely True" and "Mostly or Completely False." Had I done so, I believe a number of the ex-members who marked response Two would have marked response One, resulting in a smoother distribution of responses.

Nevertheless, even given the response pattern recorded in Table 10.10, the attitudes of this sample of ex-members are much less rejecting of MSIA's teachings than one might anticipate. We might have reasonably expected more former members to dismiss the teachings as false. This expectation is, however, overly dependent on the model of the apostate who leaves a church because she or he has lost faith in religion altogether. By way of contrast, the typical ex-member of MSIA continues to adhere to those aspects of her or his belief system that are congruent with the larger metaphysical/occult/New Age subculture – and the area of overlap between the teachings and the general ideology of the metaphysical subculture is fairly extensive. Thus, in the great majority of cases, leaving MSIA is more like dropping out of a Baptist Church and then joining a Pentecostal Church than it is like leaving religion entirely. This explains why most ex-members would describe the teachings as "More True than False."

What, then, about former members' attitudes toward John-Roger, the founder of MSIA, whose unique spiritual role is one of the principal points on which MSIA's teachings depart from generic metaphysical ideology? Might ex-members hold more negative attitudes toward J-R than toward MSIA teachings more generally? The relevant questionnaire item puts the issue in the following terms:

Which of the following best describes John-Roger Hinkins?

1. A Great Spiritual Leader
2. A Generally OK Spiritual Leader

3. A Substandard Spiritual Leader with a few good points
4. Completely Deluded or Completely False

Responses to this questionnaire item are tabulated below, in Table 10.11 – Evaluation of John-Roger.

Here we again get a pattern of responses that looks something like a normal statistical curve. Nevertheless, over two-thirds of the sample were still willing to give John-Roger a "Great" to "OK" rating, despite the fact that they left the Movement. Only two former members were willing to describe J-R as "false" or "deluded," and at least one of these ex-members converted to conservative Christianity after leaving MSIA.

This surprising statistic indicates that, although all 53 respondents had left MSIA, most felt they benefitted in one way or another from their participation in the Movement. Because they value the time they spent in the Movement, the majority feel no particular need to engage in self-justifying criticisms of either the teachings or John-Roger. This feeling of having benefited from involvement was explicitly measured by an open-ended item on the questionnaire that asked respondents if their MSIA involvement had helped or hurt them:

How has your involvement in MSIA influenced your life, for better or for worse?

Responses to this questionnaire item are tabulated in Table 10.12 – Better/Worse for the Experience.

Table 10.11 Evaluation of John-Roger

	Count	Percent
1	11	20.8
2	24.5	46.3
3	10.5	19.8
4	2	3.8
N/R	5	9.4

Table 10.12 Better/Worse for the Experience

	Count	Percent
Better	38	71.1
Worse	4	7.8
Mixed	3	5.7
Neither	6	11.3
N/R	2	3.8

With almost three-fourths of the sample willing to assert unambiguously that they feel they are better off for having been participants in MSIA, it is easy to see how so few ex-members feel a need to castigate the Movement, the teachings, or the founder. This situation is perfectly understandable if, as I have already indicated, we realize that most of the people who have left MSIA still consider themselves "on the path," in the larger sense, and continue to participate in some form of metaphysical/New Age spirituality. Such people can thus regard their membership period as part of their larger quest, and, as a consequence, positively value the time and energy they invested in MSIA. The pattern of responses to one final questionnaire item that assessed the value of the membership period further reinforces this interpretation. This item asked respondents to imaginatively place themselves back in time at the point where they initially became involved in MSIA:

If you could be transported back to the time you began your involvement with MSIA, you would probably:

1. Do it all over again with few or no changes
2. Do it all over again with many changes
3. Not get so deeply involved
4. Not get involved at all

Responses to this questionnaire item are tabulated in Table 10.13 – Would You Do It All Over Again?

Here once again we have an exaggerated pattern of response.

Conclusion

Though I feel that the positive-to-mixed attitudes toward their former organization of the ex-members discussed in this chapter and in the prior chapter can be extended to voluntary defectors from most alternative religions, there are some obvious exceptions. One prominent exception is the Church

Table 10.13 Would You Do It All Over Again?

	Count	*Percent*
1	32	60.4
2	5	9.4
3	5	9.4
4	7	13.2
N/R	4	7.5

of Scientology (CoS). While maintaining an interest in – perhaps even continuing to practice – Scientology (Rubin 2011), ex-CoS members are almost uniformly critical of their former organization. This is because of the Church's harsh policies regarding ex-members. Former members who were more than casual participants are often "declared," meaning that individuals who had been personally close to the ex-member (e.g., family members, close friends, even spouses) are required to cut off all communication. This ill-advised policy has helped transform many otherwise neutral-to-moderately-critical ex-members into devoted enemies of the Church.

I find the Church of Scientology case interesting in part because Church spokespeople uniformly dismiss the critical testimony of former members, describing them as being disgruntled apostates who are thus not objective observers. However, while defectors obviously have a point of view, this viewpoint need not be negative – as I have systematically documented in these concluding chapters. In this case as in other cases that could be cited, CoS has been its own worst enemy. J. Gordon Melton once observed that Scientologists "turn critics into enemies and enemies into dedicated warriors for a lifetime" (quoted in Frantz[1]) to which should be added, "ambivalent ex-members into hostile ex-members."

---

1. Quoted in Frantz (1997). The quote is from an interview with J. Gordon Melton. Cited in Douglas Cowan, *Researching Scientology: Perceptions, Premises, Promises, and Problematics*. In: Lewis (2009a: 73).

Afterword – Directions for Future Research

Because I hope my studies will prompt others to undertake related research, it seemed appropriate that I wind up this volume with some reflections on future research. First, a few paragraphs for the students of Religious Studies who might not have been trained in quantitative methods and who might have mild cases of math phobia.

There are plenty of introductory books available on survey design; and one need not even read the entire volume to get basic information. If one is researching a specific religious group or movement and one just wants to supplement a larger study with demographic data on group members, a simple questionnaire can be constructed using an online service such as Survey Monkey (www.surveymonkey.com). I do not know about other such ventures, but Survey Monkey provides services in 15 different languages. As for the criticism that not everyone has access to the Internet: in any "first world" country potential respondents can utilize an Internet café, a public library computer or a friend's computer to respond to a questionnaire if they do not have their own computer. (The representativeness of online questionnaires has been argued in, e.g., Stenbjerre & Laugesen 2005). Other kinds of criticisms that can be leveled against this approach apply equally to paper-and-pencil questionnaires, so I will not try to address them here. Entering data from hard copy questionnaires is much too time-consuming, unless one has a large grant from which data-entry workers can be paid.

In the United States, the General Social Survey (GSS) – a bank of questions maintained by the National Opinion Research Center at the University of Chicago – is available for researchers to utilize in their own research (http://www3.norc.org/GSS+Website/). The GSS is administered to a random sample of US residents every two years. What this means is that anyone constructing a profile of the membership of a specific group using GSS questions can then compare/contrast their profile with the characteristics of the general population. I do not know exactly what the situation is like in other countries, but in Norway where I currently work, one can obtain demographic questions and certain attitude items from the Norwegian Social Science Data Services (NSD), which contains Norwegian data from the International Social Science Programme and from the European

Social Survey. Similar to the GSS, anyone using questionnaire items from a national data service like the NSD has, in effect, a quasi-control group against which to compare findings on the group they are researching. For expanded examples of how one might utilize GSS items, the reader can refer to William Sims Bainbridge's *The Endtime Family* (2002) and to Christine Johnson's chapter in my and Nicholas M. Levine's *Children of Jesus and Mary* (2010). Helen Berger et al. also make selective use of GSS items in *Voices from the Pagan Census* (2003).

As for future research involving some of the approaches I have utilized in the preceding pages: Though I often refer to census data, in fact I have actually made minimal use of census information – mostly age and sex, along with a brief mention of ethnicity in Chapter Three. Censuses collect huge quantities of demographic information on everything from marital status to income. So within the limitations imposed by the kinds of information censuses collect, a researcher could conceivably develop innumerable studies on the basis of census data. One could, for example, examine data on education (a variable labeled "highest qualification" in some national censuses) and test the generalization that NRM members are typically more educated than average. In addition to comparing educational attainments with the general population, one could also make comparisons with the educational levels of members of mainstream religions like the Anglican Church and/or members of Christian sectarian movements like Pentecostalism. The major problems with this kind of study are, as we have seen, that the number of NRMs covered in national censuses is limited, and that purchasing relevant census data is expensive.

As for collecting data directly from religious groups, one should first note that there are primarily two kinds of NRMs, namely organized groups such as MSIA and OCS, and decentralized movements like Satanism and Paganism. Additionally, there is a third, more diffuse form of spirituality often referred to as "New Age" that can also be measured and analyzed. A significant issue with the second and third categories is the question of the representativeness of one's sample. Unless one focuses on a specific group (e.g., a particular Pagan organization or a particular New Age organization), one is never going to be able to gather a truly random (in the statistical sense) sample. Given the impossibility of compiling a random sample, I nevertheless feel that one can draw cautious conclusions from a sample of reasonable size. In the specific cases of Satanism and Paganism, it helps if the demographic characteristics of one's sample align reasonably well with the same traits represented in national census data.

Beyond the use of census data from multiple nations (as in Chapter Three) and juxtaposing questionnaire data with census data (as in Chapter

Six), my primary innovation in this volume was the quasi-longitudinal approach I took in Chapters One and Two. This was an approach I developed only after data had already been collected, focusing on the two different items that could be backdated to the point in time when the participant was recruited – age at conversion and point of first contact with the movement that the participant eventually joined. What is clear to me in retrospect is that one could develop a questionnaire which asked respondents to supply information on their educational level, marital status and the like at the time they converted, in addition to supplying information on their current educational level, marital status etc. This would allow a researcher to explore the issue of how membership in an NRM had impacted participants in these areas. The weakness with this approach, of course, is that one has no baseline (no quasi-control group) against which to determine whether individuals might have followed similar educational, professional *et cetera* paths anyway, even had they not joined an NRM. However, I think that creative researchers would be able to find ways to at least partially compensate for this weakness.

As I have previously discussed, a quasi-longitudinal approach is less desirable than a properly longitudinal approach, but it can be useful nevertheless. One must also bear in mind that this type of quasi-longitudinal methodology is particularly apt for movements that initially attracted youthful converts four or five decades ago because relatively few participants would have passed away in the intervening years. (I discuss this issue in Chapter One in footnote eight; also refer to my discussion in footnote ten in the same chapter). This approach would be far more problematic if applied, for example, to the New Zealand Anglicans who, as we saw in Chapter Three, pass away in large numbers during every five-year census period.

Finally, I hope that my research on NRM members is suggestive enough to stimulate other researchers to develop their own unique approaches or, at least, their own unique twists on such research. One can make original discoveries – or, at least, discoveries that serve to confirm or disconfirm existing generalizations – by reflection on (and by what I sometimes refer to as "playing around with") quantitative data. Thus, for example, though Roy Wallis noted that he found more male than female members when he conducted his Scientology research back in the 1970s, discovering that this pattern has continued down to the present as evidenced in census and survey data emerged from simply examining and reflecting on national census figures. To take another example, it was my ongoing contact with Order of Christ Sophia members in combination with the youthfulness of their organization that originally prompted me to hypothesize that NRMs in general might be recruiting more older members in the present time than in the past.

Then later, after the Pagan Census Revisited data had been collected, I at some point realized that I could test this hypothesis with data from contemporary Pagans. This in turn led to the discovery of the time period/age at recruitment relationship that I termed the E-Correlation. There is, in other words, no formula beyond having a relevant background, the hard work of collecting and reflecting upon data, plus an additional, intangible factor that some might call creative inspiration and others dumb luck.

In NRM studies, where in recent years so few researchers have availed themselves of quantitative methods, the field is wide open for numerous kinds of original research – even if one just collects basic data on previously unstudied or understudied religious groups. Researchers need to take up this challenge, even if only to shake the cobwebs off the conventional wisdom of the past and to keep our generalizations up to date.

Appendix –
Anglophone Census and National Survey Data on New Religious Movements

General estimates of the extent of the New Religions phenomenon vary considerably. The two basic quantitative questions in this area are: How many groups? And, How many people? These questions are not as simple as they might at first appear. A more fundamental question involves classification: Where does one draw the line between alternative and non-alternative religions? What one finds when one actually tries to determine where to draw such a line is that the difference between "mainstream" and "alternative" is a matter of degree rather than a sharply-defined distinction.

The indeterminacy of this dividing line allows anti-cultists like the late Margaret Singer to assert, without fear of direct contradiction, that as many as 20 million people have been involved in 3,000 to 5,000 cults in the United States (Singer and Lalich 1995). In contrast, Gordon Melton has estimated 500 to 600 alternative religions in the United States (Melton 1992). Similarly, Peter Clarke estimated 400 to 500 new religions in the United Kingdom (Clarke 1984). The situation is rather different in Japan, where New Religions have been thriving since the end of World War II. Japanese sociologists estimate anywhere from 800 to several thousand (Arweck 2000) such groups. And finally, Eileen Barker puts forward a figure of 2,000 or more New Religions in the West, and a figure in the lower tens of thousands worldwide (Barker 1999).

As discussed throughout this volume, an important source of information bearing on the question of numbers of adherents to alternative religions is national census data. The censuses of four English-speaking countries – New Zealand, Australia, Canada and the United Kingdom – collect information on religious membership that included select New Religions. There has also been an important series of religion surveys conducted in the United States, the American Religious Identification Survey (ARIS).

Though a few scholars of New Religions have referred to one or more of these censuses, no one has attempted a general survey except this writer (Lewis 2004). Following an examination of one estimate of world religious adherents, this appendix examines census data for the light such data sheds on participation rates in alternative religions. In the final section, relevant data from the ARIS survey will also be examined.

World Membership in Alternative Religions

An example of how the ambiguity between what is, and what is not, a New Religion can produce incongruous results can be found in David Barrett and Todd Johnson's "A Statistical Approach to the World's Religious Adherents" (2002). In terms of worldwide membership, these statistics appear to be the best figures available.

Barrett and Johnson divide the world's religions into 19 categories, with three subcategories for Christianity: Christian (Catholic, Protestant, Independent), Muslim, Baha'i, Hindu, Sikh, Jain, Buddhist, Zoroastrian, Jewish, Confucian, Taoist, Chinese Folk Religion, Shinto, Spiritist, Ethnoreligionist, Atheist, Nonreligious, Neoreligionist, and Other. They describe the Neoreligionist (New Religionist) as "twentieth-century new religions, new religious movements, radical new crisis religions, and non-Christian syncretistic mass religions, all founded since 1800 and most since 1945, mostly Asian in origin and membership but increasingly with worldwide followings." The "Other" category is described as "a handful of smaller religions, quasi-religions, pseudo religions, parareligions, religious or mystic systems, religious and semireligious brotherhoods of numerous varieties." Though I sharply question the designation "pseudo religion," it otherwise appears that most of the religions classified as Other are also New Religions. Finally, they neglect to define the Spiritism category. However, because, according to their statistics, 12,039,000 of the world's 12,334,000 Spiritists are located in Latin America and the Caribbean, it is clear that this category is meant primarily to encompass Afro-Caribbean and Afro-Brazilian New Religions like Santeria and Umbanda.

Out of a total world population of 6,055,049,000 people, Barrett and Johnson find that 102,356,000 are members of New Religions, 12,334,000 are Spiritists and 1,067,000 are in the Other category, meaning about 1.9% of the world population belong to alternative religions. This figure does not sound unreasonable, until one discovers that almost all of the people in New Religions – 100,639,000 members – are Asian. In order to analyze and critique their statistics, it will be useful to lay out all of Barrett and Johnson's relevant figures for the year 2000, continent by continent (refer to Table 11.1).

Their figure for Asian New Religions immediately strikes one as suspect. Even after being adjusted for population difference, the data still seems to indicate over ten times as many members of New Religions in Asia as in

Table 11.1 Numbers of Members in New Religions Worldwide

	New Religions	Spiritism	Other	Total Population
Africa	28,400	2,500	65,700	784,445,000
Asia	100,639,000	1,900	62,100	3,682,550,000
Europe	158,000	133,000	236,000	728,887,000
Latin America	622,000	12,039,000	98,000	519,138,000
North America	845,000	151,000	597,000	309,631,000
Australia (& Oceania)	66,500	7,000	9,400	30,393,000

[Table reproduced courtesy of ABC-Clio. From Melton and Baumann 2002: xxx.]

North America. This is probably the result of using different criteria for these two areas of the world. Barrett and Johnson almost certainly classified certain large groups like Soka Gakkai (Soka Gakkai has 9 million members) as New Religions rather than as Buddhists. In contrast, they almost certainly classified the many new Protestant sects that are constantly coming into being in the United States as Christian rather than as New Religions.

Given the large number of New Religions in sub-Sahara Africa, their low figure for African New Religions is clearly off-base. Because African New Religions tend to draw heavily on traditional Ethnoreligions, Christianity, or both, Barrett and Johnson must have classified most of these religious groups as either Ethnoreligious or Christian.

The European figure also seems quite low. Because of the concern over alternative religions in Europe since the first Solar Temple tragedy in 1994, there have been a number of official government surveys, though results have been less satisfactory than one might have hoped. For example, in 1998 the German Parliament's Enquete Commission reported the results of a national survey which indicated that 8 to 9 million people considered themselves members of non-traditional religious groups. In contrast, the Swedish Government Report of 1998 put forward a national figure of 50,000–60,000 (about 0.15% of the population), exclusive of New Age groups – a considerably lower proportion than the German figure.

As for North America, using only the New Religions figure gives us slightly less than 0.3%. Alternately, adding all of the data from the New Religions, Spiritism and Other categories results in slightly more than 0.5%. As it turns out, the 0.3%–0.5% range receives support from the national census statistics of certain other English-speaking countries, though in some countries this estimate is on the low end.

New Zealand National Census Data

A number of countries have begun to include religious affiliation as part of their national censuses. One of the most useful is the New Zealand census because of the large number of distinct groups enumerated between 1996 and 2006 (refer to Table 11.2).

The total of 21,465 members represents 0.53% of the 4,027,947 people who responded to the 2006 census, which compares favorably with the 0.3% to 0.5% participation rate for North America derived from the Barrett and Johnson data. This is, however, being extremely conservative. One could also make a reasonable argument for including Vineyard Christian Fellowship (sometimes called a "cult," with 1,605 members in the 2006 census), some of the 756 people who self-identified as Taoist, and some of the 4,830 people who the census classified as simply "Other Religion." This would bring the participation rate up to 0.7%. However, the New Zealand census allowed people to report more than one affiliation, and as a consequence the census collected many extra responses. Though not all of these additional responses could have been supplied by individuals self-identifying as members of New Religions, it is reasonable to infer that there were enough double responses by participants in alternative religions to undermine the solidness of the 0.53% figure.

There is, however, at least one more consideration to take into account. Though almost all major alternative religions have an outpost in New Zealand, few were explicitly included on the census. In particular, there are numerous Buddhist groups beyond Zen Buddhism that appeal primarily if not exclusively to Westerners. If one goes to the New Zealand Buddhist Directory (http://www.buddhanet.net/nzealand.htm), one will find groups like Soka Gakkai, Shambhala Center plus a wide variety of Vipassana meditation and Tibetan Buddhist organizations. These groups are usually classified in the alternative religions category in general survey books on New Religions (e.g., Chryssides 1999; Lewis 2001; Ellwood and Partin 1998). Participants in these groups were not distinguished from the other Buddhists constituting the 52,158 Buddhists reported in the 2006 census.

One way of understanding and evaluating the number of people involved in Western-oriented Buddhist groups (groups usually considered New Religions in the West, despite their lineage) is the ethnic backgrounds of participants. Because the website for the 2006 New Zealand census includes a table correlating ethnicity and religion, this information is readily available. The Ethnic Group and Sex by Religious Affiliation table records that 10,755 New Zealand Buddhists are of European heritage. Although some of these European Buddhists are converts because of marriage and other factors, it is

Table 11.2 Alternative Religion Membership Statistics from the New Zealand Census

Census Year	1991	1996****	2001	2006
Religion				
Satanism	645	909	891	1167
Hare Krishna	375	258	363	372
Rastafarianism	696	585	1,296	1383
Sufi**	324	156	195	177
Scientology	207	219	282	357
Spiritualism	3084	5097	5,853	7740
Unification Church	84	135	153	105
Christian Science	318	294	258	
Pantheism**	318		342	363
Heathen		579		
Theosophy		246		
Brahma Kumaris		30		
Aetherius Society		18		
Transcendental Meditation		15		
"Spiritualism & New Age Religion"		675		
New Age		669		
Animism**		138	213	207
Zen Buddhism*		81	126	78
Sukyo Mahikari		48	111	135
Tenrikyo		3	12	12
Yoga		345	414	297
Nature and Earth-based Religions		669	2,961	4527
Wiccan		789	2,196	2085
Druidism		126	150	192
Other New Age Religion		528	1,485	1488
Liberal Catholic Church		174	135	111
Total	6,876	11,289	17,436	21,465

* Like the Hare Krishna Movement, Zen Buddhism is considered a New Religion when Westerners become involved.

** Both the New Zealand and the Australian Census identify Animism and Pantheism as (neo) Pagan religions for statistical purposes (e.g., in Table 11.3, the 2001 figure for the Nature and Earth-Based category represents the sum of the Animism, Pantheism, Nature and Earth-based Religions, Wiccan and Druidism figures in Table 11.2). The religions of indigenous peoples were represented by other categories.

*** Few contemporary Muslims would self-identify as Sufis, indicating that all or most of the members of the Sufi category are members of one of several Sufi groups appealing primarily to Westerners. Like Western Zen Buddhism, Western Sufi groups are considered New Religions.

**** One can see that 1996 was the big year for adding new group categories. There were actually a half-dozen or so other groups listed that I did not include because their memberships were so tiny; these also disappeared the next year.

[Courtesy: New Zealand Statistics.]

reasonable to infer that the majority are involved in Western-oriented Buddhist groups.

There are also Swedenborgian and Unity School of Christianity churches in New Zealand, the members of which were lumped in with the 186,234 generic Christians recorded in the 2006 census. Unfortunately, estimating participation in alternative Christian groups cannot be addressed via ethnicity. Additionally, there are followers of Satya Sai Baba, Maharaji, and a wide variety of other South Asian groups who might have been lumped in with the 63,540 Hindus noted in the 2006 census. The census reported 3,300 Ethnic Europeans who self-identified as Hindus. As with the Buddhists, most of these people are likely involved in Western-oriented Hindu groups. Finally, one wonders what happened to members of other groups like the Raelians, Eckankar, Falun Gong, and Theosophy, all of which have a presence in New Zealand. When all of these organizations are considered, raising the estimated participation rate to at least 0.6% – or even 0.7% – is probably legitimate. However, even the most generous estimate would have to conclude that less than 1% of the population is actively involved in an alternative religion.

Australia National Census Data

The Australian census contains information similar to the New Zealand census although, as mentioned in Chapter Three, Australia includes some groups that New Zealand does not and excludes other groups that New Zealand includes. Unlike New Zealand, for which we have data from the 1991 census to the 2006 census, the Australian census has reported NRM numbers from 1996 up to the most recent census in 2011. Also unlike New Zealand, none of their NRM categories have changed since the 1996 census.

Between 1996 and 2001, the rise from 30,501 members to 45,829 members represents slightly more than a 50% increase in five years. (Religions in the Pagan categories experienced the most rapid rate of growth – on average, a 250% increase). However, after 2001 the rate of growth falls off to something approaching the same rate of increase as the Australian population as a whole. Thus, for example, Australia's growth rate between the 2006 census and the 2011 census was 8.32%. Comparatively, the rate of growth for the 20 NRMs cited in Table 11.3 was 7.96%, meaning that this selection of groups is falling behind the national rate of growth by about a half of 1%.

Australians' rate of participation in NRMs is also considerably less than New Zealanders'. Using just the above listed groups, 0.26% of Australians participate in NRMs compared with New Zealand's 0.53% – or about half

Table 11.3 New Religion Statistics from the 1996–2011 Australian Census

Census Year	1996	2001	2006	2011
Religion				
Animism	727	763	870	782
Caodaism	964	819	652	678
Christian Science	1,494	1666	1469	1356
Druidism	554	697	1022	1047
Eckankar	829	747	680	674
Gnostic Christian	559	723	1097	1032
Liberal Catholic Church	596	498	385	305
Nature Religions*	1,734	2225	2745	3596
Swedenborgian	504	427	365	331
Paganism	4,353	10,632	15,514	16,850
Pantheism	835	1085	1031	1393
Rastafarianism	1,023	1066	984	1391
Religious Science	634	417	347	293
Satanism	2,091	1798	2248	2453
Church of Scientology	1,488	2032	2507	2162
Spiritualism	8,140	9279	9844	11,554
Sukyo Mahikari	668	513	467	422
Tenrikyo	46	60	89	101
Theosophy	1,423	1627	1636	1485
Wiccan/Witchcraft	1,849	8755	8213	8414
Total	30,501	45,829	52,165	56,319

* I infer that "Nature Religions" refers to Paganism.

[Based on Australian Bureau of Statistics data.]

of New Zealand's percentage. However, unlike New Zealand, the Australian census did not allow people to respond to more than one item. Like New Zealand, Australia also has an abundance of alternative religion groups that "slipped through the cracks" of the above categories because they were recorded as generic Christians, Buddhists, and Hindus. Unfortunately, an Australian census table correlating religious membership with ethnicity is unavailable without paying a large fee, so I was unable to obtain the same kind of figures for Western participation in Asian Religions as I did for New Zealand. But I think we can nevertheless say that, because of the many New Religions missed by the census, a 0.3% - 0.4% participation rate for 2011 would be a reasonable but still conservative estimate.

One problem with this estimate is that it contrasts so significantly from the corresponding 0.6% estimate for New Zealand. Is there really such a marked difference in participation rates between these two sister countries? In terms of numbers of people responding to their respective national censuses, there were five times as many Australians in 2011 as New Zealanders in 2006. Of the comparable religions in the two censuses, only Christian Science had more than five times as many members in Australia than in New Zealand. Australian Mahikari and Tenrikyo members were almost five times as numerous as corresponding New Zealand members. But all of the other groups fell well below the one-to-five relationship. In the case of Rastafarianism, there were actually more total members in New Zealand than in Australia. So it seems there is a genuine difference in participation rates between these two countries.

It could be counter-argued that there are probably more alternative religions in Australia than in New Zealand and thus more Australian participants who missed the census net. And it could be further argued that, being a larger country, there are a greater number of religious "species" in Australia that draw away some of the people who would have joined other groups, thus explaining why the one-to-five ratio does not hold for most of the religions found in both censuses. However, even if a greater variety in religious fauna between the two countries is a factor to consider, it seems highly unlikely that it would be enough to account for the comparatively large difference between the two participation rates.

If we restate the data from Australia and New Zealand as 0.3% - 0.6%, then we have a statistic comparable to the Barrett and Johnson data for North America. Adding together their New Religions, Spiritism, and Other data, Barrett and Johnson's participation rate for Australia and New Zealand works out to 0.34%, which is in the same range, depending on how much weight one wants to give New Zealand relative to Australia.

United Kingdom National Census Data

The United Kingdom conducted a census with a religion identification item in 2001. The census recorded a reasonably good spread of different groups outside of the fold of the major religious groups. Regretfully, religious participation was not measured in previous censuses. I also wish the UK would drop its focus on the so-called "world religions" (a point I discussed in prior chapters) and allow respondents to fill in their specific denomination or other affiliation (refer to the figures for the England and Wales part of the census in Table 11.4).

As with the New Zealand census, missing numbers mean that data on a specific group was not gathered in that year. I would guess that members of

Table 11.4 New Religion Statistics for England and Wales from the 2001–2011 British Censuses*

Census Year	2001	2011
Religion		
Spiritualist	32404	39,061
Pagan	30569	56,620
Wicca	7227	11,766
Rastafarian	4692	7906
Scientology	1781	2418
Druidism	1657	4189
Pantheism	1603	2216
Satanism	1525	1893
New Age	906	698
Eckankar	426	379
Animism	401	541
Brahma Kumaris	331	442
Unification Church	252	452
Vodun	123	208
Occult	99	502
Hare Krishna	637	834
Raja Yoga	261	225
Christian Spiritualist Church	1461	
Christian Scientist	578	
Celtic Pagan	508	
Heathen**	278	
Asatru	93	
Sant Mat	53	
Divine Light Mission	21	
Santeria	21	
Shamanism	650	
Thelemite	134	
Witchcraft	1276	
Total	87,189	129,291

* Crown copyright material is reproduced with the permission of the controller of HMSO.

** This is a term of self-reference used by certain Pagans.

[Office for National Statistics © Crown Copyright 2013.]

the Christian Spiritualist Church, for example, clicked "Other" and wrote in the names of their distinct movements in the 2011 census, but that census officials decided (rather arbitrarily, to my way of thinking) to group them with generic Christianity. What I find useful about these examples is how clearly they demonstrate how decisions within census agencies can submerge relevant NRM data. This not only makes it impossible to provide accurate data on total numbers of NRM members, but it also shows why I can legitimately raise estimates that are otherwise based solely on listed groups.

With respect to a population of 56,100,000, a total of 129,291 members represents a participation rate of slightly more than 0.23%, the great majority of whom are Pagans or Spiritualists. The disappearance of a number of categories obviously means that quite a number of respondents were absorbed into the statistics for their parent traditions. Hindu-related New Religions (with the single exception of the Brahma Kumaris) and Buddhist New Religions are noticeably absent. Additionally, Christian-related groups like Unity and Swedenborgianism are also not represented as separate categories, as well as many other groups that have a presence in Great Britain.

An important factor influencing the outcome of the religion aspect of the census was that someone decided it would be a fine bit of fun to encourage people to write "Jedi Knight" in the religion category. As a consequence, 176,632 people in England and Wales responded that they belonged to the Jedi Knight religion. Although this really is quite amusing, I would guess that proportionally more of these self-designated Jedis were involved in some form of alternative spirituality than the general population, though how much more is impossible to determine.

Like the New Zealand census, the UK census provides information on ethnicity and religion, though I have not yet seen the relevant figures for the most recent census. In the 2001 census in England and Wales, 0.12% of the "white" population was Buddhist and .02% Hindu. This gives 57,024 Western Buddhists and 9,504 Western Hindus. There are also Christian New Religions that have slipped through the census categories. When all of these factors are taken into account, even a cautious estimate would place the participation rate in the UK in the 0.4%–0.5% range.

Canada National Census Data

Although the religion categories (which were expanded slightly in 2011) for the Canadian censuses are even less satisfactory than the categories used in the Australian, New Zealand, and British Censuses, they are nonetheless useful for comparative purposes. In a country with a population of

Table 11.5 New Religion Statistics from the 1991, 2001 and 2011 Canadian Censuses

Census Year	1991	2001	2011
Religion			
Gnostic	765	1165	870
New Age	1200	1525	2230
Rastafarian	460	1135	1055
Satanism	340	850	1050
Scientology	1215	1525	1745
Spiritualist	3735	3295	4315
Swedenborg	1425	1015	830
Unity/New Thought	4610	4000	2565
Paganism	5530	21085	25495
(Wicca; subset of Paganism)			(10225)
Pantheist			1000
Eckankar			2255
Total	19,280	35,595	43,410

[Courtesy: Statistics Canada.]

33,476,688 in the 2011 census, Canada recorded 43,410 members of alternative religions, or a participation rate of slightly less than 0.13%.

However, similar to the New Zealand and Australian censuses, Buddhist and Hindu groups regarded as New Religions were not separated for statistical purposes. And unlike New Zealand and Australia, even non-traditional Christian groups, like Christian Science, were apparently collapsed into Christianity. The addition of the classifications "Gnostic" and "New Age" appear to have been for the purpose of including alternative religious groups that did not fall handily into other categories. The New Age as a more general spiritual influence escapes straightforward efforts at measurement, as will be discussed in the conclusion. It would be quite reasonable to estimate much higher participation rates for Canada than indicated by these truncated census figures, more in the 0.4% - 0.5% range at least.

Religion Survey Data for the United States

Unfortunately, the US census does not collect religion membership data. However, in 1990, the Graduate Center of the City University of New York conducted a National Survey of Religious Identification (NSRI) via randomly dialed phone numbers (113,723 people were surveyed). Eleven years later, in 2001, the same center carried out the American Religious Identification

Survey (ARIS) in the same manner (over 50,000 people responded), though callers probed for more information than the earlier NSRI. For the most recent questionnaire (in 2008), the ARIS was administered by the Institute for the Study of Secularism in Society & Culture in Connecticut, though some of the key personnel from the City University have remained the same. Categories were developed post-facto. The results were quite interesting (refer to Table 11.6).

Although it would have been much more useful had the researchers broken down their data into more subcategories, their results are nevertheless striking. In the period of 11 years between 1990 and 2001, the overall participation rate in alternative religions appears to increase sevenfold, and then more than double between 2001 and 2008. Once again, however, we are plagued by the collapsing of important New Religions into their parent traditions. Had the various Christian alternative religions been separately categorized, the results would likely have been much different.

For the Buddhist and Hindu traditions, we can obtain a rough estimate of participation in New Religions by separating ethnic Buddhists and Hindus from Western converts. Although the NSRI did not record ethnicity, the ARIS

Table 11.6 New Religion Data from NSRI and ARIS

	1990	*2001*	*2008*
Religion			
Scientologist	45,000*	55,000	25,000
New Age	20,000	68,000	15,000
Eckankar	18,000	26,000	30,000
Rastafarian	14,000	11,000	56,000
Wicca	8,000	134,000	342,000
Druid**		33,000	29,000
Santeria**		22,000	3,000
Pagan**		140,000	340,000
Spiritualist**		116,000	426,000
Totals	79,000	583,000	1,266,000

*Numbers have been rounded off to the nearest 1,000. Unlike a census, which attempts to reach the entire population, these figures represent statistical extrapolations.

**The final four categories did not emerge as significant in the 1990 NSRI survey.

[Source: Kosmin and Keysar 2001; Kosmin and Keysar 2004; and Barry A. Kosmin, personal communication, February 2, 2012. Adapted table used with permission.]

did. I was able to obtain estimates for the percentage of "white" (Euroamerican) participants in Asian religions for the 2001 survey. Out of an estimated 766,000 Hindus in the 2001 survey, 2% were white. And out of an estimated 1,082,000 Buddhists in 2001, 28.5% were white. Calculating these percentages gives 15,320 Euro-American Hindus and 308,370 Euro-American Buddhists. Adding these numbers to the 583,000 figure and dividing the sum by a US population estimate of 207,980,000 gives a participation rate of slightly less than 0.44% in 2001. This percentage likely rose to 0.5%-0.6% by 2008. (Other non-Asians were also participants in Asian religions, but the rate of their participation was statistically miniscule).

Had all alternative religions – including the Christian, Buddhist and Hindu groups missed by the two surveys – been considered together, the growth rate of alternative religions in the United States would almost certainly have been less spectacular. Like the Australian and New Zealand census data, the NSRI-ARIS data has been sharply affected by the meteoric growth of Paganism (here represented by the Wicca-Druid-Pagan figures). Also, if Christian alternative religions had been distinguished so that they could have been included in the final total, the 0.5%-0.6% participation rate derived from the ARIS data would have been higher. How high this rate would rise if we had more complete data again depends on where one decides to draw the line between what is and what is not an "alternative" religion. If we take a conservative approach, a 0.6%-0.7% participation rate represents a reasonable estimate. Of course, if we adopted looser criteria for what constitutes a New Religion, much higher estimates would be possible.

Concluding Remarks

Generalizing from the data presented in the prior sections brings us to the conclusion that participation in alternative religions is quite low. In the Anglophone world, the participation rate is in the 0.5%-0.6% range. And though certain countries might have a lower rate than 0.3%, I would speculate that the participation rate in Western Europe as a whole probably falls into the same range. The statistical picture of New Religions reflected in this data is that of a small-scale phenomenon involving a fraction of a percent of the population. For religious groups that have formal memberships, this is probably an accurate portrait.

However, informal spiritual trends such as the strand of spirituality referred to as "New Age" often cross taken-for-granted boundaries between religions. For example, in the late 1990s, George Gallup and Michael Lindsay found that a surprising number of self-identified born-again Christians in North America held "New-Ageish" beliefs. Out of their sample, 20% believed in reincarnation and 26% believed in astrology. Although these statistics do *not* mean that 20% or more of all Evangelicals are really "New Agers," they *do* indicate that alternative spirituality has infiltrated society in ways that are missed when the population is measured in terms of mutually exclusive religious categories, and thus slip through the net of surveys and censuses.

Bibliography

Adler, Margot.
 1979 *Drawing Down the Moon*. Boston, MA: Beacon Press.
American Psychiatric Association
 1980 *Diagnostic and Statistical Manual of Mental Disorders*. Washington, DC: American Psychiatric Association, 3rd edn.
Andersen, Peter B.
 2012 Modernitetens pæne kønsroller som de kendes fra Scientologi. *Chaos: Dansk-norskTtidsskrift for Religionshistoriske Studier* 57: 129–40.
Andersen, Peter B., and Rie Wellendorf.
 2009 Community in Scientology and among Scientologists. In: *Scientology*, ed. James R. Lewis, 143–63. New York: Oxford University Press.
 2002 Kilder til et ikke eksisterende fællesskab. *Chaos, Dansk-norskTtidsskrift for Religionshistoriske Studier* 37: 9–20.
Arweck, Elisabeth.
 2002 New Religious Movements. In: *Religions in the Modern World*, edited by Linda Woodhead, Paul Fletcher, Jiroko Kawanami, and David Smith, 264–88. London: Routledge.
Australian National Census 96: Religion. http://www.aph.gov.au/library/pubs/rn/1997–98/98n27.htm
Bainbridge, William Sims.
 2002 *The Endtime Family: Children of God*. Albany, NY: State University of New York Press.
 1987 Science and Religion: The Case of Scientology. In: *The Future of New Religious Movements*, edited by David G. Bromley and Phillip E. Hammond, 59–79. Macon, GA: Mercer University Press.
Barley, Steven R.
 1990 Images of Imaging: Notes on Doing Longitudinal Field Work. *Organizational Science* 1(3): 220–47.
Barker, Eileen.
 2010 Twenty Years After: Ageing of and Ageing in the New Religions. Twenty Years After: Secularization and Desecularization in Central And Eastern Europe, ISORECEA Conference, Brno, Czech Republic, 16–18 December.
 1999 New Religious Movements: Their Incidence and Significance. In: *New Religious Movements: Challenge and Response*, edited by Bryan Wilson and Jamie Cresswell, 15–31. London: Routledge.
 1998 Standing at the Cross-Roads: The Politics of Marginality in "Subversive Organizations." In: *The Politics of Religious Apostasy: The Role of Apostates in the Transformation of Religious Movements*, edited by David G. Bromley. Westport, CT: Praeger Publishers, 75–93.
 1984 *The Making of a Moonie: Choice or Brainwashing?* Oxford: Blackwell.
Barrett, David B., and Todd M. Johnson.
 2002 A Statistical Approach to the World's Religious Adherents. In: *Religions*

of the World: A Comprehensive Encyclopedia of Beliefs and Practices, edited by J. Gordon Melton and Martin Baumann, xxvii–xxxviii. Santa Barbara, CA: ABC-Clio.

Beatty, Chuck.
 2013 Communication with author. February 12, 2013.

Beckford, James A.
 2003 *Social Theory & Religion*. Cambridge: Cambridge University Press.

Belisle, Orvilla A.
 1855 *The Prophets; or, Mormonism Unveiled*. Philadelphia, PA: W.M. White Smith.

Berger, Helen A.
 2011 Goddess Worship and Political Activity. Presented at the Eastern Sociological Society Meeting, February 24–27, Philadelphia, PA.
 2010a Pagan Men and Gender Equity by the Numbers. Presented at the American Academy of Religion meeting, October 30–November 1, Atlanta, GA.
 2010b Preliminary Finds from the Pagan Census Revisited. Eastern Sociological Society meeting, March 18–21, Boston, MA.
 1999 *A Community of Witches: Contemporary Neo-paganism and Witchcraft in the United States*. Columbia, SC: University of South Carolina Press.

Berger, Helen A., and Douglas Ezzy.
 2007 *Teenage Witches: Magical Youth and the Search for Self*. Piscataway, NJ: Rutgers University Press.

Berger, Helen A., Evan A. Leach, and Leigh S. Schaffer.
 2003 *Voices from the Pagan Census: A National Survey of Witches and Neo-Pagans in the United States*. Columbia, SC: University of South Carolina Press.

Bergesen, Albert.
 1984 *The Sacred and the Subversive: Political WitchHunts as National Rituals*. Storrs, CT: SSSR Monograph Series.

Beynon, John.
 1993 Computers, dominant boys and invisible girls: or, "Hannah, it's not a toaster, it's a computer!" In: *Computers into Classrooms: More Questions than Answers*, edited by John Beynon and Hughie MacKay, 160–89. Bristol, PA: Palmer Press.

Bibby, Reginald W., and Merlin B. Brinkerhoff.
 1974 When Proselytizing Fails: An Organizational Analysis. *Sociology of Religion* 35: 189–200.

Bobineau, Olivier, Ed.
 2008 *Le Satanisme. Quel danger pour la société?* Mesnil-sur-l'Estrée, Normandy: Pygmalion.

Bromley, David G.
 2009 New Religions as a Specialist Field of Study. In: *Oxford Handbook of the Sociology of Religion*, ed. Peter C. Clarke, 723–41. New York: Oxford University Press.
 2006 Affiliation and Disaffiliation Careers in New Religious Movements. In: *Introduction to New and Alternative Religions in America*, edited by Eugene V. Gallagher and W. Michael Ashcraft, 42–64. Westport, CT Greenwood Press.

Bromley, David G. and James T. Richardson.
   1983   *The Brainwashing/Deprogramming Controversy*. Lewiston, NY: Edwin Mellen.
Byrne, Paul
   1988   *The Campaign for Nuclear Disarmament*. London: Croom Helm.
Canadian National Census
   2001   http://ww.statcan.ca
Cerulo, Karen A.
   1997   Identity Construction: New Issues, New Directions. *Annual Review of Sociology* 23: 285–409.
Chryssides, George D.
   1999   *Exploring New Religions.* London: Cassell.
Chue, Glen.
   2008   Born-Again: Continuity and Subjectivity in Pentecostal Conversion. Paper presented at the Religion, Humanitarianism, and World Order conference held at the American University in Cairo, June 3–5.
Clark, John G., Jr., Michael D. Langone, Robert E. Schecter and Roger C.G. Daily.
   1981   *Destructive Cult Conversion: Theory, Research and Treatment*. Weston, MA: American Family foundation.
Clarke, Peter B.
   1984   New Paths to Salvation. *Religion Today* 1(1): 1–3
Coleman, James W.
   2001   *The New Buddhism: The Western Transformation of an Ancient Tradition*. New York: Oxford University Press.
Conway, Flo, and Jim Siegelman.
   1982   Information Disease: Have Cults Created a New Mental Illness? *Science Digest* (January): 86–92.
Cowan, Douglas E.
   2009   Researching Scientology: Perceptions, Premises, Promises, and Problematics. In: S*cientology*, ed. James R. Lewis, 54–79. New York: Oxford University Press.
   2004   *Cyberhenge: Modern Pagans on the Internet*. Oxford: Routledge.
Christensen, Natasha Chen.
   2006   Geeks at Play: Doing Masculinity in an Online Gaming Site. *Reconstruction* 6.1. Available at: http://reconstruction.eserver.org/061/christensen.shtml
Cox, Harvey.
   1978   Deep Structures in the Study of New Religions. In: *Understanding the New Religions,* edited by Jacob Needleman and George Baker, 122–30. New York: Crossroad.
Cult Observer.
   1986   IRS Seeks Information from Ex-Members on Way International's Political Involvement. *The Cult Observer* 3(3): 21.
Currie, Sean.
   2013   Communication with author. 9 February 2013.
Cusack, Carole M.
   2010   *Invented Religions: Imagination, Fiction and Faith*. Farnham: Ashgate.
Cush, Denise.
   2007   Wise Young Women: Beliefs, Values and Influences in the Adoption of

Witchcraft by Teenage Girls in England. In: *The New Generation Witches: Teenage Witchcraft in Contemporary Culture*, edited by Hannah E. Johnston and Peg Aloi, 139–60. Surrey, UK: Ashgate.

Dawson, Lorne L.
- 2006 *Comprehending Cults: The Sociology of New Religious Movements*. New York: Oxford University Press, 2nd edn.
- 2003 Who Joins New Religions and Why: Twenty Years of Research and What Have We Learned? In: *Cults and New Religions: A Reader*, ed. Lorne L. Dawson, 116–30. Oxford: Blackwell.
- 1998 *Comprehending Cults: The Sociology of New Religious Movements*. Ontario, CA: Oxford University Press, 1st edn.
- 1996 Who Joins New Religious Movements and Why: Twenty Years of Research and What Have We Learned? *Studies in Religion* 25(2): 141–61.

Dawson, Lorne L., and Douglas E. Cowan, eds.
- 2004 *Religion Online: Finding Faith on the Internet*. New York: Routledge.

Denzler, Brenda.
- 2003 *The Lure of the Edge: Scientific Passions, Religious Beliefs, and the Pursuit of UFOs*. Berkeley, CA: University of California Press.

Dewan, William J.
- 2006 Anomalous Experiences in North Carolina: A Survey. *The Journal of Popular Culture* 39(1): 29–43.

Driscoll, Neil.
- 1983 Can't Follow the Way. *Syracuse Herald-Journal*. Friday, October 7.

Dunbar-Hester, Christina.
- 2008 FM Radio Geeks, Meta-Geeks, and Gender Trouble: Activism, Identity, and Low-power. *Social Studies of Science* 38: 201–32.

Durkheim, Emile.
- 1960 *The Division of Labor in Society*. Trans. George Simpson. Glencoe, IL: Free Press.

Dusenbery, Verne A.
- 1988 Punjabi Sikhs and Gora Sikhs: Conflicting Assertions of Sikh Identity in North America. In: *Sikh History and Religion in the Twentieth Century*, edited by Joseph T. O'Connell, Milton Israel, and Willard G. Oxtoby, 334–55. Lewiston, NY: South Asia Books.

Dyrendal, Asbjørn.
- 2008 Devilish Consumption: Popular Culture in Satanic Socialization. *Numen* 55: 68–98.
- 2009 Darkness Within: Satanism as Self-Religion. In: *Contemporary Religious Satanism*, ed. Jesper A. Petersen, 59–74. Surrey, UK: Ashgate.

Einstein, Mara.
- 2008 *Brands of Faith: Marketing Religion in a Commercial Age*. New York: Routledge.

Ellwood, Robert S., and Harry B. Partin.
- 1998 *Religious and Spiritual Groups in Modern America*. Essex: Pearson Education, 2nd edn.

Elsberg, Constance Waeber.
- 2003 *Graceful Women: Gender and Identity in an American Sikh Community*. Knoxville, TN: University of Tennessee Press.

Engberg-Pedersen, Troels.
- 2000 *Paul and the Stoics*. Louisville, KY: Westminster John Knox.

Ezzy, Douglas, and Helen Berger.
  2009   Witchcraft: Changing Patterns of Participation in the Early Twenty-First Century. *The Pomegranate: Journal of Pagan Studies* 11(2): 165–80.
  2007   Becoming a Witch: Changing Paths of Conversion in Contemporary Witchcraft. In: *The New Generation Witches: Teenage Witchcraft in Contemporary Culture*, edited by Hannah E. Johnston and Peg Aloi, 25–40. Surrey, UK: Ashgate.

Farny, Lynn.
  2013   Communication with author. February 15.

Frantz, Douglas.
  1997   Boston Man in Costly Fight with Scientology. *The New York Times*, 21 December, 24.

Fügmann, Dagmar.
  2009   *Zeitgenössischer Satanismus in Deutschland.* Marburg, Germany: Tectum Verlag.

Gaines, M. Josephine, Mary Ann Wilson, Kerry J. Redican and Charles R. Baffi.
  1984   The Effects of Cult Membership on the Health Status of Adults and Children. *Update* 8(3–4): 9–11.

Gallagher, Eugene.
  1994   A Religion Without Converts? Becoming a Neo-pagan. *Journal of the American Academy of Religion* 62(3): 851–67.

Gallup, George, Jr. and D. Michael Lindsay.
  1999   *Surveying the Religious Landscape.* Harrisburg, PA: Morehouse.

Gardner, Martin.
  1957   *Fads and Fallacies in the Name of Science.* New York: Dover.

Giddens, Anthony.
  1991   *Modernity and Self-Identity.* Palo Alto, CA: Stanford University Press.

Gilhus, Ingvild Sælid and Lisbeth Mikaelsson.
  2005   *Kulturens Refortrylling.* Oslo, Norway: Universitetsforlaget.

Gilman, Sander L.
  1985   *Difference and Pathology.* Ithaca, NY: Cornell University Press.

Gooren, Henri.
  2010   *Religious Conversion and Disaffiliation: Tracing Patterns of Change in Faith Practices.* New York: Palgrave MacMillan.

Gruenschloss, Andreas.
  2009   Scientology: A "New Age" Religion? In: *Scientology*, ed. James R. Lewis, 225–43. New York: Oxford University Press.

Hakim, Catherine.
  2000   *Research Design: Successful Designs for Social Economics Research.* New York: Routledge, 2nd edn.

Hardacre, Helen.
  1999   *Marketing the Menacing Fetus in Japan.* Berkeley, CA: University of California Press.

Hardyck, Jane Allyn, and Marcia Braden.
  1962   Prophecy Fails Again: A Report of a Failure to Replicate. *Journal of Abnormal and Social Psychology* 65: 136–41.

Harvey, Graham.
  2009   Satanism: Performing Alterity and Othering. In: *Contemporary Religious Satanism*, ed. Jesper A. Petersen, 27–40. Surrey, UK: Ashgate.

1999 *Contemporary Paganism: Listening People, Speaking Earth.* New York: New York University Press.
1995 Satanism in Britain Today. *Journal of Contemporary Religion* 10: 283–96.

Heelas, Paul.
2002 The Spiritual Revolution: From "Religion" to "Spirituality." In: *Religions in the Modern World*, edited by Woodhead, Linda et al., 412–36. Oxford, UK: Routledge.

Hjelm, Titus, ed.
2009 Special Issue on Satanism. *Social Compass* 56: 4.

Hughes, Philip, and Sharon Bond.
2003 Nature Religions. *Pointers: Bulletin of the Christian Research Association* 13(2): 1–6.

Jakobsh, Doris.
2008 3HO/Sikh Dharma of the Western Hemisphere: The "Forgotten" New Religious Movement? *Religion Compass* 2: 385–408.

Jennings, M. Kent.
1987 Residues of a Movement: the Aging of the American Protest Generation. *American Political Science Review* 81(2): 367–82.

John-Roger and Peter McWilliams.
1993 *Wealth 101: Wealth is Much More than Money.* Los Angeles, CA: Prelude Press.

Johnston, Hannah E., and Peg Aloi, eds.
2007 *The New Generation Witches: Teenage Witchcraft in Contemporary Culture.* Farnham, UK: Ashgate.

Jones, Constance A.
1998 Metaphysical Religious Movements in the United States: A Comparison of Church Universal and Triumphant, Ramtha's School of Enlightenment, and Movement of Spiritual Inner Awareness. Paper presented at the 12th annual meeting of the CESNUR: Religions and Spiritual Minorities: Towards the 21st Century. Turin, Italy. September 10–12.

Jorgensen, Danny and Scott Russell.
1999. American Neopaganism: The Participants' Social Identities. *Journal for the Scientific Study of Religion* 38(3): 325–38.

Khalsa, Kirpal Singh.
1986 New Religious Movements Turn Towards Worldly Success. *Journal for the Scientific Study of Religion* 25(2): 233–45.

Kilbourne, Brock K.
1983 The Conway and Siegelman Claims Against Religious Cults: An Assessment of their Data. *Journal for the Scientific Study of Religion* 22(4): 380–85.

Kilbourne, Brock and James Richardson.
1988 Paradigm Conflict, Types of Conversion and Conversion Theories. *Sociological Analysis* 50(1): 1–21.

Köse, Ali.
1996 Religious Conversion: Is It an Adolescent Phenomenon? The Case of Native British Converts to Islam. *International Journal for the Psychology of Religion* 6(4): 253–62.

Kosmin, Barry A., and Ariela Keysar.
2004 *Religion in the Marketplace.* Ithaca, NY: Paramount Books.

2001 American Religious Identification Survey. New York: City University of New York.

Krogh, Marilyn C., and Brooke Ashley Pillifant.
   2004 The House of Netjer: A New Religious Community Online. In: *Religion Online: Finding Faith on the Internet*, edited by Lorne L. Dawson and Douglas Cowan, 189–203. New York: Routledge.

Lamb, Christopher, and M. Darrol Bryant.
   1999 *Religious Conversion: Contemporary Practices and Controversies*. London: Continuum.

Latkin, Carl, Richard Hagan, Richard Littman and Norman Sundberg.
   1987 Who Lives in Utopia? A Brief Report on the Rajneeshpuram Research Project. *Sociological Analysis* 48(1): 73–81.

Laue, Thorsten.
   2007 *Kundalini Yoga, Yogi Tee und das Wassermannzeitalter. Religionswissenschaftliche Einblicke in die Healthy, Happy, Holy Organization (3HO) des Yogi Bhajan*, Münster: LIT.

LaVey, Anton Szandor.
   1969 *The Satanic Bible*. New York: Avon.

Levine, Saul V.
   1984 *Radical Departures: Desperate Detours to Growing Up*. New York: Harcourt Brace Jovanovich.

Lewis, James R.
   forthcoming New Religious Movements. In: *Vocabulary for the Study of Religion*, edited by Robert Segal and Kocku von Stuckrad. Leiden: Brill.
   2014 The Youth-Crisis Model of Conversion: An Idea Whose Time Has Passed? *Numen: International Review for the History of Religions*, 61(5-6): 594-618.
   2012a Cracks in the Conversion Network Paradigm. *International Journal for the Study of New Religions*. 3(2): 143–62.
   2012b Conversion to Satanism. In: *The Devil's Party: Satanism in Modernity*, edited by Jesper Aagaard Petersen and Per Faxneld. New York: Oxford University Press, 145–66.
   2012c *Cults: A Reference Guide*. 3rd Edition, Sheffield: Equinox Publishing.
   2012d The Pagan Explosion Revisited: A Statistical Postmortem to the Teen Witch Fad. *The Pomegranate: The International Journal of Pagan Studies* 14(1): 128–39.
   2012e Scientology: Up Stat Down Stat. In: *The Cambridge Companion to New Religious Movements*, edited by Mikael Rothstein and Olav Hammer, 133–49. Cambridge, UK: Cambridge University Press.
   2011 The Devil's Demographics: Changes in the Satanic Milieu, 2001–2009. *Alternative Spirituality and Religion Review* 2(2): 248–86.
   2010a Fit for the Devil: Toward an Understanding of "Conversion" to Satanism. *International Journal for the Study of New Religions*. 1(1): 117–38.
   2010b Autobiography of a Schism. *Marburg Journal of Religious Studies*, Vol. 15: 1–19.
   2010c Review of Chris Mathews, *Modern Satanism: Anatomy of a Radical Subculture*. *Alternative Spirituality and Religion Review* 1(1): 109–13.
   2009a The Growth of Scientology and the Stark Model of Religious "Success." In: *Scientology*, ed. James R. Lewis, 117–40. New York: Oxford University Press.

2009b Infernal Legitimacy. In: *Contemporary Religious Satanism*, ed. Jesper Aagard Petersen. Surrey, UK: Ashgate.
2007 The Pagan Explosion. In: *The New Generation Witches: Teenage Witchcraft in Contemporary Culture*, edited by Hannah E. Johnston and Peg Aloi, 13–23. Hampshire: Ashgate.
2006 New Data on Who Joins NRMs and Why: A Case Study of the Order of Christ/Sophia. *Journal of Alternative Spiritualities and New Age Studies* 2: 91–104.
2004 New Religion Adherents: An Overview of Anglophone Census and Survey Data. *Marburg Journal of Religious Studies* 9(1). Available at: http://archiv.ub.uni-marburg.de/mjr/pdf/2004/lewis2004.pdf
2003 *Legitimating New Religions*. New Brunswick, NY: Rutgers University Press.
2002 Diabolical Authority: Anton LaVey, *The Satanic Bible* and the Satanist Tradition. *Marburg Journal of Religious Studies 7:1*.
2001a Who Serves Satan? A Demographic and Ideological Profile. *Marburg Journal of Religious Studies*, Vol. 6: 1–25.
2001b *Odd Gods: New Religions and the Cult Controversy*. Amherst, NY: Prometheus Books.
1997 *Seeking the Light*, Los Angeles, CA: Mandeville Press.
1994 *From the Ashes: Making Sense of Waco*. Lanham, MD: Rowman & Littlefield.
1989 Apostates and the Legitimation of Repression: Some Historical and Empirical Perspectives on the Cult Controversy. *Sociological Analysis* 49(4): 386–96.
1986 Reconstructing the "Cult" Experience: Post-Involvement Attitudes as a Function of Mode of Exit and Post-Involvement Socialization. *Sociological Analysis* 42(2): 151–59.

Lewis, James R., and Andreas Baumann.
2011 New Religions and the New Zealand Census: Are Meaningful Generalizations About NRM Members Still Possible? *International Journal for the Study of New Religions* 2(2): 179–200.

Lewis, James R., and Nicholas M. Levine.
2010 *Children of Jesus and Mary*. New York: Oxford University Press.

Lewis, James R., and Jesper Aagaard Petersen, eds.
2008 *Encyclopedic Sourcebook of Satanism*. Amherst, NY: Prometheus Books.

Lewis, James R., and David G. Bromley.
1987 The Cult Withdrawal Syndrome: A Case of Misattribution of Cause? *Journal for the Scientific Study of Religion* 26(4): 508–22.

Lofland, John, and Rodney Stark.
1965 Becoming a World-Saver: A Theory of Conversion to a Deviant Perspective. *American Sociological Review* 30: 862–75.

Lucas, Phillip.
2002 Holy Order of MANS. In: *The Encyclopedia of Cults, Sects and New Religions*, ed. James R. Lewis, 400–402. Amherst, NY: Prometheus Books.
1995 *The Odyssey of a New Religion*. Indianapolis, IN: Indiana University Press.

Machalek, Richard, and David A. Snow.
1993 Conversion to New Religious Movements. In: *Religion and the Social Order, Vol. 3: The Handbook on Cults and Sects in America*, Part B, edited

by David G. Bromley and Jeffrey K. Hadden, 53–74. Greenwich, CT: JAI Press.

Magliocco, Sabina.
2004 *Witching Culture: Folklore and Neo-Paganism in America*. Philadelphia, PA: University of Pennsylvania Press.

Mathews, Chris.
2009 *Modern Satanism: Anatomy of a Radical Subculture.* Santa Barbara, CA: Praeger.

Mattausch, John.
1989 *A Commitment to Campaign.* Manchester: University of Manchester Press.

Melton, J. Gordon.
1992 *Encyclopedic Handbook of Cults in America.* 2nd edn. New York: Garland.

Melton, J. Gordon, and Martin Baumann, eds.
2002 Religions of the World: *A Comprehensive Encyclopedia of Beliefs and Practices, Vol. 1.* Santa Barbara, CA: ABC-Clio.

Melton, J. Gordon, and Robert L. Moore.
1982 *The Cult Experience: Responding to the New Religious Pluralism*. New York: Pilgrim Press.

McLean, Kate C.
2008 The Emergence of Narrative Identity. *Social and Personality Compass* 2(4): 1685–702.

Miller, Russell.
1987 *Bare-faced Messiah: The True Story of L. Ron Hubbard*. London: Michael Joseph.

Monk, Maria.
1977 *Awful Disclosures of the Hotel Dieu Nunnery of Montreal*. New York: Arno.

Moody, Edward J.
1974 Magical Therapy: An Anthropological Investigation of Contemporary Satanism. In: *Religious Movements in Contemporary America*, edited by Irving I. Zaretsky and Mark P. Leone, 355–82. Princeton, NJ: Princeton University Press.

Moriarty, Anthony.
1992 *The Psychology of Adolescent Satanism: A Guide for Parents, Counselors, Clergy, and Teachers*. Santa Barbara, CA: Praeger.

Neitz, Mary Jo.
1987 *Charisma and Community: A Study of Religious Commitment within the Charismatic Renewal*. Piscataway, NJ: Transaction.

Nordquist, Ted A.
1978 *Ananda Cooperative Village*. Uppsala, Sweden: Borgstroms.

Oleson, Ted, and James T. Richardson.
2007 The Confluence of Research Traditions on Terrorism and Religion: A Social Psychological Examination. *Psicología Política* 34: 39–55.

Otten, Allen, and Rick Myers.
1998 *Coping with Satanism: Rumor, Reality, and Controversy*. Revised Edn. New York: Rosen Publishing Group.

Palmer, Susan J.
1993 Rajneesh Women: Lovers and Leaders in a Utopian Commune. In: *The*

Rajneesh Papers: Studies in a New Religious Movement, edited by Susan J. Palmer and Arvind Sharma, 103–35. Delhi: Motilal Banarsidass.

Partridge, Christopher.
   2004   *The Re-Enchantment of the West, Vol. 1*. New York: T & T Clark, International.

Partridge, Christopher, & Eric Christianson, eds.
   2009   *The Lure of the Dark Side: Satan and Western Demonology in Popular Culture*. Sheffield: Equinox Publishing.

Patrick, Ted, and Tom Dulack.
   1977   *Let Our Children Go!* New York: Ballantine.

Petersen, Jesper Aagard.
   2013   From Book to Bit: Enacting Satanism Online. In: *Contemporary Esotericism*, edited by Kennet Granholm and Egil Asprem. Sheffield: Equinox Publishing.
   2009a   Satanists and Nuts: The Role of Schisms in Modern Satanism. In: *Sacred Schisms: How Religions Divide*, edited by James R. Lewis and Sarah M. Lewis, 218–47. Cambridge, UK: Cambridge University Press.
   2009b   *Contemporary Religious Satanism*. Surrey, UK: Ashgate.
   2005   Modern Satanism: Dark Doctrines and Black Flames. In: James R. Lewis and Jesper A. Petersen, eds. *Controversial New Religions*, 423–57. New York: Oxford University Press.
   2002   Special Issue on Satanism. *Syzygy: Journal of Alternative Religion and Culture* 11.

Pike, Sarah M.
   2001   *Earthly Bodies, Magical Selves: Contemporary Pagans and the Search for Community*. Berkeley, CA: University of California Press.

Possamai, Adam, and Alphia Possamai-Inesedy.
   2012   *Battlefield Earth* and Scientology: A Cultural/Religious Industry *a la* Frankfort School? In: *Handbook of New Religions and Cultural Production*, edited by Carole M. Cusack and Alex Norman, 583–98. Leiden: Brill.

RavenWolf, Silver.
   1999   *Teen Witch: Wicca for a New Generation*. Woodbury, MN: Llewellyn.

Reid, Síân.
   2009   "A Religion Without Converts" Revisited: Individuals, Identity and Community in Contemporary Paganism. In: *Handbook of Contemporary Paganism*, edited by Murphy Pizza and James R. Lewis, 171–91. Leiden: Brill.
   2001   Disorganized Religion: An Exploration of the Neopagan Craft in Canada. Ottawa, ON: Carleton University, Department of Sociology and Anthropology.

Reitman, Janet.
   2011   *Inside Scientology: The Story of America's Most Secretive Religion*. Boston, MA: Houghton Mifflin Harcourt.

Richardson, James T.
   1985   Studies of Conversion: Secularization of Re-enchantment? In: *The Sacred in a Secular Age*, ed. Phillip E. Hammond, 104–21. Berkeley, CA: University of California Press.

Richardson, James T., Joel Best and David G. Bromley.
   1991   *The Satanism Scare*. Berlin: Aldine de Gruyter.

Richardson, James T., and Mary W. Stewart.
   1977   Conversion Process Models and the Jesus Movement. *American Behavioral Scientist* 20(6): 819–38.

Rigal-Cellard, Bernadette.
   2009   Scientology Missions International: An Immutable Model of Technological Missionary Activity. In: S*cientology*, ed. James R. Lewis, 325–34. New York: Oxford University Press.

Rochford, E. Burke.
   2011   Email communication to author, May 16.
   2007   *Hare Krishna Transformed*. New York: New York University Press.
   1985   *Hare Krishna in America*. New Brunswick, NJ: Rutgers University Press.
   1982   Recruitment Strategies, Ideology, and Organization in the Hare Krishna Movement. *Social Problems* 29: 399–410.

Rose, Stuart.
   2001   New Age Women: Spearheading the Movement? *Women's Studies: An Inter-disciplinary Journal* 30(3): 329–50.
   1998   An Examination of the New Age Movement: Who is Involved and What Constitutes its Spirituality. *Journal of Contemporary Religion* 13(1): 5–22.

Ross, Michael W.
   1998   Effects of Membership in Scientology on Personality: An Exploratory Study. *Journal for the Scientific Study of Religion* 27(4): 630–36.

Rubin, Elisabeth Tuxen.
   2011   Disaffiliation among Scientologists: A Sociological Study of Post-Apostasy Behavior and Attitudes. *International Journal for the Study of New Religions* 2(2): 201–24.

Schmidt, Joachim.
   1992   *Satanismus: Mythos und Wirklichkeit*. Marburg, Germany: Diagonal Verlag.

Shepherd, Gordon, and Gary Shepherd.
   2010   *Talking with the Children of God: Prophecy and Transformation in a Radical Religious Group*. Champaign, IL: University of Illinois Press.

Siegler, Elijah.
   2010   "Back to the Pristine": Identity Formation and Legitimation in Contemporary American Daoism. *Nova Religio: The Journal of Alternative and Emergent Religions* 14(1): 45–66.

Singer, Margaret Thaler.
   1979   Coming Out of the Cults. *Psychology Today* 12(8): 72–82.

Singer, Margaret Thaler, with Janja Lalich.
   1995   *Cults in Our Midst: The Hidden Menace in our Everyday Lives.* San Francisco, CA: Jossey-Bass.

Skjoldli, Jane.
   2014 (Forthcoming) "God is Blowing Everybody's Mind": Charismatic Controversies in the Jesus People, Calvary Chapel and Vineyard Movements. In: *Controversial New Religions*, edited by James R. Lewis and Jesper Aagaard Petersen. New York: Oxford University Press. 2nd Edn.

Smith, Christian, Melinda Lundquist Denton, Robert Faris, and Mark Regnerus.
   2002   Mapping American Adolescent Religious Participation. *Journal for the Scientific Study of Religion* 41(4): 597–612.

Snow, David A., and Richard Machalek.
  1984. The Sociology of Conversion. *Annual Review of Sociology* 10: 167–90.
Snow, David A., Louis A. Zurcher, Jr. and Sheldon Ekland-Olson.
  1980 Social Networks and Social Movements: A Microstructural Approach to Differential Recruitment. *American Sociological Review* 45(5): 787–801.
Solomon, Trudy.
  1981 Integrating the "Moonie" Experience: A Survey of Ex-Members of the Unification Church. In: *In Gods We Trust*, edited by Thomas Robbins and Dick Anthony, 275–94. New Brunswick, NJ: Transaction.
Stark, Rodney, and William Sims Bainbridge.
  1985 *The Future of Religion: Secularization, Revival and Cult Formation.* Berkeley, CA: University of California Press.
  1980 Networks of Faith: Interpersonal Bonds and Recruitment to Cults and Sects. *The American Journal of Sociology* 85: 1376–395.
Stenbjerre, Mads and Laugesen, Jens N.
  2005 Conducting Representative Online Research. Paper presented at ESOMAR Worldwide Panel Research Conference, Budapest, 17–19 April.
Sundby-Sørensen, Merethe.
  1988 Masser af myter om de nyreligiøse. *Humaniora* 1: 4–7.
Tipton, Steven M.
  1982 *Getting Saved from the Sixties.* Berkeley, CA: University of California Press.
Tobey, Alan.
  1976 The Summer Solstice of the Healthy-Happy-Holy Organization. In: *The New Religious Consciousness*, edited by Charles Y. Glock and Robert N. Bellah, 5–30. Berkeley, CA: University of California Press.
Tøllefsen, Inga B.
  2012 Notes on the Demographic Profiles of Art of Living Practitioners in Norway and Abroad. *Alternative Spirituality and Religion Review* 3(2): 225–52.
  2011 Art of Living: Religious Entrepreneurship and Legitimation Strategies. *International Journal for the Study of New Religions* 2(2): 255–79.
Trzebiatowska, Marta, and Steve Bruce.
  2012 *Why are Women More Religious than Men?* Oxford: Oxford University Press.
Turner, Bryan S.
  2006 *The Cambridge Dictionary of Sociology.* Cambridge, UK: Cambridge University Press.
Victor, Jeffrey.
  1993 *Satanic Panic: The Creation of a Contemporary Legend.* Chicago, IL: Open Court.
Wallis, Roy.
  1977 *The Road to Total Freedom: A Sociological Study of Scientology.* New York: Columbia University Press.
Walter, Tony, and Grace Davie.
  1998 The Religiosity of Women in the Modern West. *British Journal of Sociology* 49(4): 640–60.
Watts, Mother Clare.
  2003 *Giving Birth to God: A Woman's Path To Enlightenment.* New York: iUniverse.

Whitehead, Harriet.
   1974   Reasonably Fantastic: Some Perspectives on Scientology, Science Fiction and Occultism. In: *Religious Movements in Contemporary America*, edited by Irving I. Zaretsky and Mark P. Leone, 547–87. New York: Oxford University Press.

Wilson, Bryan, and Karel Dobbelaere.
   1994   *A Time to Chant: The Soka Gakkai Buddhists in Britain*. Oxford: Clarendon Press.

Wright, Stuart A.
   1987   *Leaving Cults: The Dynamics of Defection*. Washington, DC: Society for the Scientific Study of Religion.
   1984   Post-Involvement Attitudes of Voluntary Defectors from Controversial New Religious Movements. *Journal for the Scientific Study of Religions* 23(2): 172–82.

Zonta, Michela.
   1998   A Socio-Demographic Profile of the Membership of MSIA. Paper presented at the 12th annual meeting of the CESNUR: Religions and Spiritual Minorities: Towards the 21st Century. Turin, Italy. September 10–12.

Index

Adidam
  age at recruitment 19, 22, 29
  history of 19–20, 42
  means of recruitment 42–43
  survey of 19
American Religious Identification Survey (ARIS) 102–103, 106, 187–89
Ananda Cooperative Village 32, 39
Anglican Church 51–53, 131–32, 174–75
Anti-cult movement (ACM), anti-cultists 70, 144–46, 148–51, 153–57, 165–67, 177
Art of Living Foundation (AoLF) 28, 33–34, 132

baby boomers 16, 18–19, 72, 85–6
brainwashing 14, 143, 145–47, 150–51, 153–54, 167–68
Buddhism, Buddhists
  age at conversion 66
  age profile 66
  in census data 65, 180
  means of involvement 122
  numbers identifying as 65–66, 181, 189
  Western-oriented groups 180–83, 186–89

Calvary Chapel 28
Church of Jesus Christ of Latter-day Saints (LDS)
  age profile 54–55
  as deceptive 150
  gender ratio 54, 131–32
  in census data 49
  numbers identifying as 53–54

conversion *see also* age at & means of recruitment/involvement under individual NRMs
  E-correlation 18–20, 22–29, 107–108, 176
  Lofland-Stark model 33
  or identity construction *see* Paganism; Satanism
  reasons for 111–12
  via social networks 4–5, 31–33, 44, 78, 125
  via the Internet *see* Paganism; Satanism
  youthful, youth-crisis model 4–5, 11–17, 20, 26–27, 29–30, 67
Cult Awareness Network 165–66

deprogramming 143–57
Divine Light Mission 144, 185
Druidism, Druidry, Druids
  age at recruitment/conversion 62–63, 116
  age profile 63, 104, 116
  gender ratio 62–63, 104, 116, 133
  numbers identifying as 102–104, 106, 181, 183, 185, 188
  Teen Witch effect on 63–64, 104
E-correlation *see* conversion, E-correlation
Eckankar, Eckists 15, 50, 60–61, 182–83, 185, 187–88
EnlightenNext (EN) 26–29

Family International, The 44, 71, 111

General Social Survey (GSS) 173–74

Hare Krishna Movement
   age at recruitment/conversion 16, 20–22
   age profile 60
   ex-members 144
   gender ratio 135
   history of 21
   International Society for Krishna Consciousness (ISKCON) 21–22, 40–41
   means of recruitment 22, 39–41
   numbers of participants 59–60, 181, 185
   survey of 20
Healthy, Happy, Holy Organization (3HO) 12, 14, 144
Hinduism, Hindus 60, 178, 182–83, 186–89
Holy Order of MANS (HOOM)
   age profile 16
   economic structure 74
   history of 69–70
   religious background of members 76

International Society for Krishna Consciousness (ISKCON) *see* Hare Krishna Movement
Internet surveys *see* online questionnaires
Internet-based religions *see* Paganism; Satanism

Jesus movement 28, 53, 76–77

LDS church *see* Church of Jesus Christ of Latter-day Saints

Moonies *see* Unification Church
Mormonism, Mormons *see* Church of Jesus Christ of Latter-day Saints (LDS)
Movement of Spiritual Inner Awareness (MSIA)
   data from ex-members
      education 160–61
      income 162–63
      length of membership 163–64
      marital status 159
      occupation 161
   history of 83–84
   longitudinal study of 5–6
   membership data
      age at recruitment 15, 24–25, 86
      age profile 85–86
      educational background 88
      gender/sex ratio 85
      initiatory level 93–94
      length of membership 93–94
      marital status 86–87
      means of recruitment 33–34, 80
      number of members 84
      participants with children 87
      political affiliation 91–92
      religious background 92–93
      social class 88–91
      survey of 24, 84–85, 91
   post-involvement attitudes
      to anti-cult groups 165–67
      to deceptive recruitment 168
      to MSIA involvement 170–71
      to MSIA teachings 168–69
      to the MSIA leader 169–70
      to whether brainwashed 167–68

National Survey of Religious Identification (NSRI) 102–103, 187–89
Neopaganism *see* Paganism
New Age
   defining 189–90
   in census data 49, 133
   movement, demographics of 132–33
   NRMS, sex ratio 85
   numbers identifying as 181, 185, 187
   spirituality 120, 174

Index 207

New Religious Movements (NRMs)
  conversion to *see* conversion
  defining 2, 11, 174, 177–78
  educational background of
    participants 72, 174
  ex-members *see* deprogramming
  gender balance of
    participants 131–33
  in ARIS 100
  in census data 49–51, 132–33
  means of recruitment 31–33, 44
  misperceptions of
    participants 3–4, 67
  participation rates 177–89
  post-involvement attitudes
    to anti-cult groups 148–49
    to means of
      recruitment 146–47
    to group involvement 143–44
    to group teachings 148
    to the group leader 147–48
    to whether brainwashed 147
  post-involvement survey
    methodology 144–46
  post-involvement
    syndrome 154–58
  religious background of
    participants 76
  research problems 1–4, 19, 22, 30,
    44, 67
  social class of participants 74
  study of conversion to 111–12
  youthfulness of recruits *see*
    conversion, youthful
Norwegian Social Science Data
  Services (NSD) 173–74

online questionnaires
  as a research tool 28, 81, 113, 173
  EnlightenNext 26
  MSIA 24, 84
  OCS 27
  Pagan 17, 36
  Satan 113–14
Order of Christ Sophia (OCS)

  as a spiritual fit 119
  economic structure of 74, 81
  history of 69–70
  longitudinal study of 5–6
  membership data
    age at recruitment 15–16, 27, 71
    age profile 15–16, 71–73
    educational background 74–75,
      88
    gender ratio 75–76, 85
    length of membership 15, 71
    means of recruitment 78–80
    number of members 71
    religious background 76–77
    social class 72, 74
    survey of 70–71

Paganism, Pagans
  age of first involvement 17–18,
    29, 107
  age profile 18, 107–108
    and identity construction 118,
      128–29
  as an Internet religion 4,
    16–20, 35, 106, 117
  as 'a religion without converts'
    or 'coming home' 25–26,
    117–18, 128
  gender ratio 63–64, 133
  history of 117
  interaction with co-religionists 4,
    35, 117, 125–27
  means of involvement 36–39,
    117, 121, 124–25
  numbers identifying as 18, 29,
    99–109, 182–83, 185, 187–88
  surveys
    academic studies 100
    author's group studies 127–28
    national censuses and NSRI-
      ARIS 99–101,182, 189
    Pagan Census 16–17, 37
    Pagan Census Revisited
      (PCR) 17–20, 36–37, 106–
      109, 122

Teen Witch effect on 6, 18, 63–64, 106
Pentecostalism 53, 55, 174
Presbyterianism, Presbyterians 51, 53, 131–32

Rajneeshpuram, Rajneesh movement 74, 112
Rastafarianism, Rastafarians 62–63, 67, 133–34, 181, 183–85, 187–88
recruitment *see* conversion; *also* age at and means of recruitment/involvement under individual NRMs
Religious Science 50, 183

Sant Mat 6, 24, 84, 185
Satanism, Satanists
  Anton LaVey 35, 117, 121
  age of first involvement 62, 122
  age profile 61–62, 115–16
    and identity construction 121, 128–29
    as an Internet religion 35, 125
    as a spiritual fit 119
    as self-religion 119–20
  educational background
  gender ratio 61–62, 115, 133–34
  interaction with co-religionists 125–27
  means of involvement 6, 35–36, 121–23
  numbers identifying as 115, 181, 183, 185, 187
  surveys
    national censuses and NSRI-ARIS 49–50, 133
    Satan Survey One (SS-1) 35–36, 113–14
    Satan Survey Two (SS-2) 35–36, 111, 114, 119, 125–26
    Satan Survey Three (SS-3) 114, 122, 125
Scientology (CoS)
  age profile 58
  age at recruitment 23, 29
  and science fiction 138
  ex-members 172
  gender ratio 56, 133–39
  in census data and ARIS/NSRI 6–7, 49–50, 59, 133
  means of recruitment 41
  numbers identifying as 29, 56, 58–9, 181, 183, 185, 187–88
  Sea Org 136
social networks *see* conversion, via social networks
Spiritualism, Spiritualists
  age at recruitment 67
  age profile 56–57
  gender ratio 56–57, 133
  in national censuses and NSRI-ARIS 49, 186
  numbers identifying as 56, 181, 183, 185, 187–88

Teen Witch *see* Druidism; Paganism
Theosophy 50, 181–83
Transcendental Meditation (TM) 34, 132, 181

Unification Church
  age at recruitment 14, 16, 72
  age profile 14, 72
  as a spiritual fit 112
  gender ratio 135
  means of recruitment 41
  numbers identifying as 135, 181, 185
  political affiliation 92
  post-involvement attitudes 143–45, 147, 152–53
  surveys
    academic studies of 15–16, 33
    national censuses and NSRI-ARIS 135

Vineyard Christian Fellowship (VCF) 49–50, 53, 55–56, 180

Way International, The 144
Wicca, Wiccans
   age profile 104–105
   gender/sex ratio 64, 104–105, 133
   in national censuses and NSRI-ARIS 49, 100–103, 133
   numbers identifying as 65, 101–106, 108–109, 181, 183, 185, 187–88
   Teen Witch effect on 63–64, 104

youth-crisis model (YCM) *see* conversion, youthful

www.ingramcontent.com/pod-product-compliance
Lightning Source LLC
Chambersburg PA
CBHW071842230426
43671CB00012B/2037